The World of Birds

A Layman's Guide to Ornithology

———

"Comprehensive, readable . . . a feast for the inquisitive."
— **The Indianapolis News**

*"Corral shines in his ability to present difficult and technical concepts
with a captivating, entertaining style."*
— **Berkshire Eagle**

*"Learn the answer to many fundamental questions
about birds with this book."*
— **Wildlife Conservation**

*"A fascinating reference book . . . very comprehensive . . . it could
well entice newcomers into the field of ornithology."*
— **Baton Rouge Sunday Advocate**

*"This well written book goes beyond bird identification. . . . it also
answers the most basic questions about ornithology."*
—**Indiana Audubon Quarterly**

"Clear, well-written, enticing."
—**SciTech Book News**

The World of Birds

A Layman's Guide to Ornithology

by Michael Corral

illustrated by Keith Hansen and Jean Stover

The Globe Pequot Press

Excerpt from *The Outermost House,* by Henry Beston, copyright © 1928 by Holt, Rinehart, and Winston, Inc. Reprinted by permission. Excerpt from *Shearwaters,* by R. M. Lockley, copyright © 1942 by Devin-Adair Publishers, Inc., Old Greenwich, Ct. Reprinted by permission. Illustration from "The Stellar-Orientation System of a Migratory Bird," by S.T. Emlen, *Scientific American,* 1975, vol. 233 (2). Redrawing of figure by permission.

Library of Congress Cataloging-in-Publication Data

Corral, Michael.
 The world of birds: a layman's guide to ornithology/by Michael Corral; illustrated by Keith Hansen and Jean Stover.—1st ed.
  p. cm.
 Includes bibliographies and index.
 ISBN 0-87106-236-4
 1. Birds. I. Title.
 QL673.C67 1989
 598—dc20   89–34785
                                                              CIP

Manufactured in the United States of America
First Edition/Third Printing

To Mary and the boys.

FOREWORD

The works of Shakespeare abound with their images, as do the works of writers from other cultures. Mythology evokes the grace of the swan; poetry, the song of the nightingale or the curlew's mournful cry. On Chinese porcelain appear those marvelous pheasants; in old Egyptian drawings, the storks. Truly, birds have long been the most conspicuous of animals; so it is predictable that a science, ornithology, has been founded to study them.

Currently birding and bird watching, the popular aspects of this science, are where the action is. People are interested in feeding birds as well as sighting, identifying, and counting them. Indeed, in the United States the interest in birds continues to grow; according to the U.S. Fish and Wildlife Service, nearly one person in four both watches and feeds birds. Why all this interest? One reason is that people have a need to understand the natural world, to have some contact with nature. Another reason is that birds themselves are so diverse, so interesting. They range in size from the hummingbird, weighing only three grams, to the male ostrich, weighing in at 157,000 grams. Birds are colorful, too—witness the brilliant red of the cardinal or the bright blue of the blue jay. Birds also sing a wide variety of songs, and many species accommodate people's efforts to attract them to food or shelter.

This interest in birds has produced copious literature on the scientific study of birds, the identification of bird species by both sight and sound, and the methods for attracting and feeding birds. There are also a number of textbooks on bird biology. Generally, these have been written for college courses in ornithology and are heavy reading for a nonbiologist interested in exploring what is interesting and exciting about birds. In this book, though, Michael Corral has put together a highly readable account of what is known about bird biology. Mike's account stresses what is interesting and unique about birds. We learn about bird adaptations (colors and feathers), how birds fly, how and why they sing, why penguins' and ducks' feet neither freeze nor melt their way through ice, how geese can fly high above the altitudes where human aviators sitting in comfortable seats require supplemental oxygen, and how barn owls catch mice by listening to their sounds. The list is long and covers the whole range of bird biology in a well-organized, balanced account. Mike's interest and enthusiasm for his subject weave their way throughout the text and are infectious. Consequently, this book will prove fascinating for the myriad birders who want to know more about the intriguing animals they watch.

Ornithology, Mike believes, certainly has room for the nonprofessional. In addition to simply watching and enjoying birds, there are a multitude of opportunities to participate in ornithology. Activities range from going on the National Audubon Society's Annual Christmas Bird Count and counting the birds coming to your feeder for the Cornell Laboratory of Ornithology's Project

FeederWatch to more sophisticated activities like the Breeding Bird Survey run by the U.S. Fish and Wildlife Service.

It is possible, in other words, to make worthwhile contributions to bird biology without being a professional. My father, a busy family doctor, kept track of the changes in the number of bird species that visited or nested on our place in Cambridge, Massachusetts, over a period of forty years. He not only derived a great deal of satisfaction from doing it and from looking over his results, but his efforts also resulted in a published paper. Other nonprofessionals have devised standard methods for conducting research. If your interests lie in that direction, therefore, this book will whet your enthusiasm and help get you started.

It is a special pleasure to write this Foreword because Mike was a colleague of mine when he was a graduate student at the State University of New York at Stony Brook. Mike not only took our courses in animal behavior, he also participated in research, with me, on homing pigeons and, with other faculty, on how important the songs of red-winged blackbirds are in maintaining their territory. In the course of his years with us, we all, faculty and students, discussed and argued about what was interesting in biology and in animal behavior. Then I left Stony Brook for Cornell, and Mike got his degree and began to teach. Receiving his manuscript in the mail brought back memories of those old discussions—now put in context by an obviously enthusiastic and experienced teacher.

I am told that Mike's students are excited about birds. Now I know why.

CHARLES WALCOTT
Executive Director
Cornell Laboratory of Ornithology
Ithaca, New York

CONTENTS

PREFACE

The immediate origin of this book dates back to an article I wrote for *The Science Teacher* in which I described the ornithology course I have taught at Darrow School for the last eight years and suggested that other schools include this course in their curricula. In the article I told of the difficulty I had in finding an appropriate text, stating that I often thought of writing one for the course myself. The book, I envisioned, would be relatively short, informative, readable, and scientific; in it I would attempt to explain birds and also convey a certain, undefinable passion I feel for them. Shortly after the article was published, Mary Kennan, who was then an editor at Prentice-Hall, asked if I really wanted to write such a book. Naively, I said yes.

Yet the book really began on the bow of a ship headed for Nova Scotia almost twenty years earlier, when I stood next to a birdwatcher who was doing a census of marine birds. The shearwaters, petrels, and gannets that he showed me (for I must admit he always spotted them first) were something from another world, and to this day I am still impressed by these marine species. From this one experience I was hooked on birds.

After spending a year or two learning my species, I became a graduate student at Stonybrook. Here I was involved with an exceptional group of scientists and had a good deal of freedom to work on a number of different projects, such as filming at a gull colony, banding, recording bird song, and tracking homing pigeons. Along with this I was exposed to the exciting ideas of evolutionary biology, physiology, behavior, and ecology.

In teaching ornithology, I found my ideas on the subject becoming more organized. I also found that the study of birds was a good means of teaching science, for birds are attractive and accessible creatures that could be studied in the field as well as in the classroom. Their abundance and visibility facilitate identification and allow for projects, such as a census and experimentation at a feeder, to be conducted in a relatively short space of time in which meaningful data can be collected. From a teacher's point of view, this course is a pleasure because there are so many varied things to do; and it is also gratifying because, by the end of the year, one or two students develop that strange and undefinable glint in their eyes. They, too, have seen another world and leave in the spring as fledgling ornithologists.

I would like to thank a number of people who helped me in writing this book: my wife, Mary, for taking on innumeral tasks related to the book and for putting up with a husband who has been more distractable than usual; Keith Hansen and Jean Stover for their fine work on the illustrations; Mary Kennan for having the confidence in me to write this book; Dr. Charles Walcott for reading parts of the text; and, particularly, Sheldon Flory for reading every word, helping me with my writing, and being a source of enthusiasm and encouragement. His assistance is reflected in every part of this book.

INTRODUCTION

My approach in this book is very similar to that in class—that the principles and methods of science can be taught through birds. And as in class, I am not particularly interested in the learning of long strings of facts about birds but rather the reasons and underlying forces that give rise to the various forms, behaviors, and distributions we see in birds. In doing so I follow the format of more scholarly texts in a number of areas: The metric system is used exclusively in the presentation of measurements [See the table of conversions following this Introduction.—Ed.], species names are capitalized and followed in italic by their scientific name, and the text is referenced by giving the author and date of publication. The referencing, I feel, is important for a number of reasons: It recognizes the authors from which I take information, adds a certain credibility to the text, and most importantly, allows the reader to find out more about a particular area of ornithology. Knowing that many of these references are rather obscure and available only in university libraries, I have ended each chapter with suggested reading of more accessible works. I encourage the reader to continue the study of ornithology and hope that my text and additional sources will be helpful to this end.

The projects presented at the end of chapters are also there to encourage the reader to find out more about birds. Probably more than any other science, ornithology has a strong tradition of contribution by the nonscientist. Some of these projects suggest no more than becoming more systematic in the observations you probably make already, while others require a good deal of time and patience. I have tried most of them with my classes with varying degrees of success, finding that even the best laid plans don't always work out. Don't get discouraged if your experimental designs don't work, either; but if they do, you should consider your work for publication. Ornithological journals such as *Wilson's Bulletin, Condor, Kingbird,* and *Journal of Field Ornithology* all give the specifications for publication in every issue, and all accept both longer articles and shorter contributions. So become an ornithologist.

TABLE OF CONVERSIONS

1 centimeter (cm)	=	0.39 inches
1 inch	=	2.54 cm
1 meter (m)	=	3.28 feet
1 foot	=	0.30 m
1 kilometer (km)	=	0.62 miles
1 mile	=	1.61 km
1 kilogram (kg)	=	2.20 pounds
1 pound	=	0.45 kg
1 gram (g)	=	0.03 ounces
1 ounce	=	28.35 g
1 liter (l)	=	1.05 quarts
0° C (Celsius)	=	32° F (Fahrenheit)
37°C	=	98.6° F

- 1 -

Introducing the Birds

BIRDS HAVE ALWAYS FASCINATED PEOPLE. Captured in paintings or photographs, they are pleasing in form, with clean, sleek lines, bright in color, and bold in pattern. Although the artist depicts the beauty and vitality of these creatures on canvas, their forms are accessible to anyone who has the patience to seek them out. At one time many saw the birdwatcher as a lonely figure on a deserted winter marsh, an oddball seeking a prize unknown to most. Over the past quarter century, however, this figure rarely walks the marsh alone.

Marsh

In the 1920s Henry Beston chose to spend a year alone on the Great Beach on Cape Cod. He set out to observe nature, for he felt that people had been separated from the elementary forces by the environment we had created. Chronicling that year in *The Outermost House*, Beston expresses very clearly that, insulated from nature, we cease to be human.

The phenomenal rise of interest in birds over the past twenty-five years has been coincidental with the leisure time created by a technology that is becoming increasingly strange and artificial. Those of us who join the birdwatcher on the windy marsh seek not only the beauty of birds, but a glimpse of creatures that, Beston says, "move finished and complete, gifted with extensions of the senses we have lost or never attained, living by voices we shall never hear." For many of us, birds are the link with a world that is still in our genetic makeup, a wilder world, a simpler and more complete world than we know today.

The beauty of birds can be traced to their ability to fly. Flight requires them to be sleek and gives them the opportunity to be bright in color and bold in pattern. Birds' forms are pleasing to the eye, but that pleasure mixes with envy when we see how easily they move through a world fraught with obstacles. How many people over the ages have wished to simply fly over the barriers the world presents? In this century we have realized this dream of flight, but our machines do not offer the freedom to rise above it all on some sunny afternoon; we will never be as free as a bird.

Ornithology is the scientific study of birds. Like all science, it is an inquiry into nature, seeking an answer to a question. We know more about birds than about any other group of organisms, and yet the inquiry has just begun. Scores of species have yet to be discovered, and of the birds already described, only a small percentage are known in detail. For many species, avian ecology, physiology, and social behavior are just beginning to be explored, and in many ways migration of birds remains as mysterious to today's ornithologist as it did to the ancients.

Ornithology is like other sciences in that it is based on questions, but it is unique in that many of the answers come from the nonscientist. Ornithology has traditionally profited by contributions from those with a passion to know more about birds and willingness to follow the scientific method to that end. The most recognizable name in ornithology in the United States is John James Audubon, an artist by training, like the familiar Roger Tory Peterson. A monumental work in twenty-three volumes, *The Life Histories of North American Birds*, was written by Arthur C. Bent, a businessman; and the definitive work on the life history of the Song Sparrow, *Melospiza melodia*, was done by Mrs. Margaret M. Nice, a housewife and mother of five.

For those of us who leave the marsh unsatisfied with a brief glance at these fellow inhabitants of the earth, our need to know more about them leads us to the first step in the science of ornithology, and we need not stop there.

DEVELOPMENT OF ORNITHOLOGY

A natural science, ornithology specializes in studying birds but delves into many aspects of avian research. Like all other sciences, ornithology has evolved through the ages, concentrating its efforts here at one time and there at another but always striving to advance our overall understanding of birds.

Aristotle, with whom we may start, was interested in birds and listed 140 species, speculating on their migration, parental care, and relationships with their environment. The first great ornithologist was Emperor Fredric II (1194–1250). A falconer, Fredric was familiar with Aristotle's work and extended it, writing seven books on birds, exploring flight, migration, molt, and classification, and describing internal organs.

As the Western European countries began to explore the world, natural scientists were confronted with new creatures in bewildering numbers. Exotic tropical species such as parrots, toucans, hummingbirds, and birds of paradise captured imaginations, fueling many expeditions to seek still more intriguing species. By the 1750s biological scientists endeavored to put these creatures in order by applying the modern system of classification and later to explain their place according to evolution. Up to 1900, ornithology was preoccupied with describing and classifying these new creatures. In America, Alexander Wilson and John James Audubon advanced our understanding of native species. Centers of ornithological research built up around museum collections first in Philadelphia and Washington, then in New York, in Cambridge, Massachusetts, and in Chicago, laying the foundation for the explosion of study filling the twentieth century.

Professional ornithologists between 1750 and 1900 cared about the lives of birds but spent most of their energy on obscure descriptions, as in characterizing hummingbirds as schizognathous anisodactyle Apodiformes, and contributed little to the amateur's understanding. In America, however, professional ornithologists did not come on the scene until 1915, when Cornell University began granting a degree in the subject. Before then, science was left to the nonspecializing naturalist. Among these was Frank Chapman of the American Museum of Natural History in New York, whose interest went beyond the lives, description, and classification of birds and undertook to educate the public with exhibits displaying common and exotic species in their natural habitat. In 1899 Chapman started the periodical *Bird-Lore*, which in this century evolved into *Audubon*. At Harvard University Louis Agassiz promoted ornithology and from the Museum of Comparative Zoology the prestigious Nuttall Ornithological Club and the American Ornithologist's Union originated. This era was influenced as well by the naturalists Aldo Leopold and John Muir, whose writing seems remarkably prophetic today. By the time the first Ph.D. in ornithology left Cornell the course was already set: the study of birds would have a broad base and would be tied to the environment and public interest. This interest was reinforced by *A Field Guide to the Birds*, published by Roger Tory Peterson in 1934, a tool that would help the amateur on the way to becoming an expert.

Today ornithology is in the forefront of research in natural history. Migration, ecology, behavior, and evolution are almost synonymous with avian research. Many conservation efforts in this country have also been close to species of birds about to succumb to extinction: the Whooping Crane, *Grus americana*, and Bald Eagle, *Haliaeetus leucocephalus*, gave us insight into the environmental problems we have created and led us to rethink our way of interacting with this planet.

The trend in ornithology has been to incite the general public to greater understanding and involvement. This impetus is likely to continue as accurate census and distribution of birds in geographic areas come to depend more and more on participation by the birdwatcher. Birds will continue to contribute to our understanding of our environment. Our ability to assess stresses that a habitat undergoes will come in part from changed populations among critical species. This knowledge matters particularly in developing nations, where extent of habitat use may be indicated by well-being of the birds that live there.

THE BIRDS

Knowing that we cannot understand an organism or group of organisms in isolation, we open our study of the birds by examining their relationship to other creatures that inhabit earth. Birds are organisms that consume food; we therefore classify them among other consumers in the Kingdom Animalia. This kingdom is further subdivided into different phyla, each phylum of which includes animals that share specific basic characteristics. We place all organisms with external skeletons in the phylum Arthropoda, and all segmented worms among the Annelida; some twenty-seven phyla make up the animal kingdom. The group that interests us here is made up of animals with spinal cords and backbones, phylum Chordata, subphylum Vertebrata. In this subphylum are seven major groups, or classes: the fish (composed of three classes, sometimes grouped in the superclass Pisces), the amphibians—class Amphibia, the reptiles—class Reptilia, the birds—class Aves, and the mammals—class Mammalia. Fossil evidence tells us that the fish evolved first some 450 million years ago. Amphibians, evolving from fish, were able to exploit the land but needed to return to water to breed. Reptiles evolved from amphibians and became fully terrestrial. Both birds and mammals came from reptiles. Each group has characteristics that distinguish it from the others. The birds' exclusive characteristic is feathers. They are egg layers like fish, amphibians, and reptiles, and warm-blooded like mammals, but the feather sets them apart.

If we compare these vertebrate groups, we discover that fish have succeeded best, as judged by survival and adaptation, achieving a worldwide distribution of more than 20,000 species. Because of their limited ability to control their body temperature, amphibians and reptiles are most common in the tropical regions of the world, where they are represented by 3,000 and 6,000 species respectively. About 4,100 species of mammals are distributed throughout the world and some 8,700 species of birds. By this measure we must consider birds as the most successful group of terrestrial vertebrates.

Judging by distribution, we find that birds are the most far-flung among the vertebrates, for they inhabit every part of the earth—from isolated oceanic islands to overcrowded urban areas. They have been sighted at the South Pole, observed from the lofty heights of the Himalayan Mountains; they are not uncommon on the open ocean and are present in the driest desert. In short, they are the commonest and most easily observable organism in almost any environment.

Looking within the class Aves, we see that birds range in length from the 2.5-meter Ostrich, *Struthio camelus*, to the .065-meter hummingbird. The heaviest birds are flightless, the Ostrich weighing some 150 kilograms (the extinct elephant birds of Madagascar weighed up to 450 kilograms). Among flying birds, about 15 kilograms seems to be the upper weight limit of the largest species of swans, pelicans, and vultures. At about .0025 kilogram, the smallest species of hummingbirds are the lightest birds. The longest wingspans support the Wandering Albatross, *Diomeda exulans*, at 3.5 meters, the New World Condors at 3 meters, and possibly the Marabou Stork, *Leptoptilus crumeniferus*, at 3.5 meters. The long-extinct condor, *Teratornis incredibilis*, had an estimated wingspan of some 5 meters. As a group birds are the fastest creatures on earth. The Spinetail Swift, *Hirundapus caudacutus*, has been timed in level flight at more than 170 kilometers per hour. The Peregrine Falcon, *Falco peregrinus*, which relies on its

The Ostrich, at 2.5 meters tall, is the largest bird, while the hummingbird, at 65 centimeters, is the smallest.

speed to overtake its prey, has been observed in a dive at well over 250 kilometers per hour. Others, like shorebirds that travel long distances to and from their breeding grounds, cut the travel time by flying regularly in excess of 100 kilometers per hour. And these speeds can be sustained for long periods. Racing pigeons can move at 90 kilometers an hour for twelve to fifteen hours at a time, for an elapsed distance of some 1,000 to 1,400 kilometers a day. This ability makes birds not only the fastest of creatures but the most traveled as well.

The Arctic Tern, *Sterna paradisaea*, probably logs more kilometers than any other species. Breeding close to the Arctic Circle, they spend their winter in the high latitudes of the Antarctic Ocean, only to return in the spring to the Arctic, a round trip of at least 33,000 kilometers in a year. Many small birds make nonstop flights over bodies of water ranging from 700 to 2,000 kilometers in length in less than three days. As for altitude, many birds never venture much above the treetops. But during migration birds commonly fly at up to 1,500 meters; on more than one occasion flocks have been observed by radar as high as 6,500 meters. Birds in the Himalayas have been seen at 8,700 meters, and in an incredible accident a Ruppell's Griffon, *Gyps ruppelli* (a type of vulture), collided with a jet plane at more than 11,000 meters in altitude (Laybourne, 1974). A number of species that have adapted to life in water have mastered their environment. The Gentoo Penguin, *Pygoscelis papua*, reaches swimming speeds of up to thirty-six kilometers per hour (Murphy, 1936); loons and penguins can remain underwater for fifteen to eighteen minutes; and loons and ducks can achieve diving depths of sixty meters—the Emperor Penguin, *Aptenodytes forsteri*, an amazing 265 meters (Kooyman et al, 1971).

Life spans of birds in the wild vary predictably with size. Small birds like hummingbirds and wrens rarely live more than five years, and larger songbirds like robins and jays live from ten to twenty years. Gulls live up to thirty years, a few species reaching a maximum age of forty years. We have numerous records of captive birds living much longer—a number of species of hawks and owls live into their fifties and sixties, and cockatoos survive for more than one hundred years. It is interesting to observe these oldsters in captivity, for their feathers become sparse, their colors dull, and their behavior subdued, all alterations never observed in the wild, for the environment makes swift work of those that are slow to react to its vagaries.

Although we find 8,700 types of birds in almost every conceivable size, shape, and color, their general body makeup is remarkably consistent. Mammals range in size and shape from the enormous whale to the flying bat, and reptiles from four-legged to varieties with no legs at all, but all birds show strong similarities. Any child who has learned to group objects with similar characteristics would put most, perhaps all birds together in one group. For all birds possess feathers, have forelimbs modified to wings, and walk on their hindlimbs. Their teeth have been replaced by two horny bills, and all lay eggs; their internal anatomy shows shared characteristics. All have similar skeletons and large, powerful four-chambered hearts, and all are warm-blooded. Birds' very efficient respiratory systems are totally different in structure from those of reptiles or mammals, and most birds have excellent vision and hearing.

The class Aves, then, consists of a large group of terrestrial vertebrates that at first glance seem diverse, but on closer inspection they show many similarities. Our study of birds begins by examining the differences and similarities between birds as we apply systematics, or the science of classification. I hope that you will come to appreciate that systematics is much more than assigning a species to a group and giving it a name that is impossible to pronounce; it is also an orderly method for studying a group of organisms that reveals something about the evolutionary history of the animals we call birds.

CLASSIFICATION AND EVOLUTION

Science is a human invention that helps in our quest to understand nature. Nature is so large and at times chaotic that it seems to defy understanding. Its phenomena range from the big bang of ultimate creation and unimaginable effects of warped space to microscopic mitochondria and chemical energy of adenosine triphosphate. Science, though, has looked for and found indications of order. Great minds like those of Aristotle, Galileo, Newton, Mendel, Linnaeus, Darwin, and Einstein have seen order in the seemingly infinite diversity and have shown us the underlying principles and forces that shape our universe and all within it.

So too have we looked among living forms for order, and, failing that, we have imposed the order we wanted. Through the ages, we have grouped animals and plants in almost every conceivable way: where they lived, their number of appendages, and whether or not they were useful to us. Not until 1758 did the Swedish naturalist Carl von Linné devise a system of classification that began to uncover a meaningful order in the apparently limitless diversity of life. Linné assumed that there were ideal species, to which he assigned two Latin or Latinized names, the first being the genus, the second the species. He could now assign to the organism a unique name that would be understood by speakers of all languages. This method of referring to a species by two names is called binominal nomenclature. Through the years, Linné's own name was transformed by his own system to the Latinate Carolus Linnaeus. The Linnaean System of Classification compares similar species to the ideal. If the species share many characteristics they are grouped in the same genera but given a different species name. The familiar Song Sparrow, for example, is named *Melospiza melodia*, but the very similar Swamp Sparrow is *Melospiza georgiana*. Not only are they two species but, because they share the same genus name, they are also similar species. Comparing the Song Sparrow to the White-throated Sparrow, *Zonotrichia albicollis*, differences are sufficient to grant the latter bird its own genus, in this case *Zonotrichia*. But the Song Sparrow and White-throated Sparrow are closer in form than the Song Sparrow and the Herring Gull, *Larus argentatus*. To show the degree of similarity above the genus level, the classification system groups all sparrows in the family Fringillidae (which includes grosbeaks, finches, and buntings, as well as sparrows), and all gulls in the family Laridae. The names of families always end in *-idae*. The 170 families of birds include almost 2,000 genera. Families are further grouped into a more inclusive category: *order*. The family Fringillidae is in the order Passeriformes, which is a very large division that includes sixty-three families, all considered perching birds, whereas the family Laridae is included in the order Charadriiformes, which includes ten families of shorebirds. The characteristic ending of all names of orders is *-iformes*. All orders of birds are gathered in the class Aves.

This system of classification is more than two hundred years old and has been modified somewhat over that time. Many species, particularly those occupying a large range, show variation in form through that range. Where this variation occurs the species is further divided into subspecies and given a third name. The Eastern Song Sparrow, which breeds away from the coast, from eastern Canada to Maryland, is not as gray as the Atlantic Song Sparrow that is found along the coast. Here the Eastern Song Sparrow, being the first described, is considered the type specimen and is given the name *Melospiza melodia melodia;* and the Atlantic Song Sparrow becomes *Melospiza melodia atlantica.* Another modification adds categories to the system: divisions such as subclass, superorder, suborder, superfamily, subfamily, and subgenus show closer degrees of relatedness between groups.

The original Linnaean system of classification assumed not only that some species were ideal but also that the number of species in the world was unchanging, a belief that was prevalent in the 1700s. We now know that the number of species is in constant flux, that some are being formed and some are becoming extinct. It is more than a coincidence, though, that the system of classification that Linnaeus set down shows the evolutionary history of life, but its originator never knew that evolution was at work.

EVOLUTION

If nature has a theme, it is change. All matter created at the first moment in time is still with us today, but its form is now very different. This relentless change in the form of matter is called evolution. Swirling gaseous clouds condense to stars as smaller bits of matter are caught in gravitational fields around these giants and held during the star's lifetime. The star, converting matter to different forms and releasing energy at fantastic rates, eventually fades, its fuel spent. The lifespan of this sun and its system of orbital bodies is in billions of years, during which matter can assume very complex forms.

Of the nine planets that orbit the sun in our solar system, only the third planet, Earth, absorbs enough solar energy to promote significant modifications of matter. Liquid water allowed carbon-rich chemicals to accumulate, accelerating chemical evolution. Chemical reactions in this primordial soup produced ever more complex forms. These chemicals also grew more and more complex, climaxing in compounds that by making copies of themselves could begin to control their own destiny. Like all matter before, these living forms were subjected to change as they multiplied and diversified. So greatly did later products of this organic evolution differ from their original ancestor that the kinship between them was difficult to see.

Scientists in the 1700s maintained that the universe and all within were produced by special creation, and that human beings were most special of all. But an evolution in thought was beginning to change our sense of time and place in the universe.

Geological scientists began to document how natural processes could account for the changes observed in land forms. Their calculations suggested that earth was much older than anyone had imagined, providing a long enough time to allow for these changes. As the nineteenth century began, science had accepted the evolving earth, explained by volcanoes, earthquakes, and erosion. Organic evolution was more difficult to explain and accept. Fragments of ancient life forms were known, but did not by themselves suggest kinship among living things; those who did believe in evolution could not adequately explain how the changes in life took place.

With this historical background, HMS *Beagle* left England in 1831 on a worldwide scientific expedition. On board was a twenty-two-year-old naturalist, Charles Darwin. Although familiar with ideas about evolution and geology, Darwin began the voyage accepting special creation as the source of life. During the five-year expedition, this keen and systemic observer of nature had a unique opportunity to see how diverse the forms of life on this planet could be.

Darwin's most significant observations were from the thirteen small Galápagos Islands. Lying on the equator in the East Pacific Ocean, a thousand kilometers from South America, they are geologically young, hot, and dry, and inhabited by curiously assorted plants and animals. The whole place inspires one question: How did this come to be? The islands themselves are remains of volcanoes that rose from the sea floor between one and four million years ago, the evidence being that they still show black basaltic lava.

But how did the plants and animals come to live there? The only answer is: by accident. Insects and birds were blown by the wind, seeds were washed up by ocean currents, and land animals were carried on driftwood rafts from the mainland. If these were some of Darwin's answers, further examining the life forms brought only more questions. The giant land tortoises that inhabit the islands (their Spanish name is Galápagos) had long been used for fresh meat by sailors. The governor told Darwin that the tortoises' shells were distinctively shaped on each island or region on an island. Could successive accidents have brought land tortoises to these lonely islands, stranding a slightly different tortoise on each island?

Fourteen species of small finches on the islands were all closely related but lived nowhere else in the world. Again, could fourteen flocks have been blown off course, having no choice but to make these islands their home? If so, what was the probability that all the immigrants would be finches? Darwin was forced to interpret his observations in the most probable way, that the land tortoises were descended from one stranding, and that the different types he observed were related to that original group. The finches probably were from one flock blown off course from the mainland, the progenitor of the fourteen species that were there when Darwin arrived.

For this very cautious man these answers were unsettling. If these life forms

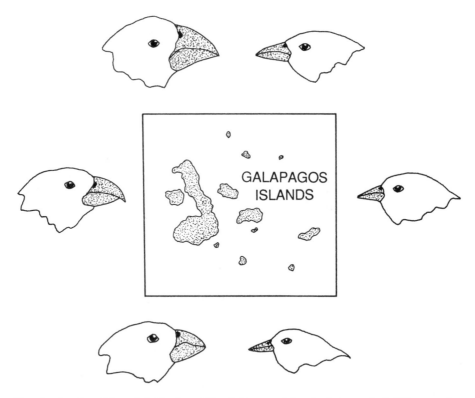

The closely related Darwin's Finches of the Galapagos Islands show marked differences in the size and shape of their beaks.

did represent evolution, then what was the mechanism for change? Not until twenty years after returning to England was Darwin sure enough in his explanation to venture a hypothesis, probably the greatest statement in biology: the theory of natural selection.

During those twenty years back in England, Darwin became interested in domestic breeding of plants and animals. He was impressed by the diverse forms a breeder could bring about in relatively few generations. By selecting offspring with desired characteristics and cross-breeding them, breeders would get larger, stronger stock, or descendants showier or more colorful than their ancestors. Did nature thus select offspring with characteristics that better equipped them to survive in their environment? And if the environment changed, would nature alter the choices, giving rise to a new form of the species? After studying twenty years, Darwin said yes.

Darwin presented *On the Origin of Species* in 1859 as a statement of logical ideas supported by observation. All organisms have enormous potential to reproduce, but any environment can accommodate only a fixed number of individuals of a species. Therefore competition arises among members of a species, in any species there is variety. The individuals that survive the competition and breed are the fittest or best adapted to the environment, and these adaptations are handed down from generation to generation. Over long periods, these inherited characteristics can change the species. This was a remarkable statement, especially in the mid-1800s, when nothing was known of chromosomes, genes, or DNA and genetics was yet to be established. A universal statement, it makes all creatures related. Darwin, son of a minister, has been described as everything from an ape to a God-killer, but he saw natural selection as the Creator's subtle but powerful tool.

Appropriately, the fourteen Galápagos finch species that have come to bear Darwin's name are a good example of how species form. The founding species must have arrived on the islands some time after plants came, possibly being blown off their migratory route. Ships on the open ocean are often swamped by flocks of land birds during migratory periods. The original arrivals found food and very little competition. As the colony grew, some group or groups spread to other habitats or islands and in time became isolated from the original colony. These isolated breeding populations might be subjected to quite different environmental pressures, such as different sources of food. In an arid region these seed-eating birds might have to contend with larger and harder seeds than in a habitat with more rainfall. Here offspring with larger, more powerful beaks would be favored by natural selection. Also, the breeding season is usually coincidental with maximum availability of food. These groups might have begun to look for different environmental signals to initiate the breeding season. After successive generations of being isolated, they would differ enough in appearance and behavior that they would no longer recognize each other as potential mates; a new species was formed.

This radiation of species from an original group was possible because the islands harbored no competitive species. Some finch populations then began to fill the roles or niches that other species occupied on the mainland, including insect eaters and one distinctly warblerlike variety. Two species filled the woodpecker niche by searching for insect grubs in rotting wood. The Woodpecker Finch, *Camarhynchus pallidus*, does not have the woodpecker's chisel-shaped bill or long tongue, but breaks off cactus spines or twigs of trees to probe for grubs in tree holes. No warbler or woodpecker finch had ever evolved on the mainland because warblers and woodpeckers already occupied these niches.

How long does it take for species to form? Here, fourteen new species arose in less than one million years. From some observations it seems that natural selection may work more rapidly than originally thought. During a very dry period one of Darwin's finches, the Medium Ground Finch, *Geospiza fortis*, increased bill size and thickness during the three-year study in response to exceptionally hard seeds (Boag and Grant, 1981). Gould and Eldridge (1977) hypothesized that evolution might work quickly during rapid environmental change and then level off for long periods. They call these spurts punctuated equilibria, basing the theory on absence of fossils of many transitional species or missing links they would expect to find if evolution was slow and steady.

Evolution by means of natural selection is a major statement with religious and philosophical implications that alter our way of seeing humanity and the universe. The theory gives meaning and unity to many areas of biology and has refined systemics.

CLASSIFICATION REFLECTS EVOLUTION

The Linnaean system of classification does not explain why the world has 300 species of pigeonlike birds. It grouped them in the family Columbiformes simply because they were alike. The understanding brought by evolution gave life to classification. The 300 species of pigeons and doves form a true family because they have a common ancestor. A subspecies can now be seen as a possible step toward formation of a species. If two subspecies remain geographically isolated long enough, different selection pressures may eventually make them sufficiently different to inhibit interbreeding. You can see good examples in any field guide. In the warbler family, the Black-throated Green Warbler, *Dendroica virens,* in the eastern states is very similar to the Townsend's Warbler, *Dendroica townsendi,* which breeds west of the Rocky Mountains. An interesting speculation is that some time ago they were subspecies, but through isolation they developed into separate species. This type of species formation is divergent evolution.

Natural selection can also mold unrelated species until they look remarkably similar, a process named convergent evolution. Diving ducks and loons have webbed feet and the same general body shape because both have had to adapt to similar selection pressures, not because they are closely related. Convergent evolution, then, occurs when originally dissimilar organisms independently adapt to similar environments.

Organisms need not look alike to be closely related, but they must have structures showing common ancestry that are called homologies. The hair on a bat and birds' feathers keep the organisms warm, but they are not homologous structures. Hair and feathers are both produced by convergent evolutionary pressure to maintain a constant internal temperature and therefore are considered merely analogous. Diving petrels in the southern oceans are very similar in size, color, and behavior to auklets in the North Pacific, but the petrels have a tube covering the upper mandible that is homologous with the other tube noses—shearwaters and albatrosses. The diving petrels are thus more closely related to these birds many times their size than to species that seem very similar. Homologous structures can change during evolution, but their presence is the key to classification as determined by evolution.

Our modern classification system is based on the number of homologous structures shared by two species. The more homologous features they have, the more closely related the two species are. But how does a systematist know whether structures are homologous or analogous? Only by observing in detail external and internal structures of many organisms can the determination be made. In birds, such key features are number and arrangement of feathers, foot structure, and embryonic development, as well as fossil evidence. Biochemical techniques are beginning to make this determination more accurate, especially analysis of blood proteins, which shows degree of relatedness between species and families. Another new technique is DNA-hybridization, analyzing arrangement of genes on chromosomes; this may be the ultimate method in arranging the avian tree.

The Wandering Albatross (flying) and the Common Diving Petrel (left), although very different in size and shape, are related species. Cassin's Auklet (right) and the Common Diving Petrel, while not closely related, are similar in size and shape because they inhabit the same type of environment.

With this knowledge of evolution and classification, we now begin our study of those organisms that share the same homologous structure, feathers.

ARCHAEOPTERYX

Eon by eon, the planet's natural history is etched on its surface, only to be covered, often obliterated by successive chapters. The story, revealed in great canyons and rift valleys that split the book down the middle, reveals a word here and a sentence there, often out of context, its meaning scrambled. Because we need to understand our origin and place in nature, we have kept looking for clues, continually rewriting the script. In many ways we have gained an impressive fund of knowledge. This planet, which seems so stable and unchanging, has a history of change. Bathed in tropical lushness, frozen in arctic ice, filled with hordes of strange creatures, its continents have formed and moved as shallow sea beds were lifted to mountaintops.

The birds' evolutionary story too has been written on the face of the earth, but this story is more fragmented than most because relatively few avian fossils have been found. The same features that made birds the premier fliers also made them poor subjects for preservation. Because they are light, they float and are seldom buried and fossilized in rock formations, their delicate skeletons

An artist's rendition of the lizardlike bird Archaeopteryx

decomposing quickly. For now the story of birds begins with a remarkable fossil find called *Archaeopteryx*. It is a true transitional species between reptiles and birds. Found first in 1861 embedded in a Bavarian limestone quarry, this crow-sized bird lived 160 million years ago during the Jurassic period. It was a contemporary of the large dinosaurs and the primitive egg-laying mammals. In fact the fossil probably would have been classified as a small dinosaur if not for the well-defined imprints left by feathers surrounding the creature's tail and fore-limbs, for it had a reptilian jaw and teeth, a long bony tail, three clawed fingers, and walked on its hind legs. It had opposable toes for perching in trees, probably climbed using its clawed fingers and, if it could not fly, at least it could glide on the large surface area the feathered wings provided.

Archaeopteryx leaves little doubt that birds evolved from a group of small dinosaurs and that the feathers derived from the reptilian scale. But, if the fossil answers some questions, it poses many more. What were the immediate ancestors of *Archaeopteryx*? Did the feather evolve primarily for flight or for warmth? And was *Archaeopteryx* alone in those ancient treetops and therefore the original ancestor of all birds? Answers to these questions lie hidden in fossils yet to be unearthed.

For the next twenty million years nothing is known of avian evolution. But fossil finds dating from 140 million years ago in the Cretaceous period indicate that birds had spread and diversified. Fossils of six species of gull-like birds in the genus *Ichthyornis* have been unearthed in North America. These birds are the first species we know of that could truly fly. They were very modern in appearance, except that they retained reptilian teeth. Another species from this period was the large, flightless, loonlike *Hesperornis*. Nearly two meters long, it had wings reduced in size, webbed feet, and teeth. Along with these species, fragments of eighteen other species have been found from this period, some ancestral to families we know today.

When dinosaurs became extinct at the end of the Cretaceous, a major period in birds' evolution began. Many large, flightless, and predatory species evolved, probably filling the niches left vacant by the large dinosaurs. By now the reptilian jaw was replaced by the avian beak and many modern families were arising. Some thirteen million years ago, in the Pliocene, diversification among birds was at its peak. Natural selection produced spectacular forms: giant condors with 5-meter wingspans, penguins the size of a man, petrel-like seabirds with 4.5-meter wings, and giant elephant birds that weighed up to 450 kilograms and laid eggs with a volume of seven liters.

As the Ice Ages began the number of species declined, songbirds became the dominant group, and by the beginning of the recent epoch, 11,000 years ago, all modern species were established. We know about 1,700 species from fossils; of these, 900 are extinct forms. Adding these to the 8,700 species alive today gives us a cast of 9,600 characters in the 160-million-year-old story of birds. But most authorities agree that the cast was much larger; Brodkorb (1960) estimates that more than 1.5 million species of birds will eventually join the list.

A WORLD OF BIRDS

In classifying birds we attempt to show not only relationships among species but also their place in evolutionary time. Therefore species are listed in sequence from the most ancient to the most recently evolved. Because of the great gaps in the avian evolutionary record, authorities present orders and families in different sequences. Most agree that the order Passeriformes is the most recently evolved group, but the arrangement of families is still open to question. The American Ornithologists' Union (A.O.U.) places the family Fringillidae last because they see the birds' reduced numbers of primary feathers as a product of recent evolution, whereas European ornithologists place the family Corvidae at the end because they consider these birds the most intelligent and therefore the most recently evolved. With these problems in mind, we briefly survey the orders of living birds, using the 1983 A.O.U. checklist for North American birds and Perrins and Middleton (1985) for birds outside North America.

CLASS **AVES**

Order **Struthioniformes**—Ostriches

These largest living birds, inhabiting the arid and savanna regions in Africa, have four distinct subspecies.

Order **Rheiformes**—Rheas

Rheas are large flightless birds that live in South American scrublands and grass-lands. Each of the two species is in its own genus.

Order **Casuariiformes**—Emus and Cassowaries

The Emu, *Dromaius novaehollandiae,* is a large flightless bird in open areas of Australia; the one species is in the family Dromiceidae. Cassowaries inhabit forested regions in northern Australia and New Guinea. They are flightless birds with highly colored necks and bony structures on their heads. The three species are in one genus, family Casuariidae.

Order **Apterygiformes**—Kiwis

Found only in New Zealand, kiwis are small flightless birds with only vestigial wings. They live in brushy habitats and are nocturnal. The three species are all in the same genus.

These first four orders, all flightless and ancient, have a flat sternum. Because of this feature they were once grouped in the family Ratidae; these species are not now considered closely related, but they are still collectively called ratites.

Order **Tinamiformes**—Tinamous

Tinamous live in Central and South American forests and grasslands. The one family, nine genera, and forty-six species are ground birds and weak fliers.

Order **Sphenisciformes**—Penguins

The familiar penguins inhabit the colder oceans in the Southern Hemisphere, though one species breeds at the equator on the Galápagos Islands. All are flightless, but "fly" underwater searching for fish, crustaceans, and squid. The sixteen separate species are in nine genera, all in the family Spheniscidae.

Order **Gaviiformes**—Loons

The aquatic loons breed in the colder regions in the Northern Hemisphere. Their webbed feet, set well back on the body, make them swift swimmers and divers, but very clumsy on land. The four species are grouped in the same genus. All are highly migratory and all occur in North America.

Order **Podicipediformes**—Grebes

Grebes are similar to loons in appearance and in their aquatic lifestyle. They are worldwide in distribution. Many species have elaborate feathering on the head. Of the twenty-six species in six genera in the family Podicipedidae, six species occur in North America.

Order **Procellariiformes**—Albatrosses, Shearwaters, and Petrels

All these birds of the open ocean are decidedly wary of land. They range in size from the 3.5-meter wingspan of the albatross to the diving petrel with a .3-meter wingspan. All have tubular external nostrils, and are collectively called tube noses. Among the four families, twenty-three genera, and ninety-two species are twenty-two species that are found off the North American coast at different times of year.

Order **Pelecaniformes**—Pelicans and Allies

The birds in the diverse group of six families that includes pelicans, gannets, trop-icbirds, cormorants, frigatebirds, and anhingas are all aquatic, many of them oceanic, living mainly on fish. Most species are confined to tropical and sub-tropical regions, with only the cormorants and gannets regularly breeding in the temperate zones. Of the fifty-two species in seven genera, seventeen species occur in North America.

Order **Anseriformes**—Swans, Ducks, and Geese

The Anseriformes are divided into two families, Anatidae and Anhimidae. Anhimidae is a small group of three South American species referred to as screamers. Anatidae, a very large family of 149 species in forty-one genera, includes swans, ducks, and geese. They are mostly aquatic birds with webbed feet, and are distributed worldwide, fifty-five of the species occurring in North America.

Order **Falconiformes**—Vultures, Hawks, and Falcons

These birds of prey are divided into four families: New World vultures, the Secretary Bird, *Sagittarius serpentarius*, falcons, and accipiters. Seven species of New World vultures occur in North and South America. One species of Secretary Bird occurs in Africa. Falconidae is the family of caracaras and falcons. Caracaras are reptile- and carrion-eating birds in the Western Hemisphere, with nine species, and falcons are strong, fast fliers that eat birds, mammals, and insects, with thirty-seven species in one genus. The family Accipitridae is a diverse group of 217 species in sixty-four genera and includes kites, hawks, harriers, eagles, Old World vultures, and Osprey, *Pandion haliaetus*. Falconiformes have worldwide distribution, thirty-four species of this order occurring in North America.

Order **Galliformes**—Game Birds

The large Galliformes group of 263 species in seventy-five genera and six families is adapted to life on the ground. The largest family is Phasianidae, including 183 species of pheasant and quail. Living mostly on seeds, these birds are generally nonmigratory. Twenty-two species occur in North America.

Order **Ciconiiformes**—Herons, Bitterns, Storks, and Ibises

Most of the long-legged, wading Ciconiiformes have long necks and pointed or down-curved beaks. The 114 species in forty-five genera and six families are distributed worldwide, and species that breed in the temperate zones are migratory. Many species are aquatic and eat fish, amphibians, and insects. Seventeen species occur in North America.

Order **Phoenicopteriformes**—Flamingos

The large, familiar pink flamingos with extremely long necks and legs are included by some in the preceding order. All nest near shallow water, some at high altitude, and they feed by straining the water for small marine life. Flamingos feed their young on crop milk. Of the four species in three genera, one species occurs occasionally in North America.

Order **Gruiformes**—Cranes and Allies

In many ways the Gruiformes is an order of misfits that range dramatically in size and form from the graceful crane to the drab rail and button quail. These birds are in a very ancient group that has brought species diversification to the extreme. Of the 190 species in sixty-six genera and twelve families, thirteen species occur in North America.

Order **Charadriiformes**—Shorebirds, Gulls, and Alcids

The large and diverse Charadriiformes are divided into three suborders: Charadrii, including twelve families of waders and sandpipers, plovers, avocets, and oystercatchers, all highly migratory. The suborder Lari has four families of gulls, terns, skimmers, and skuas, all webfooted and strong flyers. Suborder Alcae consists of one family of auks, Alcidae, the Northern Hemisphere counterpart of the penguins in the southern oceans. In North America, 137 species of this order occur.

Order **Pteroclidiformes**—Sandgrouse

This order consists of a small group of sixteen species in two genera that superficially resemble doves. They inhabit arid regions in the Old World. Males of these species bring water to their chicks by soaking their belly feathers at a watering hole.

Order **Columbiformes**—Pigeons and Doves

This familiar order of birds has 300 species in forty-two genera of one family. Their distribution is worldwide, but they are absent at the higher latitudes. Along with flamingos, they are the only birds that feed their young with milk secreted in their crop. Twelve species occur in North America.

Order **Psittaciformes**—Parrots, Lorries, and Cockatoos

Only one of the 328 species in this order has occurred in North America, the now-extinct Carolina Parakeet, *Conuropsis carolinensis*. As a group these birds occur in the tropics and Southern Hemisphere. All have hooked beaks, two toes facing forward and two backward, and most are brightly colored. They are fruit and seed eaters. Many have been artificially introduced into North America.

Order **Cuculiformes**—Cuckoos, Turacos, and Hoatzin

The largest of the three families in this order are the Cuculidae, the cuckoos, with 127 species in twenty-eight genera. The most notable feature in forty-five members of this family is that instead of making a nest or caring for young, the female lays her eggs in other birds' nests. In this family is the roadrunner of the North American deserts and the anis. The family Musophagidae, the turacos, have twenty-two African species; Opistocomidae, the Hoatzin, *Opisthocomus hoazin,* is the one species in this South American family. Only five species of this order are found in North America.

Order **Strigiformes**—Owls

These worldwide nocturnal predators are represented by 133 species in twenty-four genera and two families. The family Tytonidae includes ten species of barn and bay owls, and Strigidae, the typical owls, includes 123 species in twenty-two genera. All share many characteristics, such as large head, forward-facing eyes, and two toes directed forward and two to the rear. In North America nineteen species of owl occur.

Order **Caprimulgiformes**—Nightjars and Frogmouths

A nocturnal group of mostly insect eaters with very large mouths. Most of the ninety-eight species are confined to the tropics. Of the five families, only one, Caprimulgidae, is represented in North America by seven species, including the familiar nighthawk and poor-will.

Order **Apodiformes**—Swifts and Hummingbirds

This order of small-footed, fast-flying birds is divided into two suborders: Apodii, the swifts, and Trochili, the hummingbirds. Swifts are a group of birds that catch insects on the wing. They are strong fliers and many species are highly migratory; all secrete a sticky fluid from their salivary glands, with which they glue their nests together. Among the seventy-four species in ten genera, four species occur in North America. Hummingbirds all inhabit the New World and are concentrated in tropical South America. These smallest of birds live on nectar, small insects, and spiders. Many species are brilliantly colored. The 315 species of hummingbirds are in 112 genera, sixteen species occurring in North America.

Order **Coliiformes**—Mousebirds

Mousebirds are represented by six African species, all gregarious. The small brown and gray birds have a distinguishing arrangement of toes, the first and fourth being very mobile and directed backward.

Order **Trogoniformes**—Trogons

In this tropical group of brilliantly colored birds the males are more brightly colored than the females. They have short, stout beaks and eat mainly fruit, but
supplement their diet with insects, frogs, and lizards. Most species nest in tree
cavities. The thirty-seven species are in seven genera, with one species in North
America.

Order **Coraciiformes**—Kingfishers and Allies

The ten families in this order are oddly assorted: all have strong, prominent beaks
and the third and fourth toe is jointed at the base. The kingfisher family,
Alcedinidae, is probably the most familiar group, with eighty-six species in fourteen genera, of which three species are found in North America. The other families are tropical and include todies, motmots, bee-eaters, rollers, hoopoes, and
hornbills.

Order **Piciformes**—Woodpeckers and Allies

This group of birds is defined by highly specialized beaks and arrangement of toes
(typically two in front and two facing backward). Of the six families, only
Picidea, the woodpeckers, are found in North America. Some 200 species of
woodpecker are in twenty-eight genera, of which twenty-one species occur
north of Mexico. The other families include jacamars, puffbirds, barbets, honeyguides, and toucans.

Order **Passeriformes**—Perching Birds

These most recently evolved birds are by far the most diverse group, with more
than 5,000 species. All have toes adapted for perching in trees, with three toes in
front and one behind. All have either nine or ten primary flight feathers and
usually twelve tail feathers. The young of all species are naked and helpless on
hatching. The four suborders and sixty-three families include more than 1,000
genera. The first three suborders are generally called subocines because of their
limited vocal ability. The suborder Oscines are perching birds with highly developed vocal ability, including the familiar backyard songbirds. North America
has 289 passerine species in twenty-four families.

Suggested Reading

The Encyclopedia of Birds, edited by Perrins and Middleton, is a complete survey
of the world's birds. Books such as *Hummingbirds,* by Skutch; *Life Histories of
North American Birds,* by Bent; *The Secret Islands,* by Russell; *Loon Magic,* by Klein;
Ocean Birds, by Lofgren; *The Owl Papers,* by Maslow; and *Hawks,* by Peterson are
more limited in scope, but they give a good deal of information about different
orders and families of birds. For the development of ornithology, see
Ornithology from Aristotle to the Present, by Stresemann. The best text on ornithol-

ogy I know is *The Life of Birds,* by Welty; other good texts are *Ornithology in Laboratory and Field,* by Pettingill, and *An Introduction to Ornithology,* by Wallace. Ideas on evolution seem to endlessly flow from Stephen J. Gould in his articles in *Natural History,* collected in *Ever Since Darwin, The Panda's Thumb,* and *The Flamingo's Smile.*

Projects

Start a notebook on the birds you see, assigning a page or two for each species on your list, and set out other sections for your feeder and for places where you go birding. In the species section, head the page with the bird's common name and also its scientific name and its family and order. These names may be unfamiliar, but the more you use them the easier they become; names may also reveal relationships you might not be aware of. Observations in these sections might include when and where you see a species; if it is migratory, its arrival and departure dates each year; numbers of males and females, adults, and immatures; behaviors; location of nests; and so on. Also include any questions that might occur to you about a species or a behavior, and later find the answer, or perhaps design observations so that you can answer it yourself.

For those of you with computer fever, field notes can be recorded on disks; database and spreadsheet are extremely helpful in managing large amounts of information. See *A Field Guide to Personal Computers for Bird Watchers and Other Naturalists,* by Mair.

- 2 -

Feathers

WHETHER THE FEATHER EVOLVED first as a form of insulation or as a means of locomotion has been debated for many years. Some authorities feel that birds evolved during a warm period in earth's history and would have benefited little from insulation; feathers, then, evolved for flight. Others argue that dinosaurs apparently had evolved ways of controlling their body temperature and that, because birds evolved from small dinosaurs, feathers were adaptations for further temperature control. *Archaeopteryx* gives little support to either hypothesis because its body was fully feathered and it had well-developed flight feathers. The question will be resolved only when our fossil history of birds predating *Archaeopteryx* is filled out.

Why feathers evolved is debatable, but this new structure certainly had potential. Feathers have higher insulating value than any other material known; they are light but strong enough to provide lift and are easily modified in form and color for protection and as a means of communication.

KINDS OF FEATHERS

Feathers are the bird's principal covering. They are protein outgrowths of cells that develop in skin follicles much as hair does. Early development of the feather is similar in many ways to that of the reptilian scale, and unfeathered parts of birds, such as legs and feet, are covered with scales. Like hair or scales, feathers arise from dermal layers beneath the skin's surface, and as the cells proliferate they erupt on the surface. Instead of flattening like a scale, however, they produce a cone-shaped sheath that enfolds a tightly rolled feather. When the sheath splits, the feather unfurls, displaying its structure. The blood supply to

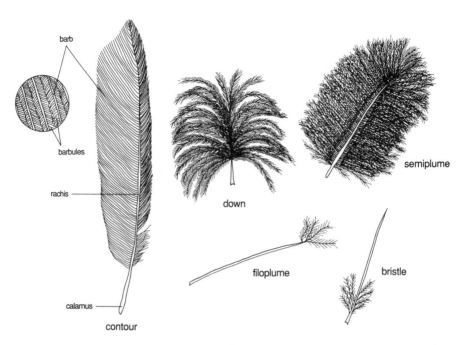

barb

barbules

rachis

calamus

contour

down

filoplume

semiplume

bristle

Different types of feathers are found on different birds. The circle at the left represents a magnified view of the surface of a contour feather, wherein interlocking barbules make up the fabric of the vane.

this external structure is then cut off, but the feather remains embedded within the skin as a dead product of the cells that formed it.

The sequence is essentially the same for all the types of feathers birds produce. For birds not only have an external covering, the *contour feathers,* but most species also have an internal layer of *down feathers,* along with other types, the *semiplume* and the *powder down.* Aside from these, most birds have seemingly incomplete types of feathers, the *filoplumes* and *bristles.*

Most typical and in many ways most nearly complete is the contour feather. This is the structure that gives the bird its streamlined shape; it includes flight feathers of wing and tail. The contour feather, constructed around a central shaft, has a vane on each side. The shaft is hollow, air-filled, and flexible, but stiff. The section of the shaft to which the vane is attached is the *rachis;* below the rachis is the *calamus,* the portion of the feather that is embedded in the skin. The calamus is roughly oval in cross-section; the rachis is rectangular. Projecting off either side of the rachis are smaller structures, the *barbs,* which lie parallel to one another, with the longest barbs at the center of the rachis. Under the microscope we see that the barbs too project finer structures, the *barbules.* At the inner edge of the barb, barbules are folded to form teeth or spines, whereas barbules on the barb's outer edge project tiny hooks. Because the barbs run parallel to each other, the two types of barbules interlock, forming the surface of the vane. This surface, then, is composed of very tightly woven fine structures that can withstand much force before the interlocking members let go. When the barbs do separate, however, they can be "zip-locked" back together simply by moving the barbs parallel again, causing the barbules to hook back up. This can be done by running two fingers along the vane (the bird would use its bill). All contour feathers are about the same, though with minor modifications. The vanes of body feathers are more symmetrical and the shafts more flexible than those of the flight feathers, and the woodpecker's tail feathers have a very stiff rachis that helps support the bird on vertical surfaces. Owls achieve silent flight partly because they have no interlocking barbs along the edge of the flight feathers, so that the wing presents a very soft edge as it moves through the air.

Down feathers, found beneath the contour feathers, have a calamus but lack a rachis; instead, individual barbs branch from a short calamus, making them soft. The barbules, lacking hooks, do not form vanes but keep the down feather fluffy. Down gives superior insulation because it traps large volumes of air between barbs and barbules. This type of feather, abundant on waterfowl such as eider ducks, is absent altogether in woodpeckers. The young of many species are covered with down feathers.

Semiplume feathers are similar to down in that they occur beneath the contour feathers and lack hooked barbules. Unlike down feathers, however, they have a rachis, and the barbs are arranged in vanes. Semiplumes are abundant on waterfowl, usually along the sides of the abdomen, where they provide insulation and buoyancy.

Filoplumes and bristles are feathers mostly composed of a shaft and very few barbs. Filoplumes have barbs at the tip of the rachis and bristle feathers have barbs at their base; both are associated with the bird's sense of touch. Filoplumes are most abundant around flight feathers and have many tactile nerve endings in their follicles. When the flight feather moves it presses against the filoplumes, apparently stimulating the nerve endings in the follicles and making the bird aware of the feather's position. Bristles are very hairlike in appearance and apparently in function. They form eyelashes in some species and can also filter dust from the air entering the *nares* (nasal openings) of others. They are most familiar in the flycatching species, surrounding the beak as both the avian counterpart of whiskers and an insect-net.

Unlike other types of feathers, powder-down feathers grow continuously and are never molted. Instead, the barbs at the tip of the rachis disintegrate into a fine powder as the feather grows. This powder is scattered by preening and helps waterproof the plumage.

Although contour feathers cover most birds' entire body, only in ratites, penguins, screamers, and colies are these feathers evenly distributed over the surface of the skin. This even distribution is considered a primitive quality, for in most species feathers grow in tracks, generally laid down in rows with areas of naked skin between them. Muscles under the skin attach to the feather sockets, allowing the bird to increase the insulation supplied by the feathers by fluffing them. These muscles are also used to raise patches of feathers for display, as in the jay's crest.

The number of feathers a bird has varies with its size. Larger birds have more feathers than smaller ones, birds living in colder climates have more feathers in winter than summer, and aquatic species have more feathers than comparably large terrestrial ones. A Ruby-throated Hummingbird, *Archilochus colubis*, has more than 900 feathers, whereas a Song Sparrow, *Melospiza melodia*, has 2,000 and a Tundra Swan, *Cygnus columbianus*, 25,000. In winter, the White-throated Sparrow, *Zonotrichia albicollis*, has 2,500 feathers but in summer only about 1,500 (Wetmore, 1936). Comparing terrestrial to aquatic species, the Bald Eagle, *Haliaeetus leucocephalus*, has 7,182 feathers and is roughly half the weight of a Tundra Swan, which has more than three times that number. The Pied-billed Grebe, *Podilymbus podiceps*, is nearly three times the weight of a Mourning Dove, *Zenaida macroura*, but has almost five times as many feathers. Because smaller bodies lose heat more quickly than larger bodies, smaller birds are generally better insulated than larger ones. Ruby-throated Hummingbirds have about 300 feathers for every gram of body weight; the swan has only four per gram.

Although feathers are designed to be light, their sheer number adds substantially to the bird's weight. Feathers account for between 5 and 14 percent of the bird's weight. An eagle's contour feathers weighed 586 grams, or more than twice as much as the bird's skeleton (Brodkorb, 1955).

FEATHER MAINTENANCE

The bird has so many feathers—its principal means for keeping warm and dry as well as its primary equipment for movement—it is not surprising that birds spend a good deal of time keeping their plumage in good order.

When not eating, flying, or sleeping, birds attend to their feathers in a number of different ways, of which *preening* is the commonest. Birds preen by using beak or feet to arrange individual feathers, repair separated vanes, or remove dirt and parasites. Preening serves other functions as well. At the base of the tail in most species is the *uropygial gland*, which secretes an oil. While preening, birds squeeze this gland with the beak and spread the oil on their feathers, legs, and feet. The oil helps preserve and waterproof the plumage. When the gland is experimentally removed, the feathers deteriorate markedly. Ornithologists suspect that this oil also helps in species-recognition in some birds and may have nutritional value as well, for the oil, when exposed to the sunlight, produces an activated form of vitamin D, which is then absorbed through the skin and which may help to control avian rickets (Thomson, 1964). Most aquatic species have highly developed uropygial glands, although, curiously, cormorants have no gland and must air-dry their feathers, which become thoroughly soaked after being in the water; their characteristic wings-spread-out posture is required because of poorly waterproofed feathers.

All birds bathe in one way or another, most of them in water, where they dunk their heads, letting water roll down their backs while vigorously flapping the wings. A number of species, like swallows, merely splash at the surface of a body of water while in flight, and swifts bathe by flying in the rain. Water baths are generally followed by extended periods of preening. Many birds, particularly in arid regions, bathe in dust as others do in water. In the preening that follows, they remove any moisture or excess oil that has trapped the dust from the bath. Dust bathing may also be a way of flushing out feather parasites. Many species of birds actively sunbathe, fluffing up their feathers, often assuming bizarre postures to expose themselves to direct rays of the sun. This little-understood behavior is thought to help rid birds of parasites, or activate vitamin D.

Probably the most peculiar form of feather maintenance is *anting*. Birds such as jays either actively pick up ants with their beaks, crush them, and rub the ant's body fluid on their plumage or they passively squat on an anthill and allow ants to crawl through their feathers. Either behavior is thought to get rid of feather lice. In active anting, formic acid in the ants' body fluid kills lice, but in passive anting the insects rid the feathers of parasites in ways not understood.

Anting *remains a peculiar type of feather maintenance. Here a jay has picked up an ant and is about to place the latter on its feathers.*

More than 200 species of birds have been observed anting, but the behavior seems to be learned because it is not practiced by all members of a species (Potter, 1970).

MOLTS

Even with the best of care, feathers become worn and must be replaced. In molting, birds shed and replace feathers. All birds molt at least once a year. The large number of feathers to be removed takes much energy, generally confining it to a time of year when other demands on the bird are low. Late summer and early fall are the commonest times for species to replace their feathers, for the breeding season is ended, migration is yet to come, food is still abundant, and the bird can thus begin the winter season with a new feather coat.

Probably the simplest molting strategy is to replace all the feathers at once and get it over with, and the Adélie Penguin, *Pygoscelis adeliae,* does just that. After breeding season, the birds come ashore to spend three weeks in inactivity while molting all their feathers. During this time they lose nearly half their body weight (Penny, 1967). A number of other water birds adopt this strategy but less extremely. Geese, ducks, loons, and others all molt their flight feathers in one period, but this method of molting is not common for two reasons: first, during this flightless period birds are vulnerable to predation; and second, though large birds can afford to lose a good portion of their body weight, small birds cannot. The Adélie Penguin increases its body weight prior to molting and its Antarctic environment is relatively predator free. Ducks and geese are some-what protected on water and can continue to feed while flightless. But even here, some species of ducks and geese seek out predator-free habitats in the Arctic, and some fly long distances to ensure that this molt is done in safety. Loons migrate to their winter saltwater habitat before they begin their molt. During this four- to six-week flightless period, many brightly colored male ducks take on a camouflage coat of body feathers, their *eclipse plumage,* to further protect against predation.

Birds that are absolutely dependent on flight for protection and locomotion must adopt less drastic molting patterns, the most usual being gradual loss and replacement of contour feathers. The wing flight feathers are lost and replaced one or two at a time in a bilaterally symmetric pattern, and tail feathers are molted in pairs, generally the inner two first. By this method, birds can still fly, but the drawback is that this molt can last a long time. Most small birds take seven to eight weeks molting in this way, but some eagles and cranes take up to two years to completely replace contour feathers. Longer molting periods introduce much variability into the timing, both between and within species. There are numerous examples of species of the same genera molting at different times of the year. For example, the Dunlin, *Calidris alpina,* molts rapidly as the arctic summer wanes before migrating, whereas the Purple Sandpiper, *Calidris maritima,* molts in the temperate zone after migrating from the Arctic in old feathers. In the Peregrine Falcon, *Falco peregrinus,* the highly migratory northern populations interrupt their molt in order to migrate, but the southern populations, with more favorable post-breeding conditions, complete their molt on the breeding grounds by October. Among the Osprey, *Pandion haliaetus,* the female molts after egg laying, but the male, who does most feeding of the female and young, must wait to molt until the young are independent.

Two factors seem to determine whether or not a bird will molt more than once a year: first, if the bird's feathers are worn down quickly by abrasion; and second, if the species color and pattern differ during the breeding season. Abrasion in migratory flight by European warblers in the genus *Phylloscopus* apparently leads to a second molt, for sedentary species of this genus molt only once. In the Short-toed Lark, *Calandrella cinerea,* the European race molts only once, whereas the Asian race, inhabiting the abrasive, windblown deserts in central Asia, molts twice.

A number of species partially molt body feathers before the breeding season, invariably leaving the male with breeding plumage that is brighter, more distinctive than the winter plumage. Familiar examples are many species of New World warblers, tanagers, and shorebirds. Some species change their seasonal appearance without going through a molt. The Snow Bunting, *Plectrophenax nivalis*, has white breeding plumage that changes to a darker winter coat as the white-tipped contour feathers wear away, revealing the brown interior of the feather. The European Starling, *Sturnus vulgaris*, undergoes much the same change, as the white feather tips of its speckled winter coat wear away by spring to leave the glossy breeding plumage.

Most passerines become sexually active at either one or two years of age; this is when they adopt the adult plumage. Gulls take from two to four years, depending on the species, to reach adult plumage. Traditional names for molts were nuptial and winter: a postnuptial molt resulted in winter plumage and a prenuptial molt in nuptial plumage. But confusion was possible: the Wilson's Storm-Petrel, *Oceanites oceanicus*, breeds in the Southern Hemisphere and winters north of the equator, where it is summer. Traditionally, the bird would appear to be in its winter plumage in summertime. A problem too are birds that breed every two years but molt yearly. Here the postnuptial molt might not follow the breeding season.

To resolve such confusion, terminology proposed by Humphrey and Parks (1959) is gradually being accepted. In this system, *basic plumage* is the feather coat when only one plumage is worn by the species or the winter plumage when it has two feather coats. The late-summer molt is called *prebasic*. Some species have different plumage during the breeding season; this coat is the *alternate plumage*. The molt that precedes it is the *prealternate molt*. *Supplementary plumage* is the name applied to a third feather coat, such as the eclipse plumage of some male ducks. *Definitive plumage*, either basic or alternate, does not change appearance in successive molts; this is the adult plumage of the species. The Rose-breasted Grosbeak, *Pheucticus ludovicianus*, adopts a definitive plumage at two years of age, whereas the Herring Gull, *Larus argentatus*, does so only by its fourth year.

Molts and plumages proceed in consistent succession in a species, in that most birds begin their lives covered with natal down. The natal down is lost in the *postnatal molt*, which leads to the *juvenal plumage*, and this form is retained after the bird leaves the nest and until the first prebasic molt in late summer or early fall. The plumage the bird then acquires for winter is the *first basic plumage*. This first prebasic molt is rarely complete because it does not include the flight feathers. If the species does acquire plumage identical to the adult winter plumage, the feather coat is not referred to as the first basic plumage, but simply as the basic plumage, because it is definitive. The first basic plumage is the immature plumage for most species and is worn at least through the first winter. In species that molt before breeding, the first basic plumage is replaced by the alternate plumage in a prealternate molt. If the feather coat is distinguishable from the adult form, this molt is referred to as the *first prealternate*, and the plumage as the *first alternate*.

After the breeding season comes the *second prebasic molt*, which usually is a complete molt; in passerines the definitive species plumage is now adopted, if it hasn't been already. Molts and plumages in these species are then no longer numbered. The Herring Gull, which does not have an alternate plumage, does undergo a second and third prebasic molt until it arrives at a definitive basic plumage at the end of its third year.

We need to know the sequence of molts and plumages a species undergoes to make correct field identification; at times knowing that sequence is the only way of correctly gauging an individual's age. The sequence also reveals something about the breeding biology of the species and the feathers' function in protection and communication.

In small birds with short lifespans, the molting of juvenal feathers generally leads to the basic species plumage. They acquire the adult form quickly and are ready to breed in their first spring. In the longer-lived Red-winged Blackbird, *Agelaius phoeniceus,* adult males engage in much competition for favorable breeding territories. With the first prebasic molt, yearlings acquire the first prebasic plumage, which is duller in color than the definitive species plumage. These first-year males can and will breed if they establish a territory, but are generally kept from doing so by more experienced and colorful adults. Among Herring Gulls, which live up to twenty years, young birds do not acquire breeding plumage until they gain enough experience to defend hotly competed-for nesting areas in the colony.

Remaining in subadult plumage is useful because the feathers are less conspicuous, giving some protection from predators. A bigger advantage, perhaps, is that young birds who lack the colors that imply competition and rivalry are tolerated on the breeding grounds.

COLOR, CAMOUFLAGE, AND COMMUNICATION

External features of all birds are made primarily of contour feathers. Unlike mammals and reptiles, whose external anatomy is usually of earthy color, most birds show bold colors and patterns, probably because of flight. Birds can afford to be brightly colored because they can easily outdistance most predators, whereas terrestrial animals protect themselves with camouflage. Plumage does, of course, have elements of concealment, but in many species the advantages of being bright dominate. Such species as the North American warblers seem to have struck a compromise between the evolutionary forces toward being bright or remaining cryptic, for their alternate plumage is bright in color and bold in pattern but their basic plumage is composed of feathers that blend with the environment.

If the feather evolved only for protection and flight, it would be difficult to explain the enormous variety in color and the extravagant structures found in plumage. One need look no further than the back yard to realize that the robin's red breast or the jay's blue back have a function beyond warmth or flight. Almost every avian order has species with feathers so striking that they are not only conspicuous but so extravagant that they counter one of the feather's primary functions, flight. The male Resplendent Quetzal, *Pharomachrus mocinno*, which some consider the most beautiful bird in the world, has extremely long tail covert feathers. In taking off, this bird is very careful not to drag these elegant plumes across its perch, or so it seems, for in starting its flight, it first turns and falls backward, and begins forward flight only when it has cleared the perch (Maslow, 1985). The male African Standard-winged Nightjar, *Macrodipteryx longipennis*, has one flight feather on each wing that projects well beyond the

Some of the spectacular plumes found in the avian world adorn, from top left, Wilson's Bird of Paradise, Large Racquet-tailed Drango, Tufted Coquette, Resplendent Quetzal, Standard-wing Nightjar, and Golden Pheasant.

others. These feathers are retained through the mating season, but the bird snaps them off when it ceases its courtship flight. Birds of paradise and hummingbirds have probably brought feathers to their highest extravagance. The two groups have colors of every conceivable hue and combination, and feathers that tax the imagination by their variety and structure. These birds are extreme examples that prove we cannot ignore how greatly color and the patterns it produces protect a species in its environment and provide signals in a system of visual and auditory communication.

Color in a feather is produced by pigmentation and structure. Pigmented feathers are products of the cells that form feathers. As the feather grows it is coated with nonsoluble organic chemicals that reflect color. Pigment colors a feather rather as indelible ink might. The pigments are melanins and lipocromes, and they usually produce black, red, yellow, orange, and violet. Blue is not found as a pigment in birds and green is very rare. These colors and others are created by structural patterns in the feather. In much the same way as the thin film forming a soap bubble shows colors when we shine light on it, the fine structure of the barbules combines with pigmented colors to produce structural colors. The blue of a jay's feather is caused by the feather's structure and contains no blue pigment. It reflects blue when light "bounces off" it, but shows gray-brown (pigmented color) as light passes through it. The iridescent colors in many species are also produced by the feather's structure, even more like the colors in a soap bubble. These structures cause different colors, depending on the angle at which incoming and outgoing light strikes the twisted barbule, whereas the structure of the jay's feather is flat, and always produces blue. The black of a grackle comes from pigmented color, but in good light these feathers make glossy browns and violets because of the barbule microstructure. In many hummingbird species, the throat area, or *gorget,* appears dark, but from head-on in the proper light these gorgets give off some of nature's most beautiful and brilliant colors.

A bird's white feathers, containing no pigment, reflect all colors of light simultaneously. They are the simplest feathers and take least energy to produce, but lacking pigment they are weaker than colored feathers. No wonder so many white-winged species have their outer feathers tipped with black.

We infer from birds' varied colors that they have color vision. Most terrestrial predators, though, lack this capacity; they must see many-colored birds only as shades of gray. Perhaps, then, bright colors are not as conspicuous as they seem. In fact even the most outlandish plumage incorporates some type of concealment, especially when seen as shades of black and white.

Color and the patterns it produces can help protect a bird from predators in several ways, most familiar of which is to match color of the plumage to the bird's environment. Sparrows and thrushes blend in with the brown, leafy forest floor. The Piping Plover, *Charadrius melodus,* is light gray like its sandy habitat. *Counter-shading* is another common type of camouflage. Counter-shaded species have shades of color opposite to those produced by sun and shade. Sunlight can lighten color and shade darken it; because sunlight is brightest on the bird's back and dullest on the belly, species counter this effect with darker backs and lighter underparts; the bird contrasts less and therefore stands out less in its environment. Thrush, sparrow, and plover plumages show a counter-shaded pattern, as do those of most species. Birds that live on the water also show this dark-on-top and light-under pattern, for a dark bird swimming on the surface is difficult to spot from above, and its light underparts match the sunlit surface when seen from under the water.

Bold patterns too can protect a species. Zebras in a zoo seem the antithesis of camouflage, but in their natural habitat these patterns break up the animal's outline, and it blends with the background. This *disruptive coloration* is found in many species of birds around neck and head. The dark neck and chest bands of the Killdeer, *Charadrius vociferus,* gives the effect of separating the body from the head, disrupting the bird's body contour. Dark or light eye lines, so common in birds, are thought to have a disruptive function, as are splotchy light colors on a dark coat.

The plumage of both the Killdeer (standing) and the Wilson's Plover (hidden) are marked with bold dark and light bands that disrupt each bird's contour.

Some species are cryptically colored when perched or on the ground, but show bold patterns when they take flight. These patterns suddenly appearing may startle a predator or at least direct attention away from the head and body region of the bird. Such *startle patterns* can be seen in the white rump of many woodpeckers or the very distinctive black-and-white wings of the Willet, *Catoptrophorus semipalmatus.* Although these patterns are generally interpreted as antipredator devices, they may alert other birds to a nearby predator. Species recognition may be yet another function of such patterns.

In external anatomy, the Lark Sparrow, *Chondestes grammacus,* combines all types of protective plumage patterns. The overall brown matches the grasslands the bird inhabits, and its dark back and rump contrast strongly with the light breast, belly, and flank. The disruptive pattern on the head, so distinctive in the drawing on page 34, blends with the dark and light pattern of tall grass, breaking up the contour of the head. The dark eye line and striped crown, with the bright startle pattern on the outer tail feathers and less on the wing bars, direct the eye away from the body's more vulnerable regions. But other colors and patterns in the plumage seem to have very little protective value. Most obvious of these on the Lark Sparrow are the dark feathers on the breast forming a "stickpin." These and other such features probably help in communication among Lark Sparrows.

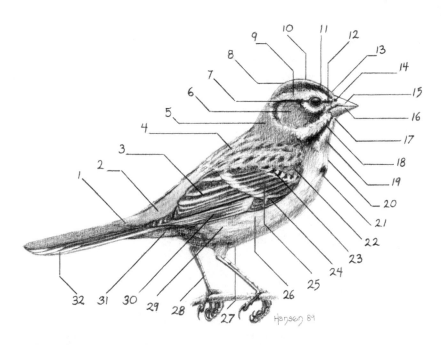

The external anatomy of a Lark Sparrow

1. **Upper Tail Coverts**
2. **Rump**
3. **Secondaries**
4. **Back**
5. **Nape**
6. **Earpatch**
7. **Eyeline**
8. **Crest**
9. **Supercilliary Line**
10. **Crown**
11. **Median Crown Stripe**
12. **Lores**
13. **Forehead**
14. **Naves**
15. **Upper Mandible**
16. **Lower Mandible**
17. **Chin**
18. **Malar Line**
19. **Throat**
20. **Chest**
21. **Breast**
22. **Lesser Wing Coverts**
23. **Middle Wing Coverts**
24. **Alula**
25. **Greater Wing Coverts**
26. **Side**
27. **Belly**
28. **Tarsus**
29. **Flanks**
30. **Primaries**
31. **Undertail Coverts**
32. **Outer Tail Feathers**

Like other organisms, birds must be able to communicate with members of their species and at times with other species. They must have a system of signals to tell of willingness to breed, to defend a territory, and to establish dominance. Their primary means of communication are sound and sight. Because birds can produce a large array of sounds, vocal communication with songs and calls can convey complex and varied messages. Visual signals are generally fixed on the birds' plumage, lacking the variability in songs and calls. Birds can augment these visual signals with body postures enhancing the signal and the message, but they can rarely alter the meaning. Although exceptions can probably be found, communication by visual elements in the plumage conveys only simple and unambiguous messages.

Feathers' primary service in communication is probably species recognition. Each species must differ enough from all others in color and pattern to signal unambiguously who they are. For our own field identification of birds, we depend at least partly on the obvious visual differences among species. Many species of birds show a difference in size and plumage between the sexes; they are *sexually dimorphic.* In species with slight sexual differences in plumage, they seem specifically or even exclusively to indicate the bird's sex. In the eastern subspecies of the Northern Flicker, *Colaptes auratus,* males and females are almost identical in plumage except that the male has a dark line of feathers bordering the chin, referred to as a moustache. When such a moustache is experimentally painted on the female in a mated pair, she is driven away from the nest by her mate as though she were an intruding male (Noble, 1936). We can readily determine sex in many species of woodpeckers by presence or absence of a patch of red feathers on the head or nape of the neck.

Other sexually dimorphic species carry clear differences between male and female. Most often the males are larger and more colorful than the females. Intense competition among males to attract females has led to elaborate plumages that convey breeding readiness to the female or warn competing males about their willingness to defend a territory. In the Red-winged Blackbird, *Agelaius phoeniceus,* territorial males sing and display their bright-red shoulder patches during the breeding season. These visual signals help the resident male maintain his territory. When the red feathers are experimentally dyed black,

Sexual dimorphism is illustrated here by the male and female Red-winged Blackbird.

intruding males all but ignore the resident's aggressive postures and song, and quickly take over his territory (Smith, 1972). In the male European Robin, *Erithacus rubecula,* the red breast is the aggressive signal, for a territorial male will attack an intruder if red-breasted and will even attack a tuft of red feathers, but will ignore a male robin on its territory if it has no red feathers (Lack, 1943).

In the cliff-nesting Black-legged Kittiwake, *Rissa tridactyla,* plumage of the young does not signal aggression but actually reduces it. During the time young Kittiwakes share their tiny ledge nest, they behave aggressively toward one another. Because they have no place to run to during an aggressive episode, one chick will adopt a behavior of turning away its beak, exposing the back of its head to its sibling. Across the nape of the neck a line of black feathers seems to inhibit subsequent aggressive impulses (Cullen, 1957).

In many male birds, the plumage seems designed only for courting the female. Among the Peafowl, *Pavo cristatus,* the cock courts the hen with his extremely long tail coverts held erect, framing his metallic blue neck and head. Each tail covert feather has eye-spot designs on it. When the male approaches the female head-on, she is confronted not with one pair of eyes, but with hundreds; all these seeming suitors are thought to bring her into readiness for breeding. As though this striking visual display were not enough to win her affection, the male vibrates these feathers producing a quivering sound.

Producing sound with the feathers is not unique to the peacock, however; a number of species use it to enhance the courtship display. The male Anna's Hummingbird, *Calypte anna,* courts a perched female by flying in steep arcs above her. He orients this flight so that on the downward power dive he is coming directly into the sun, causing his iridescent gorget to burst into color, and as he passes the female, his tail feathers make an explosive whine. The male Ruffed Grouse, *Bonasa umbellus,* assumes a display posture similar to the peacock's, and rapidly beats his wings, producing a powerful, low rhythmic roll of sound. This sound lacks the intimacy of the peacock's, for it is used to attract females to his territory from long distances. Woodcock and snipe courtship displays are performed at dusk or in darkness; therefore their courtship feathers lack striking visual components, but are designed solely to produce sound. The woodcock's outer wing feathers make a soft twittering sound as the bird ascends on its courtship flight; the snipe's stiff outer tail feathers, held at right angles to the body, vibrate with an eerie bleating sound as the bird dives toward the ground.

Swans and ducks too produce sound while flying. As the wing passes through the air, it causes sounds ranging from a distinctive whistle to a dull hum, all thought to keep the birds in contact with one another while in the air. Even the clapping and whirling sounds pigeons and other ground-feeding birds make at takeoff are thought to be more than incidental noises. They seem to be the auditory equivalent of a startle pattern and they also alert other birds to danger.

Suggested Reading

Chapters on feathers in Welty's *The Life of Birds* and Pettingill's *Ornithology for Laboratory and Field* have more detail on feathers than you have read in this description. Ideas on communication in birds and other animals are presented very clearly in chapters 16, 17, and 18 in *Animal Behavior: Its Development, Ecology, and Evolution,* by Wallace. In *Bird Behavior*, Burton describes visual communication in birds and gives many photographs of birds in display.

Projects

Molts are a rather confusing subject, all the more because labels such as summer and winter plumage are being replaced by alternate and basic feathercoats. A good way to start getting familiar with the new terminology that Humphrey and Parks explain is to notice plumages among species you can identify and record these in the species section of your notebook. Also record the date when you see a bird in molt, best told when it lacks the same flight feather on each wing; jot down whether this molt is a prebasic or prealternate molt. You can do this practicing as you observe birds at a feeder, where you can readily see species such as the American Goldfinch coming into the alternate feathercoat at winter's end.

Examine feathers that you find on the ground with a hand lens or microscope to see their internal structure. Determine the coloration by holding the feather up to the light. If the color changes to dull grays or browns, it is produced by the barbule microstructure; if not, the feather is pigmented. Go on to identify the bird species, possibly even its sex and age, from this lone feather.

- 3 -

Flight

THE UNDERSTANDING OF HOW TERRESTRIAL CREATURES MOVE is in many ways self-evident. Walking, running, and crawling all entail muscles applying a force against a surface. But movement through the air is not so easily understood. Even though Newtonian laws of motion apply to flight just as they do to walking, we have taken a long time to fully comprehend the origin behind the forces that make flight possible. After all, we depend on the power of sight, which leads us to ignore the colorless gas that surrounds us. A room not full of solids or liquids must be empty, it seems. Even though we are continually reminded that the air is present, we hardly expect this mixture of primarily nitrogen and oxygen to have substance enough to produce force.

Gases and liquids are both fluids; they flow. In the 1700s Daniel Bernoulli described very precisely how streams of fluids move. A high-school physics student learns from Bernoulli's principles that an increase in the velocity of a fluid will result in a decrease in the force of the fluid per unit area, or pressure. This velocity-pressure relationship in a fluid is the principle of flight, but not until early in the twentieth century was it successfully applied to a machine that lifted off the ground by its own power. And this first flight at Kitty Hawk, North Carolina, was by no means the first human attempt to fly.

People had always wanted to fly, we can be sure, and had looked to the birds to try to understand this form of locomotion. In mythology, Icarus used a bird's feathers to leave the earth. In our quest to understand avian flight, though, we did not see beyond feathers and flapping wings to Bernoulli's elegant principles. Many early attempts to fly thus resorted to beating the air, which only delayed our entry into the age of flight.

AERODYNAMICS

A solid object placed in a stream of fluid causes the fluid to be displaced. A teardrop-shaped object separates an airstream with its blunt leading edge, causing the air to slide over the two surfaces smoothly. The symmetrical shape forms two airstreams whose velocities and pressures are equal at every point. Laterally bisect this teardrop and you have an *airfoil*. Present that to the same stream of air and the latter will cause a very different flow than the teardrop-shaped object. As the airstream is parted by the leading edge of the airfoil, the air on the lower linear surface moves at the same speed as before, but the air across the curved upper surface must travel farther over the same amount of time to meet the airstream across the lower surface. Therefore the upper airstream increases in velocity, resulting in a decrease in pressure. The reason for the increase in velocity is not obvious, but has to do with conservation of energy by particles in the stream. The air

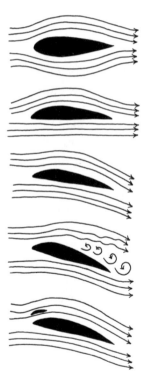

Air streams across a teardrop-shaped object uniformly in the top drawing. In the next three drawings lift is created by the air moving more quickly across the longer, upper surface. The amount of lift is determined by the shape of the object and its angle of attack to the air stream. The small airfoil in the bottom drawing (in birds' the alua feathers) can be raised for added lift.

molecules on the upper and lower surfaces remain equal in total energy throughout, but the upper airstream molecules have lost some potential energy and so increase their speed, gaining kinetic energy, to offset the loss. The airfoil has created pressure differences in the air across its two surfaces. The higher pressure on the lower surface pushes the airfoil up as the lower pressure on the upper surface pulls. The combined effect of these two forces is *lift*. The greater portion of the lifting force is created by the pull of the upper airfoil surface. If the lift developed by the stream of air is greater than the force of gravity, the airfoil will rise.

The amount of lift developed depends on factors such as shape of airfoil; angle at which airfoil meets airstream, or *angle of attack;* and relative speed of airfoil and airstream. Considering the first two factors, an airfoil that is *cambered* (convex on top and concave at the bottom) develops more lift than does a half-teardrop shape. The more obtuse the angle of attack, the greater the lift. Both these factors have limits: if the object has too much camber or too great an angle of attack, lift will decrease rapidly. This dropoff in upward force is caused by the airstream's breaking away from the surface, creating turbulence, or *drag.*

Lift always increases as relative speed of airfoil and airstream increase. A stationary airfoil will therefore develop lift when a stream of air passes across its surface; so too will a moving airfoil in still air. An object's forward motion is produced by some force, the thrust. Because any object with an airstream moving across its surface creates some turbulence, the forward motion is countered by drag caused by air resistance. If thrust is greater than drag, the airfoil will move forward, creating lift. If the lift is greater than the force of gravity, this object will not only move forward, but will rise.

Consider how these forces play on a gull that is momentarily stationary in the air. The bird's body is similar in shape to a teardrop and the air flows smoothly across its surface. Because the gull has no forward motion, it is balancing its forward thrust with the inevitable opposing forces of drag created by turbulence and air resistance. If it were to lower its feet, raise its tail, or even turn its head or fluff its feathers, increased drag would pull the bird backward and lead to a stall. The bird's wings are airfoils, slightly cambered and angled in such a way as to create lift. Contour feathers on the upper wing surface periodically flicker upward in the area of low pressure, but the long, stiff flight feathers do

Sabine's Gull in flight

not move, allowing the two airstreams to meet with minimal turbulence off the trailing edge of the wing. Because the bird is stationary, the lifting force is equal and opposite to the force of gravity and the gull is essentially weightless.

Gulls are masters at playing the nuances of these four forces. Momentarily suspended in air, they show how these forces can be balanced. For a gull, however, the sky is an avenue for travel, and to glide and soar, to turn and fly into the wind it depends on creating imbalances among these forces.

GLIDING AND SOARING

The simplest type of movement through air is a free fall. An object in free fall is accelerated by the force of gravity but supported in varying degrees by air resistance. The amount of support depends on the object's shape. A parachute's large surface area slows the fall because of resistance by the air. A bird falling with wings extended is also supported by air resistance, but because of the shape of the wings and the speed imposed by gravity, the bird moves forward and is lifted by air streaming across the wing surfaces, and the result we call *gliding*. A vulture atop a 100-meter cliff, simply by spreading its wings and falling, can travel up to 2,000 meters horizontally during its fall. This method of locomotion, used by flying squirrels and some reptiles and amphibians, was undoubtedly the forerunner of true, powered flight in birds. Gliding requires little effort and is rapid and direct, but in still air it inevitably leads to the same place, the ground; to repeat the glide, the creature must expend much energy climbing the nearest tree or cliff. But air, being a fluid, is rarely still. Its movement can provide the energy a proficient glider needs to extend indefinitely its time in the air and *soar*.

In a very simplified way, air moves in two directions relative to earth. Its horizontal flow is wind, and it also moves vertically in updrafts and downdrafts. Ultimately both these motions are caused by the sun's heat. When the sun's energy strikes earth's surface, a portion of that energy is reflected back to the atmosphere, heating the air. As the air temperature increases it expands and rises, causing thermal updrafts. Surrounding air moves in to fill the space left behind by the rising air, causing a horizontal flow of wind. At higher and cooler altitudes the rising air spreads and eventually falls, creating downdrafts and winds at different heights. These convecting currents occur on a global scale, generating the prevailing winds, but they also take place locally as the sun strikes such features as rock outcroppings, which reflect a good deal of energy back into the atmosphere. Local thermals are much more common and predictable over land than over water, whereas prevailing winds are commoner over the open ocean. These differences in wind have led to evolution of two types of soaring birds: terrestrial species that *statically soar* on thermal updrafts, and pelagic birds (seabirds) that *dynamically soar* on prevailing winds.

Static soaring species are best exemplified by the New- and Old-World vultures, large birds with very long, broad wings and ample tails. Although quite heavy, they are buoyant flyers because their wings have large surface area. The measure of buoyancy or *wing loading* is the numerical ratio of the wings' surface area to the mass of the bird. Vultures' wings typically carry about one gram of body weight for every two square centimeters of surface, whereas a loon's wings support almost four times that mass (Poole,1938). Long, ponderous wings,

Static soarers like this vulture reduce drag at their wingtips by spreading their primary feathers to form slots.

adapted for buoyancy, are relatively inefficient at flap flying, making birds such as vultures dependent on updrafts for motion. These species are thus confined to regions where the sun's heating is strongest and are found in habitats that generate local updrafts. Their time in the air is severely restricted by inclement weather, and even on sunny days they rarely fly until the sun has warmed the earth. Adaptations such as low wing loading and high camber, which enable them to develop lift on the slightest wisp of air, also create a good deal of drag. As a result these birds of prey are far too slow to capture a meal and depend almost entirely on carrion for food.

The size and shape advantage these big birds have is readily seen when they encounter a column of rising air while gliding. Their descent is arrested, and although they are still falling, now they are doing so in air rising faster than the rate of fall. The net result is that the bird gains altitude, and as it does so it uses its tail as a rudder, maneuvering to stay within the spiral that heated air forms (Pennycuick, 1972). The vulture's forward speed throughout the ascent is low and so close to stall speed that the bird must delicately balance its forward thrust with the drag created by turbulence. The major source of drag is at the wingtips, where the airstream tends to swirl into the low-pressure regions on the wing's upper surface. These wingtip vortices are reduced by spreading the outer wing feathers to form slots at the wingtips. Each large feather is itself an airfoil, providing lift; but more important, these *slotted wings* smooth out the airflow on the wingtips. As the bird gains altitude, its horizontal gliding range also increases. At 500 meters, the vulture has an effective range of up to ten kilometers if it breaks away from the thermal and simply glides to earth. This whole flight may last hours and be done without a wing beat.

This method of locomotion is regularly employed also by buteo hawks and eagles, but as their sharp talons prove, they still capture prey and require enough speed in their design to do so, even though many of the larger eagles depend on carrion to supplement their kills. Birds of prey, cranes, storks, pelicans, and geese, among others, depend on thermals during migration, using them to gain altitude, which they then abandon for a glide in the migratory direction. Flocks of geese have been observed porpoising from one thermal updraft to another during long migratory flights.

Thermal updrafts are not the only source of rising air on land. When wind strikes uneven surface features, it is deflected upward. The length and height of these updrafts depends on the direction and strength of the wind and the shape of the land feature. A familiar scene is gulls soaring along outer beach dunes on a summer's afternoon; here an onshore wind is being deflected upward as it encounters the rise of the land. These opportunistic birds take advantage of the free ride as they scout out an afternoon snack. Hawk Mountain in Pennsylvania's Kittery Range is world famous for the many birds of prey that can be seen during fall migration. But these soaring birds concentrate here only when weather conditions produce a rising cushion of air. On the best days for seeing them northwesterly winds strike the ridge and are so deflected as to produce not only an updraft but a tailwind as well. This range is part of a greater avian travel avenue extending from Maine to Georgia. Cold air flowing in from central Canada brings the temperate summer to an end, but as it does so the wind is lifted by the Appalachian Mountains, providing the soaring birds with an easy street to milder climates.

Over water only a little of the sun's energy is reflected into the atmosphere, making thermal updrafts uncommon; neither does the often flat surface of the sea deflect wind upward. Static soaring species therefore avoid flying over open bodies of water, but much wind energy there is higher in velocity and more consistent in direction than on land. Oceanic gliders exploit this energy to soar, but their design and technique are very different from those of land-soaring birds. Albatrosses are the best example, with their exceedingly long, narrow wings that are well adapted for dynamic, not static, soaring.

Unlike variable land winds, open-ocean winds travel thousands of kilometers unobstructed, flowing in broad belts. The trade winds in the tropics are

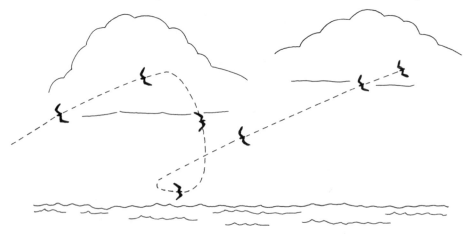

Dynamic, soaring ocean birds use the wind and their own momentum to cover long distances effortlessly.

named for the reliable and consistent flow of air that facilitated movement of goods when ships depended on wind. In the great southern oceans, these wind belts encircle the earth, blowing fast enough to produce sound. At the latitudes of the Roaring Forties and the Howling Fifties the oceanic gliding species reach their greatest diversity. Strong though these winds are at the surface, they blow at twice that speed twenty meters above the waves. Wind speed is lower at the surface because part of the wind's energy is plowed into the sea, producing waves. Oceanic gliders take advantage of these differences in velocity to soar dynamically.

On the open ocean an albatross gains height by facing into the wind. Just as it is about to stall, the bird performs a sweeping turn and heads downwind. Gravity combined with a tailwind accelerates the bird's flight as it races in a shallow glide toward the waves. When the bird falls to sea level it again executes a broad turn and faces into the wind. Momentum carries it forward and it develops lift. As the bird rises, it slips backward in the airstream, but also encounters higher wind speeds and continues to rise. At about twenty meters above the surface the wind levels off at maximum velocities and the bird can no longer gain height. To avoid a stall it again turns downwind and repeats its fast glide. The albatross exchanges altitude for speed as it moves across the ocean and, like the vulture, without flapping a wing. Unlike the vulture, however, which delicately balances the aerodynamic forces, the albatross depends for its dynamic soaring on momentum and speed. Not that the albatross is less graceful than its terrestrial counterpart; so impressed were early sailors on the southern oceans with the albatross's mastery of the wild wind that they saw these birds as embodying the seaman's soul in the state of bliss.

The most noticeable difference in shape between vulture and albatross is in width of the wings. The vulture's long wings are wide, whereas the albatross's are narrow; the relationship between a wing's length and width is its *aspect ratio*. The albatross's high aspect-ratio wings slice cleanly through the air, minimizing drag but developing relatively little lift. The wings are also low in camber, compared with the vulture's high-lift wings. Combining high aspect ratio and low camber, dynamic soaring birds develop sufficient lift only at high air speeds, like those on the open ocean. These birds are high-speed gliders that depend on strong winds for lift and reduced drag for speed. They are specialists, and in their element they are superb; but when the wind slackens, their long wings prove rather inefficient at developing forward thrust by flapping. In fact, these magnificent flyers were long ago dubbed gooney birds because of their inept and often (for us) comic attempts at takeoff and landing on the sandy atolls where some species breed. Most species, however, avoid these awkward moments by nesting on the windward side of island cliffs, where prevailing winds build high air speeds, allowing them to maintain lift and dignity in landing and takeoff.

Shearwaters, large petrels, and fulmars all soar dynamically like the albatross, but they are smaller, thus more efficient flap-flyers and less dependent on regions with strong and constant winds. Their distribution is worldwide because of their less specialized form.

POWERED FLIGHT

Most species of birds are not adapted so that they can use the wind's energy as the vulture and albatross do. To move, they must supply their own energy for forward thrust by flapping their wings. Impressive and graceful as soaring flight is, the species that employ it in locomotion are vastly outnumbered by those that generate their own power. By this index alone powered flight is an enormously successful adaptation. For unlike the vulture or albatross, species that flap-fly can move under any wind condition, live in almost any habitat, and fly when and where they please.

Powered flight is quite complex mechanically and often misunderstood. Casual observation suggests that a flap-flying bird's wings move up and down in flight. This motion, however, would result not in horizontal but vertical force. As we have seen in soaring species, the primary vertical force is lift, which is developed by the wing's shape and not its motion.

Another popular misconception is that the wing develops thrust as we do in rowing a boat or making hand motions in the breast stroke. That is, the forward force is caused by backward movement of the wing; but slow-motion photography shows it is not. Even though the motion of a bird's wing during flapping is caused by a power stroke and a recovery stroke like those of oars in rowing, the power stroke is a downward and forward motion of the wing and the recovery stroke is upward and backward. This is a complex motion, especially because all the while the wing must continue to provide the lift to keep the bird airborne. To understand better how a bird's wing provides both lift and thrust, we must study the structure of the wing.

The bird's wing is homologous with the human arm because they share the reptilian forelimb as a structural ancestor. Even though human arm and avian wing diverged long ago and have evolved for very different functions, the underlying structures are surprisingly alike: except in the hand region, wing and arm bones correspond exactly.

The upper part of the wing that connects the shoulder to the bend in the wing (elbow) is constructed around the humerus, a relatively short and thick bone in birds that does not project as prominently as in human beings. It is surrounded by muscle, tendons, and skin and covered with contour feathers, but has no flight feathers. The avian equivalent to the human forearm, also called the forearm in birds, extends from the bend in the wing to the wrist. In both human beings and birds, this region is built around two bones, ulna and radius, which meet at both ends and are slightly bowed away from each other in the middle. When the wing is fully extended the radius supports the leading edge of the wing and the ulna the trailing edge. Attached to the ulna are the flight feathers called *secondaries*. Major evolutionary modifications in structure have taken place in the hand region of the wing: it has been lengthened by fusion and extension of bones. In most birds the length of the hand is equal to or greater than that of the forearm. Although the human wrist, hand, and fingers have twenty-seven bones, birds have only six. The leading edge of the bird's hand retains a rudimentary thumb, the pollex, to which are attached the *allula* feathers. Embedded in the trailing edge of the bones of the hand are the *primary* flight feathers.

The entire wing surface is covered with contour feathers laid down in rows, the *coverts*. The coverts that cover the calami of the primary and secondary feathers on the upper wing surface are the *greater primary,* and the *greater secondary* coverts. Progressive rows of covert feathers overlap these coverts in shingle style. On the wing undersurface, covert feathers are fewer, but the arrangement is similar. The undersurface coverts are collectively called the *wing lining.*

A cross-section through the wing shows a blunt leading edge made of feathers, muscle, and bone. The upper surface is convex, the lower concave, each surface extended by the long, trailing flight feathers: in short, the section is an airfoil.

When a bird flaps its wings, the power stroke begins with the wings held at an angle above the bird's back. The wings then move down and forward. During this stroke the hand of the wing moves the greater distance; the forearm moves the lesser distance. The forearm thus remains relatively fixed and retains its airfoil qualities, providing most of the lift through the stroke. Most of the thrust developed during this stroke comes from the hand region of the wing. The primary feathers, fixed and stiff at the base, bend backward at the tips as they meet increasing pressure from the air. The resulting angle these feathers assume as they cleave the air is like that of a propeller blade. The effect is also similar, for both propeller blade and downward-moving part of the wing are airfoils. As they move through the air they create higher pressure on the trailing surface and lower pressure on the leading surface. The airfoil therefore moves ahead,

In the first three drawings from the left, the flamingo is shown in its recovery stroke, in which the outer portion of the wing is drawn into the body as the wing moves back and up. In the fourth drawing the primary feathers of the wing are extended as the bird begins its power stroke and the wing moves down and forward, pulling the bird through the air. During the entire process lift is maintained by the airfoil shape of the inner portion of the wing.

pulling the plane or bird with it. The recovery stroke develops little or no thrust in most birds. The wings are brought upward and backward until the wing angle is above the bird's back. As in the power stroke, the forearm is relatively stationary and provides lift but the hand goes through a quite different motion. At the end of the power stroke the bird abruptly changes the hand angle, bringing it closer to the body and minimizing air resistance. In this motion the primaries "open up" so that air can pass through the spaces between these feathers, further reducing drag. When this stroke is complete, the wrist angle changes again, the primaries close, and the next power stroke begins. Visually, the wing traces a downward-pointing oval or figure eight, and the most pronounced figure is traced at the wing tip.

Despite my description the dynamics of powered flight are still imperfectly understood and vary a good deal among species of different sizes and shapes. Many large birds and some small species apparently cannot afford to lose time on a recovery stroke that develops no thrust; these species change the angle of the entire wing at the bottom of the power stroke to gain some thrust from the primaries as they move to the top of their arc. Even an individual bird changes its wing motion at different stages in its flight.

As any pilot knows, the two most critical moments in flying are takeoff and landing. Both maneuvers are generally done into the wind, where the bird benefits by extra lift from higher relative air speed. Takeoff must be considered the most aerodynamically taxing moment in flight because the bird starts with no lift or thrust. And though some species, especially the hummingbirds, can develop enough thrust by wings alone to get airborne, most species need assistance from the legs. As these species begin the power stroke, they crouch, then jump into the air. The wings are now beating more vigorously and the lift-producing airstream has a tendency to break away from the upper surface of the wings. Many species spread their allula feathers during the initial part of takeoff, causing the stream of air to flow more evenly across the wing surface and maintaining lift. Many waterfowl and oceanic birds, which have relatively small wings and large bodies, need to gain more speed in order to lift off: they run along the surface of the water into the wind while flapping their wings. In some species this taxiing is quite long and waterfowl have often been reported to be trapped on a lake by a partial overnight freeze that foreshortened their runway so that they could not get airborne.

If takeoff is the most demanding part of flight, landing must be the most hazardous, for if the bird misses its mark it risks severe injury. Probably water landings require least precision with a large margin for error and a soft surface.

Many of the species that need to gain extra speed to take off from water cannot reduce their speed without stalling as they come in for a landing. These birds make final approach a high-speed glide, lower the landing gear, and ski to a stop. Birds that land on a perch or level ground have little room for error. They begin this maneuver by spreading the tail feathers and increasing the wings' angle of attack, both actions adding drag and slowing the bird. Just as they are about to land they beat their wings backward, extend the allula feathers to maintain lift, and thrust feet in front of body. The legs absorb the initial shock as the body continues to move forward until they stand upright as they close their wings. More buoyant birds can continue to reduce their landing speed to zero while maintaining lift by flying into the wind. These birds then lower their legs and simply step down onto the ground.

DIFFERENCES IN DESIGN

The environment, with natural selection, favors organisms that best fit the habitat's demands. Though all flying birds depend on aerodynamic forces—lift and thrust—to move, it is the environment that determines the method of flight for each species. Because the wing provides lift and thrust, differences in its structure primarily determine the type of flight.

Savile (1957) classifies four major wing types by structure; these types correlate highly with the way the species flies and its habitat. The types are: *elliptical, high-speed, high aspect ratio,* and *slotted high-lift.* The type of flight and associated wing structure are complemented by the tail flight feathers.

The elliptical shape is the commonest wing type, with nine or ten primary and secondary feathers; it is the typical wing among the passerines. The wing is rounded at the tip and generally broad throughout. The rounded hand of the wing is formed by the outermost primary feathers, which are reduced in length. This design does not develop a great deal of thrust, but its low aspect ratio creates lift at low speed. The advantage in this design is that the wing, which is slotted in many species, gives the bird much control over its direction and speed. This type of wing is that of a bird adapted to a forest habitat, where maneuverability matters more than speed. The passerines' feet are adapted to perch on branches, and their wings must ensure that these birds avoid branches

(left to right) The broad wings of the buteo create lift at low speed. The longer primaries of the falcon slice through the air causing this bird to fly fast. The shearwater's long, narrow wings are adapted to high-speed soaring, while the eliptical wings of the jay increase manuverability at low speed.

that are obstacles and yet land precisely on those they choose for perches. Many of these birds gain control from an ample tail that acts as rudder or air brake. This is also the wing type of henlike birds, Galliformes, the rails and gallinules. Probably because of their heavy bodies and terrestrial habits, these species are generally weak flyers. The accipiter hawks too have an elliptical wing. These forest-living hawks fly at speeds uncharacteristically high for the wing design, but their long tails give them agility for avoiding obstacles and capturing prey. Bent (1961) illustrates how fast and agile these hawks are: a Cooper's Hawk, *Accipiter cooperii,* pursued a quail into the open; just as the quail dove for cover in the brush, the hawk made its move. In an instant the hawk accelerated, turned upside-down to catch the fleeing quail in its talons, then righted itself and flew away with its prize.

The high-speed wing design is shared by many species. The outermost primary feather on this wing is the longest, with successively shorter inner primaries, resulting in a pointed wing. This design develops maximal forward thrust on the power stroke, making these birds the fastest creatures on earth. The hand's efficient, thrust-producing shape allows these species to reduce the lift-producing qualities of the wing that cause drag. This wing has shortened, often reduced numbers of secondary feathers and low camber. This pointed, high aspect-ratio wing is found on falcons, swifts, shorebirds, some waterfowl, and hummingbirds, among others. Most of these species live in habitats that are relatively open, where they do not need abrupt turns, but reduced travel time over long distances, or capturing prey on the wing, is essential. Size and shape of the tail, though, do affect control that the bird does not get from wing shape, as we see in comparing the flight of the swallow to that of the swift. Both birds capture insects while in flight, but the ample-tailed swallow does so gracefully, continually changing speed and direction, whereas the almost tailless swift flies stiffly, moving in straight lines and broad sweeping turns.

The oceanic pirates, the jaegers, depend on the speed developed by their wings to overtake fleeing seabirds. These birds would not be nearly so successful in their plunder if they could not maneuver in the ensuing dogfight. Their well-developed tail enables them to continue to harass gulls or terns long enough to force them to disgorge their food.

Falcons probably best exemplify this high-speed wing design. The swept-back posture of the wing resembles that of a jet fighter. For these bird-eating hawks, speed is essential in overtaking the prey. The Peregrine Falcon, *Falco peregrinus,* greatly increases its speed by partially folding its wings and dropping, or stooping, on its victim, often from a great height. By this method of hunting, the falcon quickly closes on its prey from above and behind, killing instantly by striking with its talons.

The high-speed wing did not evolve in many shorebirds and waterfowl as an adaptation for feeding because these birds feed on the ground or on water; rather, it is highly effective in increasing speed and reducing travel time in their long migration. The lack of a well-developed tail in these species is consistent with both their open habitat and their direct method of flight.

Gram for gram, the species that develops most thrust while flying is the hummingbird. These little jewels of birds have been reported to beat their wings up to 200 times a second, develop thrust on both strokes of the beat, and fly up to 100 kilometers per hour (Pearson, 1960). Unlike other birds with this type of wing, hummingbirds are among the most agile flyers. They can turn abruptly, accelerate to top speed in an instant, hover, and fly backward and even upside-down. These aerial feats are aided by an ample tail, but the unique attachment of wing to shoulder gives the wings this versatility. The shoulder joint is extremely supple, allowing free movement in all directions and giving these birds the unique ability to turn the entire wing 180 degrees, which enables them to fly backward.

The high aspect-ratio wing of the albatrosses, large petrels, and shearwaters is long, narrow, and pointed. The larger species have a longer forearm, with consequent increase in the secondaries, the largest albatross having up to thirty-two. The low camber and high aspect ratio of this wing reduce drag but develop adequate lift only at high relative air speeds. These birds are generally not strong flap-flyers, but glide effortlessly in strong wind. The tail feathers of these species are short, but their need for maneuverability on the open ocean is limited.

The slotted high-lift wing is designed for maximal lift at low speed; it is highly cambered, with up to twenty long secondary feathers in the larger species. The long, slotted primaries form a round wingtip, much as in the elliptical wing. This is the wing not only of terrestrial soaring birds of prey, but of large, long-legged species such as herons and cranes. This type of wing is well suited to these ground-feeding birds, which use thermal updrafts in migration but also need to land at low speed so as not to damage their long, fragile legs. The soaring birds of prey have well-developed tails that enable them to maneuver in wispy thermals.

Although these four major wing types account for many of the world's birds, a number of species have wing shapes that do not fit neatly into any category, or else they fly in a way that is uncharacteristic for the type of wing. Swans and geese have wings that are highly cambered and broad, but pointed at the end. These birds combine the high-lift wing of soaring species with the high-speed shape of fast flyers. This design enables them to move rapidly, but also to take advantage of the lift provided by rising columns of air. Similarly, the gull's wing shape is like that of the oceanic soaring species, but their lower aspect ratio and higher camber makes them strong flap-flyers as well as excellent static soarers. The American Swallow-tailed Kite, *Elanoides forficatus,* and the frigatebirds have the low aspect-ratio, pointed wing of fast-flying species, and these birds are capable of swift flapping flight, but they are most often observed soaring at low speeds, much like vultures and other static-soaring species.

In many species aerodynamic design of the wing is only one consideration. Species that use their wings to propel themselves underwater as well as in the air must compromise wing size and shape for efficient movement in these very different fluids. Although most diving birds either swim underwater, thrusting with their webbed feet or their wings partially folded, the auks and their allies swim with wings fully extended. These birds, relatives of the graceful gulls and terns, are ungainly in the air, beating their short stubby wings in a blur. Longer, broader wings would certainly improve their flying ability in air, but underwater, larger wings would decrease the speed and agility these birds must have to pursue and capture fish. The Great Auk, *Pinguinus impennis,* twice the size of the next largest auk, was far too large to maintain a wing that met the demands of flying in both air and water. This species "chose" to use its wings to fly underwater, and with that evolutionary "choice," forever lost the possibility of leaving the surface.

FLIGHTLESSNESS

Only a few among the 8,700 species of living birds are flightless. These species represent a number of orders of birds, suggesting convergent evolution. All flightless species retain many characteristics of flying birds, such as air sacs and flight muscles, which lead us to believe that these species evolved from flying forms. Although these birds are not related to one another, common factors seem to have led them to flightlessness such as size, predation, and isolation on oceanic islands.

If a species doubled its size and maintained the same type of flight, its wings would have to increase in surface area by more than a factor of two. The Great Auk's, *Pinguinus impennis,* evolutionary ancestor was limited in size while it retained the power of flight; when it became flightless it could evolve a larger form. The advantage of being larger in a cold climate is expressed by *Bergmann's rule*, by which increased size decreases the ratio of surface area to volume and results in conservation of heat. We can think about the ancestor of the Great Auk as being pushed by natural selection toward greater size as an adaptation to reduce heat loss. This alteration could probably apply to many species that live in arctic regions, but these species must also rely upon flight to escape predators and find food, pressures opposed to the evolutionary push toward large size. The Great Auk, however, spent most of the year on the open ocean and bred on isolated, predator-free islands. Its method of capturing prey by swimming underwater with wings fully extended favored a smaller wing. This bird therefore evolved into a flightless species because nature favored large size, selected against large wings, and, maybe most important, did not prohibit these variations through predation. These same environmental pressures undoubtedly led to evolution of the flightless penguins in the Southern Hemisphere. Incidental reports of encounters between penguins and people demonstrate that a land predator is completely alien to these birds. For not only are they curious of other creatures when out of the water, but probably because of their myopic vision, approach quite closely. When they are pushed or even struck, and fall into the water, these birds respond to the assault not by fleeing but by jumping out of the water, only to be struck again. Penguins have lived in an environment free of land predators so long that they react to danger by fleeing the water where the seal and whale, their only natural predators, live.

Size and predation also seem to be a factor for the Ostrich, *Struthio camelus,* Emu, *Dromaius novaehollandiae,* cassowary, and rhea. Collectively called ratites, these are all ground-feeding birds that live in habitats with powerful predators. Their large size, aggressiveness, and speed on foot are their protection against predators. For these species to retain the power of flight, their wings and supporting structures would have had to increase to ungainly proportions.

Lack of predators seems to have been a common factor contributing to evolution in a number of flightless species that inhabit isolated oceanic islands. Dodos on the Mascarene Islands, kiwis on New Zealand, and a number of grebes, rails, and cormorants all probably flew to, or more probably were blown to these islands long before any predatory species arrived. Once established, these birds evolved in a predator-free environment. This factor, coupled with the risk that flying could get them blown out to sea once again, led to reduced wing size. The history of these flightless birds, which also evolved as gentle and fearless, is quite sad. For when the creatures were again confronted with a predator—an upstart species, the human being and his associates, the feral dog, cat, pig, and the tagalong rat—many were quickly exterminated. The dodo survived only 170 years after first meeting people, and the last pair of Great Auks was clubbed to death on a rocky island off Iceland in 1844.

Suggested Reading

Every type of flying is fully described in Ruppell's *Bird Flight. Biona Report 3: Bird Flight,* edited by Nachtigall, deals with the very technical aspects of aerodynamics and birds. In *Hummingbirds,* Greenewalt discusses how the ultimate power flyers move through the air, and dynamic soaring is described in Jameson's *The Wandering Albatross.*

Projects

After you know something about the physics of flight, the best way to learn more is to watch birds in flight more closely. Setting out a hummingbird feeder will attract these impressive birds, and you can see for yourself their ability to hover and fly backward. Soaring birds can also be observed closely, and gulls at the beach provide an excellent opportunity to see the lift and drag forces in action. At fall hawk-watching areas you can see many species of these birds on the same day. Notice how different species with different types of wings use the wind to move.

- 4 -

Anatomy and Physiology of Birds

IN GREEK MYTHOLOGY DAEDALUS AND HIS SON ICARUS fashioned wings of feathers fastened with wax and thus were able to fly. Their flights together led Icarus so near the sun that the wax melted and the boy fell from the heavens to his death. Although this story is meant as a parable about impetuous youth, its literal interpretation points out how improbable it is to think that feathers alone give the ability to fly. In fact, the only probable event in the entire story is Icarus' fall, for, even with the largest flight feathers on earth, wing-loading values for the boy would be tremendously high. His ascent into the heavens would have to be not with the condor's graceful spirals, but at very high speed, with a whirl of beating wings. If Icarus could generate enough thrust, his arm muscles would soon tire from inadequate blood supply. As he left earth, his posture would have to be horizontal, continually changing the position of his legs to maintain his center of balance. As he rose higher into the sky, the wax holding the feathers would not melt, but the cold would freeze it and his extremities; before then, though, Icarus would find himself gasping for air in the rarefied atmosphere.

In short, people were not meant to fly; birds were. The feather is an adaptation for flight, but it would be of little use in this activity without major internal changes to complement the feather. The internal structure of birds and the way in which that structure works, their anatomy and physiology, all have been molded by evolution for flight. Every avian physiological system contributes in some way to the bird's ability to fly.

55

BONE AND MUSCLE

Any vertebrate's skeleton supports and protects the body and, by its connection with muscle, moves body parts. For flight, the arrangement of bone and muscle in birds has undergone major modifications from that of their terrestrial ancestors. These changes include reduced weight of the skeletal framework, fusion and hollowing of bones, and enlargement of surface area on some bones to permit attachment thereto of powerful muscle groups. These adaptations result in a bird that is light but strong enough to fly and also to so alter its center of gravity that it keeps its balance while either flying or walking.

A prerequisite for flight is lightness. The bird's weight is much reduced because parts of the skeleton are filled with air. Although not all birds show this *pneumatization,* in most species the larger bones are hollow. The advantage lightness gives is clear in the frigatebird: this 1.6-kilogram bird with two-meter wingspan has a skeleton that weighs only 114 grams, less than 7 percent of the body weight. In fact the bird's feathers are heavier than its skeleton (Murphy, 1936). These hollow bones are strong because they are supported internally by an interlacing network of fiber. These hollow bones are also part of the respiratory system, connected to the complex system of air sacs that help breathing.

Comparing a typical bird's skeleton with that of, say, a mammal, we see that among the bones of the head the heavy jaw bones are eliminated, the skull is extensively pneumatized, and the eye sockets are very large. The neck is made of individual vertebrae that protect the spinal cord, but, because these bones are free to move, the bird's neck is very flexible. Long-necked species have up to twenty-three vertebrae, and the complex attachment of muscle in this region gives the head and neck a great deal of freedom to move. Where the spinal cord enters the trunk, though, the vertebrae are fused for almost the entire length, causing the back to be rigid. The spinal cord terminates in the individual bones of the tail, the last and largest bone in which the *pygostyle* is all that is left of the long reptilian tail. In the pygostyle the flight feathers of the tail are embedded. The complex attachment of muscle to these tail bones allows the bird to move and spread the tail feathers in various directions.

Around the chest cavity, the ribs provide protection to the internal organs, fusing on the ventral surface to form the shieldlike sternum. The sternum projects a large *keel* (ratites excluded), on which arise the flight muscles. The ribs are so arranged that they permit the chest cavity to expand in normal breathing movements. Because of this flexibility these bones provide little support to the sternum; if they were its only buttress, the sternum would be driven into the chest when the flight muscles contracted. The major brace for the sternum is the *coracoid;* this stout bone firmly anchors the sternum to the bird's main frame.

The wing articulates from the shoulder region, where the head of the humerus fits snugly into the cavity formed at the junction of the coracoid and the scapula (shoulder blade). Extra support is provided by the *furcula,* which fuses

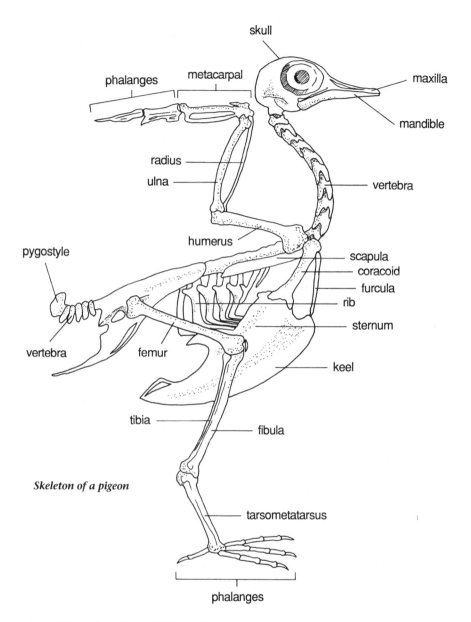

Skeleton of a pigeon

the shoulders, forming a V-shaped bone commonly called the wishbone. This arrangement of bones in the shoulders, along with the fused vertebrae of the back, causes the force imposed by the flight muscles on the sternum to be translated into movement of the wings without deforming the shape of the back.

Because muscle can only contract and relax, the two-stroke action in a wing beat requires two sets of muscles, both located on the sternum. The *pectoralis* arises on the outer portion of the keel, inserting directly onto the underside of the humerus, and is responsible for the power stroke of the wing beat. The *supracoracoideus* arises on the inner portion of the sternum and threads via a tendon through an opening in the head of the coracoid to insert onto the upper surface of the humerus. This muscle raises the wing on the recovery stroke. These two massive muscles account for as much as 35 percent of the body weight in strong-flying species such as ducks and hummingbirds (Hartman, 1961).

The wing skeletal structure is reduced in length and width of the humerus and extension and fusion of bones in the "hand." This variation from mammals is most pronounced in birds with high-speed wings, in which the bones of the "hand" make up more than half the length of the wing. In long-winged soaring species the ulna and radius are elongated. Various small muscle groups arising on the scapula, humerus, ulna, and radius, and the bones of the "hand" are

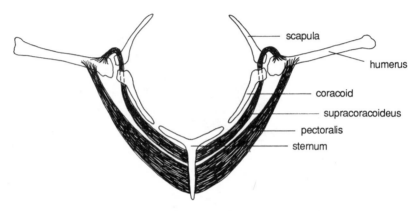

The breast muscles of a bird make possible the up-and -down movement of the wing. One end of the more massive pectoralis is firmly anchored on the keel, while the other end inserts into the lower portion of the humerus; its contraction pulls the wing down. The supracoracoideus also arises on the keel, but threads through the bone of the wing socket to insert on the upper surface of the humerus. When this muscle contracts, the wing is brought up.

responsible for extending and retracting the wing, its forward and backward movement, the angle of attack, and movement of the allula and flight feathers.

In the leg region the rigid backbone is fused to the bones of the pelvic region. The pelvic bones are fused to form one broad plate on which arise the muscles that control the upper portion of the legs. The avian hindlimb is homologous with the mammalian hindlimb and, like the wings, birds' legs have been modified by evolution in fused and extended lighter bones and reduced length for the heavier ones. The thigh region of the bird's leg is supported by the femur. This bone, generally the most massive in mammals, in birds is proportionally shorter and thinner. Because the femur articulates more toward the backbone and is angled forward, the thigh region is not readily observable in the field. The calf or "drumstick" extends from the knee to the ankle. The knee is level with the bird's flank or belly and is made by the junction of tibia and fibula with femur. These two calf bones, of which the fibula is reduced to a splinter, in many birds are angled toward the tail. The ankle joint is the most conspicuous division of the leg and is formed by the junction between tibia and tarsometatarsus, which is fused from ankle and foot bones. Watching a long-legged heron walk, we get the peculiar impression that the avian leg bends in the opposite direction from ours because the ankle (which does bend in the same direction as ours) is halfway up the leg, about in the same relative position as our knee. The foot of birds is very simple in structure, composed of the tarsometatarsus (referred to as tarsus) and the bones of the toes. Birds stand either on their toes or on the ball of the tarsus. The toes range from two in the ostrich to four in passerines and other species; no species has five toes. The arrangement of toes is generally characteristic of an order: all Passeriformes have the three middle toes facing forward and the big toe directed backward, the little toe having been lost.

Muscles that arise on the pelvic bone insert onto the femur; these muscles extend and retract the leg. Thigh muscles that control the mid-portion of the leg insert onto the tibia. Muscles on the tibia control the extremities of the leg by projecting long, slender tendons to the tarsus and toes. This arrangement of muscles and tendons centers the weight of the leg in close to the body and significantly simplifies structure in the lower portion of the leg. The bird's long foot is composed of little more than a tough scaly covering, relatively few bones, and tendons that require little blood supply, can absorb shock, and can endure cold.

The familiar dark and light meat on the Thanksgiving turkey represents two types of muscle found on birds. The color difference is caused by muscular structure, the number of energy-producing mitochondria, the number of blood vessels in the muscle, and the presence of oxygen-storing myoglobin in the muscle fibers. Dark muscle is made of thinner fibers, has many blood vessels and mitochondria, and can store oxygen, all giving the muscle the capacity to sustain contractions for long periods. White muscle, usually deficient in these characteristics, therefore can contract only for much shorter periods. In most strong-flying species the breast flight muscles are made of dark muscle and the leg muscle is white. These are opposite to the familiar chicken and turkey, which are primarily ground-dwelling and weak-flying species.

CIRCULATION AND RESPIRATION

The large flight muscles that keep wings beating for long journeys need to be supported by physiological systems that bring energy-producing materials and carry away waste products from their metabolism. Muscle is made of cells, all cells do work, and the energy to do work comes from digested food and oxygen. In the cell, food is chemically broken down in the presence of oxygen and the energy released is converted into forms useful to the cell. Heat is produced and waste products are formed. One primary function of the circulatory system is to deliver food and oxygen to the cells and to remove waste from them.

Birds are among the most active of creatures, partly because of a circulatory system that is very efficient at transporting materials to and from the cell. This efficiency is attributed to the size of the muscular pump that drives the blood through the body. The avian heart is proportionally as much as four times larger than the human heart and beats up to eight times as fast. A Black-capped Chickadee, *Parus atricapillus,* has a resting heart rate of 500 beats per minute (Odum, 1941), and a Blue-throated Hummingbird, *Lampornis clemensiae,* was observed to have a rate of 1,260 beats a minute during exercise. Not only is this organ large and powerful, but its four-chambered design completely separates oxygenated blood being pumped to the body from oxygen-depleted blood returning to the heart, ensuring a rich supply of oxygen to the cells.

The circulatory system is intimately associated with the lungs, where blood is exposed to air, allowing exchange of oxygen and carbon dioxide to take place. The two chambers on the right side of the heart receive blood from the body through the veins and pump the blood through the pulmonary artery to the lung capillaries. Because this blood is returning from the body, it is high in carbon dioxide, a cellular waste product, and low in oxygen. The capillaries in the circulatory system are very thin-walled vessels that allow materials to pass through. While the blood is in contact with air space in the lung, carbon diox-

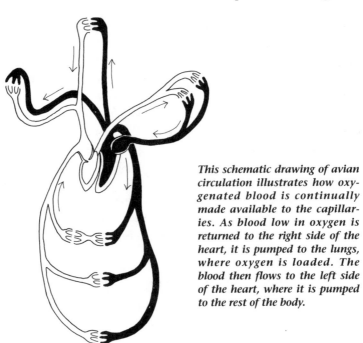

This schematic drawing of avian circulation illustrates how oxygenated blood is continually made available to the capillaries. As blood low in oxygen is returned to the right side of the heart, it is pumped to the lungs, where oxygen is loaded. The blood then flows to the left side of the heart, where it is pumped to the rest of the body.

ide diffuses out of the blood into the air space and oxygen moves from the air space into the blood. The capillaries then collect up into the pulmonary veins and return to the left side of the heart to be pumped, by the next set of contractions, to the body. In this way the avian heart is similar to the mammalian heart: it is really two pumps joined together, with the right side serving the lungs and the left the body. Because the lungs are close to the heart and carry much less blood than the rest of the body, the left side of the heart is larger than the right, developing pressures up to ten times as great.

Another factor that influences the quantity of oxygen available to the cells is the oxygen-carrying capacity of the blood. Most of the oxygen transported in blood is mediated by the hemoglobin molecules in red blood cells. The blood of strong-flying bird species is richly supplied with oxygen-carrying cells—more than six million cells per milliliter of blood, comparable to mammals but more than six times the count of most reptiles (Portmann, 1950).

Along with oxygen, blood carries the products of digestion, plus minerals and hormones, to the cells. Digested carbohydrates, proteins, and fats, along with water and minerals, are absorbed by the capillaries in the digestive tract. These compounds are then circulated through the body and are directed to active cell groups by small arteries that dilate, causing increased blood flow in that area. When blood enters the capillary network of cells that are metabolizing, rapid exchange of materials occurs.

While the blood is unloading materials useful for the cells in producing energy, it is also loading the waste products of metabolism. Carbon dioxide is carried away from the cells on hemoglobin and dissolved in the blood plasma; toxic wastes are transported to the liver to be converted to nontoxic forms, or to the kidneys to be excreted from the body; and excess heat produced by the cells is absorbed by the blood to be distributed through the body. In this way the circulatory system regulates both the bird's chemical composition and its temperature.

Animals are often referred to as cold-blooded or warm-blooded, a usage that at times is misleading, for a cold-blooded reptile sunning itself may have a higher body temperature than a warm-blooded mammal. We can more accurately describe an animal's internal temperature as homeothermic or poikilothermic, the former referring to maintenance of a constant internal temperature and the latter to internal temperature that fluctuates with the ambient temperature. Only birds and mammals are homeothermic. The evolution of homeothermy has proved to be an enormously effective adaptation because, compared with their sluggish reptilian relatives, birds and mammals are alert and active regardless of outside temperature. But for this adaptation an energy price is paid. Homeothermic animals must in effect leave their motors running all the time, even when they are not going anywhere, whereas the poikilotherms turn their cellular fires down when the air temperature drops. It is estimated that up to 80 percent of the energy produced in human beings is used to maintain a constant internal temperature. A chickadee in a northern forest must endure a fourteen-hour night, expending much energy while sleeping just to keep its tiny body as much as 40 to 80°C above the ambient temperature. Avian feathers insulate the body outside, but feathers alone do not ensure homeothermy.

Birds maintain a higher internal body temperature than do mammals, ranging from 40 to 42°C depending on the species. This is the temperature at the body core (the internal organs and the brain); temperature at the extremities can vary widely. Cellular metabolism produces heat and feathers prevent this heat from escaping, but the circulatory system is responsible for distributing the heat throughout the body.

When environmental temperatures are low, heat production must equal heat loss to maintain homeothermy. Under these temperature conditions birds increase the rate of cellular metabolism, producing more heat, and increase their insulation by fluffing up the feathers, but at unfeathered portions on the legs the potential for heat loss is high. Birds have evolved an efficient method for reducing heat loss in the legs by the structure of blood vessels in this region. Arteries, leaving the body core and carrying blood at body temperature, run next to and counter to veins that are returning cooled blood back to the body, allowing transfer of heat from artery to vein. Blood returning to the body is thus warmed before it enters the core, and lower portions of the leg are held above freezing. Pheasants exposed to a temperature of -18°C maintained 2.7°C in their toes while blood returning to the body was 35.7°C (Ederstrom and Brumleve, 1967). Low temperatures are tolerated in tarsus and toes because of the lower leg simplified structure. This countercurrent heat-exchange system accounts for the penguin's being able to stand on ice for long periods without melting the ice or freezing the toes. In fact, many species of penguins are so well insulated by feathers and layers of fat that they will overheat if their feet are not in contact with a cold surface. Even with this mechanism, a significant amount of heat is lost in the legs during cold weather, and to minimize this loss many species stand on one foot, retracting the other into the insulating feather coat, or else sit on their legs. While active, many small birds crouch more on cold days, covering their tarsi with feathers.

As the temperature rises, the normal rate of cellular heat production matches the rate of heat loss. These temperatures represent zones of thermal neutrality, at which birds need make no physiological adjustments to maintain homeothermy. The temperature range of thermal neutrality varies among species and correlates with the climate in which the species lives; for the northern Ruffed Grouse, *Bonasa umbellus*, it ranges from about 0°C to 33°C; for the Northern Cardinal, *Cardinalis cardinalis*, of the temperate zone, from 18°C to 33°C; and for the tropical Black-rumped Waxbill, *Estrilda troglodytes*, from 28°C to 38°C (Welty, 1975).

At higher environmental temperatures birds must again do work to maintain a constant internal state. Once more blood flow to the legs becomes important. By increasing flow to this region, cooling occurs, and blood returning to the body is below the body temperature. The most effective method of cooling is evaporation of water. Birds have no sweat glands, the water from which would only mat down the feathers; instead they evaporate water on the surface of the upper respiratory tract in hot weather. This method of cooling is accomplished by rapid, shallow breathing, which vaporizes the water on the moist surface of the air sacs and cools the blood under the surface of these structures. Some birds, such as the Turkey Vulture, *Cathartes aura*, further cool themselves in hot weather by excreting liquid waste, which is mostly water, on their legs; as the water evaporates it cools the blood returning to the body (Hatch, 1970).

For a number of species, long periods of inactivity in cold weather are a difficult physiological problem. Hummingbirds, especially species that live in the

Andes, have too little stored energy to maintain heat production through the cold nights in these mountains. The hummingbirds allow their internal temperature to drop, many species doing so by raising the feathers to dissipate heat quickly. As their body temperature drops the birds enter a torpid state, with drastically reduced heart and breathing rates. In the morning the birds increase their temperature and, as it approaches normal, they become active again. The advantage in such nightly hibernation is that birds reduce their energy requirement by up to 90 percent (Lasiewski and Lasiewski, 1967).

Some species have been observed extending this torpid state for as long as three months. This type of avian hibernation occurs in some swifts and nightjars that depend on insects for food and apparently is an alternative to migration.

If we think about the avian circulation system as being tinkered with by evolution to make it more efficient, we must see the changes here as only in degree; the respiratory system, though, must be considered as being completely redesigned during the evolution of birds, for in anatomy and physiology the avian lung is radically different from those of the mammalian and reptilian lung. One need think no further than the freak collision between an Old-World vulture and a jet airliner at 11,500 meters to realize that this bird had enough oxygen to be alert and active at an altitude where no reptile or mammal could survive.

To understand how the avian lung is designed we must compare it to the mammalian or reptilian lung. In these groups of animals the lung can be likened to a balloon that fills with air when the chest cavity expands and empties when the cavity contracts. But this lung never completely empties of air. The gas left behind has been in contact with the lung capillaries and as a result has more carbon dioxide and less oxygen than fresh air does. On the next inspiration, fresh air enters and mixes with the gas already present, so that the capillaries never come in direct contact with fresh air, which decreases the amount of oxygen and carbon dioxide exchange that can take place.

The avian lung, though only half the size of the mammalian lung, is much more efficient because it continually circulates fresh air. Instead of being saclike, it conducts air through itself in one direction with very fine tubes. When this air comes in contact with the lung capillaries the exchange of oxygen and carbon dioxide is rapid and complete. The exact course air takes through the lung is still open to some question, but the entire respiratory system involves a more complex arrangement of air-delivering tubes than that found in mammals or reptiles. It also includes *air sacs,* unique to birds, which have a number of functions. Aside from decreasing weight and cooling the body, these structures act like bellows, pushing air through the lung. Air sacs themselves are not involved in gas exchange with the blood, but their part in the avian respiratory system is large.

Contraction by muscles surrounding some air sacs causes air to enter the respiratory system through nares or mouth. The trachea then directs the air toward the air sacs. In most species, the trachea divides before it passes through the V-shaped clavicle (wishbone) into two air tubes, the *bronchi.* The structure of this junction is quite complex, especially in songbirds, for it is surrounded externally by muscle and internally contains the tympanic membrane. This membrane vibrates when air moves across it and produces sound. The entire structure is called the *syrinx,* or voice box, birds having no vocal cords. Air flows through the bronchi and enters the air sacs and then, in a manner not completely

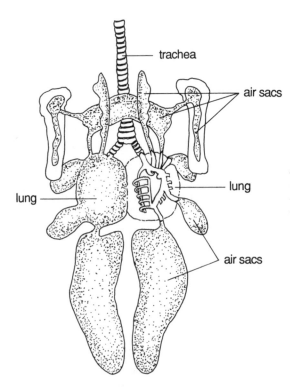

The avian respiratory system is a maze of tubes and air sacs that direct gases through the bird's relatively small, but highly efficient, lungs.

understood, passes through the lung via fine tubules, exchanging gases as it does so. The gas, now relatively high in carbon dioxide and low in oxygen, is stored in other air sacs, and when these sacs contract the gas is forced out the bronchi and trachea.

Although most birds' breathing rates are quite high—between forty and fifty breaths per minute in pigeons, compared to a normal resting rate of twelve in human beings—the rate is lower than that of comparably sized mammals. Rate of breathing is strongly influenced by activity, in that the respiratory movements increase sevenfold during flight (Lord et al, 1962). Also, because birds depend on evaporative cooling in the air sacs, breathing rates increase with temperature. When the House Wren, *Troglodytes aedon,* had its internal temperatures experimentally elevated, the rate of respiration rose from 100 breaths per minute to 300 (Baldwin and Kerdeigh, 1932).

DIGESTION AND EXCRETION

The digestive system in all animals has the same function: to bring food into the body, physically and chemically break it down, and eliminate undigested

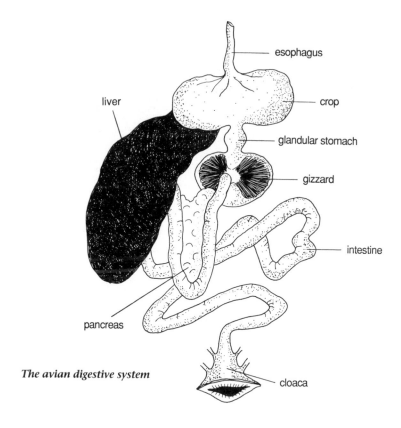

material. This system includes the mouth, the alimentary canal, which conducts food through the body, and organs that secrete digestive enzymes into the canal. The excretory system, designed to maintain a constant internal chemical environment, does so by removing from the blood cellular waste products and regulating the amount of chemicals useful to keep the body functioning properly, while retaining in the body all digested food. In birds, the major organs in the excretory system are the kidneys, the lungs, and the salt glands. Both digestive system and excretory system are designed to work in the intense avian metabolic machine, but their structures must also minimize the machine's weight.

Before we look at how the digestive system modifies the food birds eat, we must see how their food has modified them. Forelimbs are specialized for flight, and wings can do little more than help the bird overtake or approach the food, but the bird's beak, and somewhat less often the feet, are used to capture food and get it into the digestive tract.

Flesh-eating species, primarily hawks and owls, have on the toes sharp, strong nails, the *talons*, which are used to capture and kill prey. Almost all these species have strongly decurved upper mandibles forming hooked beaks that are used to tear the catch to pieces. Even species that swallow their prey whole have this equipment. Vultures show a similar beak shape but do not kill their prey and thus have lost their raptorial cousins' powerful talons.

Bills and feet (left to right)

    Sharp-shinned Hawk
    Blue-winged Teal
    Whimbrel
    Red-cockaded woodpecker
    Fox Sparrow
    Cape May Warbler
    Magnificent Hummingbird

Fish-eating birds also have beaks, feet, and legs modified to capture and eat prey. These features are tailored for efficiency, whether the bird wades, swims, or dives for fish. Probably the commonest beak type in this group is the long, pointed one of the loon, tern, and heron. These beaks are used to grasp fish and sometimes to spear them after an underwater chase propelled by webbed or lobed toes, as in cormorants or grebes, a plunge from the surface, like the king-fisher, or a quiet walk on long legs, as in the egret or stork. Mergansers have bills with serrated edge to better grasp the slippery prey. Another fish-catching type of bill is that of the pelican, whose expandable pouch on the lower mandible floods with water when opened under the surface, drawing fish into the mouth. Probably the most unusual bill among the fish-eating birds belongs to the skimmer, whose long lower mandible is plowed through the water as the bird flies just above the surface. When the sensitive tip of the lower mandible touches a fish the bird's head snaps down to grasp its prey. Also in this group is the Osprey, *Pandion haliaetus,* and some fishing eagles that plunge feet first to catch fish close to the surface.

Birds that pick and probe for small invertebrate prey show greatest variability in beak types. In this group, the commonest is the pointed beak that is used to take insects and worms from the ground, just under the surface, or underwater. This beak ranges in shape and size from the very long curlew and godwit beak to the short warbler beak, from the avocet's upward-curved one to the down-curved beak of the ibis, and includes the spatulated beak of the Spoonbill Sandpiper, *Eurynorhynchus pygmeus*. The birds that probe under the soil have laterally compressed beaks, enabling them to open the mouth while pushing a minimal amount of soil; the American Woodcock, *Scolopax minor,* has an upper mandible that is flexible at the tip, so that it can grasp worms underground without having to open its mouth. Woodpeckers also have long, pointed beaks, but with these strong bills, along with uniquely reinforced attachment to the skull, these birds can hammer away at the surface of wood to get at insects.

Insect eaters that catch their prey on the wing generally have short, flat bills that are wide at the base, providing a large trap with which to catch the prey; this equipment is most pronounced in the tropical potoos and frogmouths, which sally forth at night, but is also evident in the swallow and flycatcher. All these species have bristle feathers fringing the base of the mouth, acting as an insect net. The feet of flycatching species are generally smaller, but those of other species that feed on small invertebrates show no special adaptation except to support them as they pursue their prey.

Plant-eating species show much variability in bill shape. Swans, geese, and most dabbling ducks use their flat, round bills to tear grasses and tubers from the ground. Seed eaters have powerful conical beaks that can crush seeds with hard shells. Among these is the unique beak of the crossbill, which pries open the seed with the crossed tips of the mandibles. Fruit eaters generally have pointed beaks for picking food from trees or bushes. The estimated 1,600 species that depend on nectar as a staple food have long, pointed beaks for probing deeply into flowers.

Flamingos, some ducks, and a few tube-nose species have bills that are designed to sift small plants and animals from water. These bills are fringed with parallel plates that allow the water to leave the mouth, trapping the food behind.

Some bills are shaped specifically for just one food source, but many species eat more than one type of food, and their beak must be designed to accommodate this varied diet. The beak's length, size, and shape, though, generally give good insight into the life of the species. The beak is controlled by a complex collection of muscles; both mandibles can be moved independently; and head and beak are perched on an extremely flexible neck. For these reasons the beak performs surprisingly varied tasks, including body maintenance and nest building, as well as its most essential function, getting food into the mouth.

Once food is inside the mouth it is manipulated by the tongue, which in species such as woodpeckers and hummingbirds also helps carry food to the mouth. In species that eat dry food, salivary glands secrete fluids to moisten the food and make it easy to swallow. These glands also play an important part in nest building among swifts and swallows. During the breeding season their glands enlarge, copiously producing a sticky fluid that cements the nest together. Bird's-nest soup, a delicacy in China, is made from the saliva of swifts in the genus *Collocalia*.

At the back of the avian throat, the trachea diverts air to the lungs and the esophagus conducts food to the stomach. In many species the esophagus swells before entering the stomach, forming the *crop*. Birds are not leisurely eaters, usually gulping their food; the crop stores this food until the stomach is ready to accept it. During the breeding season, the parent birds hold food in the crop until it is fed to the nestlings, and in pigeons and flamingos the crop secretes a cheesy fluid that is fed to the young.

Muscular contractions in the digestive tract push food into the stomach. Birds have two kinds of stomachs. Food from the crop first enters the glandular stomach, which secretes enzymes and acid on the food, beginning chemical digestion. From here the food is moved into the muscular stomach, or gizzard. The gizzard in a sense has taken the place of the teeth, for it is here that food is ground up: until it reaches the gizzard, the food of many species is still whole. Grit helps in the grinding in many birds, ranging in size from grains of sand to small pebbles. The gizzard of seed-eating chickenlike birds is particularly well developed; it has been reported that turkeys can crack walnuts and bend steel needles with the gizzard. This structure also separates out indigestible parts of food. In owls and hawks as well as other species, the gizzard prevents passage of bone and fur, collecting them into a pellet that is later expelled through the mouth.

From the gizzard, food is directed to the intestines, where most of the chemical digestion and all the absorption of digested food takes place. Chemical digestion is aided by enzymes secreted by liver and pancreas as well as by the intestine itself. In species that consume hard-to-digest vegetable matter, the end of the intestine enlarges into the cecum. The cecum holds food longer so that chemical digestion can continue.

As food is digested, simple carbohydrates, proteins, and fats are absorbed by the intestinal wall and enter the capillaries to be distributed through the body. Undigested materials now enter the terminal portion of the digestive system, the *cloaca*, to be eliminated from the body.

The bird's digestive system is efficient and rapid in processing food. Powerful digestive enzymes break down the useful components in food almost completely, as attested to by the relatively small quantity of feces produced by birds, and so too does the rapid growth of nestlings, who convert more than 50 percent by weight of food eaten into body weight. The speed of digestion varies with the food eaten and with the species. Berries, which are mostly water, pass through a fruit eater's system in less than thirty minutes, but hard-to-digest grain can take up to twenty-four hours.

The admonition, "you eat like a bird," whether applied to method of eating or quantity of food eaten, has little basis in fact, for most birds, eating quickly, consume large quantities of food. The amount of food a bird eats depends on the size of the bird and the kind of food. Small birds eat more food as a percentage of body weight than large birds. Chickadees eat up to 30 percent of their body weight daily, doves about 10 percent, and chickens, 3 percent (Nice, 1938). A Bohemian Waxwing, *Bombycilla garrulus*, was estimated to eat more than 300 percent of its body weight in berries in one day. And when storing up fat for long migratory flights, many small birds will consume more than half their weight in the days before departure.

Aside from food and the minerals and vitamins therein, birds need to consume water. The water lost in eliminating waste and in normal respiration must be replaced. Although some water is formed during formation of energy in the cells, all birds must take in water.

The amount of water an organism needs varies, one of the most important factors being its method of ridding its body of salt and nitrogenous waste. Nitrogen-rich proteins broken down in the cell form ammonia, a highly toxic chemical that must be diluted with large quantities of water so as not to poison the cell. Simple organisms that live in fresh water excrete the ammonia dissolved in internal water and replace the water from their surroundings. Animals that cannot replace water so readily, such as those living in salt water or on dry land, convert the ammonia to urea, which is less toxic than ammonia and therefore can be stored and eliminated in a more concentrated solution, so that less water has to be replaced. Converting ammonia to urea, though, costs cellular energy. Reptiles, the first vertebrates freed from a watery environment, could not have escaped without further converting nitrogenous waste to a less toxic form than urea. The reptilian egg neither gains nor loses water; cellular metabolism in the egg, inevitably producing ammonia or urea, would poison the growing embryo. In response, reptiles further convert urea to uric acid, which highly concentrates the waste, but more important, is almost insoluble in water. This step again costs the organism energy, but ensures that the waste will not poison the embryo, for it can now simply be stored in the egg membrane. Conversion to uric acid also reduces the reptile's need for water, for now nitrogenous waste can be excreted from the body with little loss of water.

Both birds and mammals evolved from reptiles, but although birds lay eggs and excrete nitrogenous waste as uric acid, mammals develop their embryos internally, where exchange of waste materials takes place through the placenta, and as a consequence they excrete the less expensive but more toxic urea. Birds lack a urinary bladder, a major weight-reducing adaptation, directly because of this difference. Also, the ability to conserve water preadapts birds for living in dry environments.

The *kidney* regulates the chemical composition of the internal environment by filtering the blood plasma. Birds have paired kidneys, located behind the lungs and close to the backbone. These organs are continually supplied with blood by the renal artery. The renal vein returns filtered blood to the body and the ureter carries away excess water, salts, and uric acid to the cloaca. When the bird eliminates these wastes from the cloaca, it usually voids undigested materials from the digestive system as well. Examining the excreta, which invariably seem to fall on a newly washed car, reveals a white paste surrounding a dark, solid center. The paste is mostly uric acid, and the solid the undigestible portion of the bird's last meal.

The avian kidney is not nearly as efficient at ridding the body of sodium chloride (table salt) as the mammalian kidney. Sodium chloride is absolutely essential for proper functioning of the body, but in excess it is detrimental. Birds that live on or near salt water, however, regularly drink it with no ill effects. Drinking salt water, as any thirsty sailor knows, leads to increased excretion of salt by the kidney, and with it a good deal of water, which only increases the thirst. Birds that drink salt water, however, show no increased water loss and do not dehydrate because in birds the *salt glands* and not the kidneys are designed to excrete excess salt. The salt glands are paired structures at the front of the skull that concentrate salt from the blood. They concentrate salt water to almost twice the salinity of sea water; the water then leaves the body through ducts to the nasal openings. In Procellulariformes, salt is conducted through the tube at the base of the upper mandible, from which it is forcibly expelled.

Carbon dioxide is excreted through the lungs. Because the lungs are moist, air expelled from the respiratory system contains much water vapor. Thus birds are continually losing water as they rid themselves of carbon dioxide. In juncos, roughly one third of the daily water loss at thermal neutral temperatures was through the respiratory system (Anderson, 1970). As the temperature rises and the bird begins to actively evaporate water to decrease its temperature, the water loss doubles and even triples. This loss can be harmful during hot, dry weather because, unlike the water lost in other physiological systems, the loss in respiration is unregulated. To avoid dehydration, birds remain inactive during the hottest parts of the day.

NERVOUS SYSTEM

The body's physiological systems are not independent units functioning autonomously in the organism: their actions are coordinated. The nervous system integrates the billions of cells of a complex vertebrate into purposeful behavior by controlling and regulating these systems. The nervous system is made up of the brain, spinal cord, and peripheral nerves, whose influence over the cells and body systems is direct and rapid.

The nervous system is divided by structure into two regions: the central nervous system, composed of the brain and spinal cord, and the peripheral nervous system, with the sensory and motor nerves. The whole system's functioning is based on electrochemical impulses that travel through the nerve cells, representing bits of information. Nerve impulses generated by external stimuli are directed toward the brain through the sensory nerves and the nerves in the spinal cord, and impulses that affect behavior are conducted away from the brain to the muscles, through the spinal cord and motor nerves. The brain, then, receives incoming information and can initiate signals that command the body to act. The brain, however, is not just a relay station passively making connections between sensory and motor nerves; its function is more properly seen as assessing the messages it receives against factors such as motivation, memory, and experience, and then issuing orders in a coordinated sequence to the body's motor units, all in a fraction of a second. How the brain does this work is still not completely understood, but we know that the brain is equipped with a battery of sensors, numerous neurotransmitters, and arrays of nerve tracks that connect its functional units. These interconnections make the brain the most complex organ in the body.

The brain itself is divided into regions by its structure and function. In human beings the most prominent portion in the brain is the cerebrum. This structure, with its outer layer, or cortex, greatly enlarged by being folded in on itself many times, is the seat of reason, voluntary action, memory, perception, and intelligence. Evolution has favored expansion of the cerebral cortex in us because our physiology was rather ill equipped for the environment we first found ourselves in. To survive, we had to rely on cooperative hunting, communication, and use of tools, all of which necessitated a larger cortex. Birds, though, when confronted with a stressful environmental situation, rarely

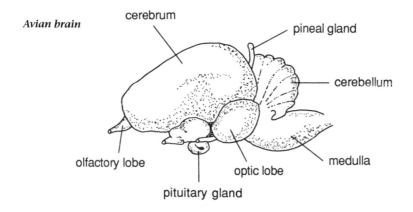

Avian brain — cerebrum, pineal gland, cerebellum, medulla, optic lobe, olfactory lobe, pituitary gland

paused long enough to solve the problem; their solution was simply to fly away. As a consequence, the cortex of the bird's cerebrum shows no enlargement by folding, leaving birds as a group with limited ability to learn or reason. Much of avian behavior is based on instinct and conditioning, whose centers are in the lower portion of the cerebrum.

If birds have limited problem-solving ability, the brain's anatomy confirms that they are superior in perceptual ability and reaction to problems in the making. On each side of the midbrain are the optic lobes, which are very large and attest to the bird's well-developed sense of sight. Behind the cerebrum is the cerebellum, which controls coordinated movement. In birds, as we would expect, this structure is also large and well developed.

The lower midbrain in the hypothalamus region is the seat of the bird's basic drives, such as hunger, thirst, pain, and aggression. At the base of the brain, before it forms the spinal cord, is the medulla, which regulates many physiological systems in the body by controlling heart rate, movements of the digestive system, and respiration.

We can illustrate how the avian brain works with a hawk perched on a branch examining a field. When the hawk's eyes detect movement in the grass and then a mouse, the information is coded in electrical impulses and relayed through sensory nerves to the optic lobes of the brain. In the optic lobes, the sequences of impulses might be decoded to perception of a mouse. From here, nerve tracks share this perception with other parts of the brain. In the cerebrum this perception is checked against stored images of prey species, and possibly the prior success ratio in catching this prey species is called on. Lower brain centers advise whether the hawk's physiological needs, such as hunger, might be served if it attempted a strike. If the bird is not hungry the pending commands from the cerebrum might be halted in favor of tracking the mouse for any new information that might be beneficial in future encounters. Even if the hawk is not hungry, the time of day must be taken into account, or an attack might be called for by a "memory" of hungry chicks back in the nest. To launch an attack, the medulla must begin to elevate heart and breathing rates, and cut back on digestive and kidney functions. Commands from the cerebrum are sent to the cerebellum, where motor impulses are coordinated and relayed to the flight and leg muscles via the spinal cord and motor nerves. All the while, new information is being gathered: movement of the prey, wind direction, and speed are needed to determine how to approach it. As the bird is about to strike, the behavioral pattern becomes more stereotyped, as if the hawk switches to an instinctual program. At the final second, the wings beat backward and the talons close, ending a typical hunting episode, whose underlying complexity is merely hinted at in this rather anthropomorphic description.

The sensory cells in the nervous system are unique in that they can transduce external stimuli into electrical impulses. These electrical events are then conducted through the sensory nerves to regions in the brain where images of sight, sound, touch, taste, and smell are processed. The sensory cells are either spread more or less evenly throughout the body or region of the body, as with touch, or centralized and organized in an organ such as the eye. Of all the sensory systems, sight has the potential for yielding the greatest amount of information about the environment, and, in birds, vision is relied on more than any other sense.

VISION

The avian eye is probably the most efficient and best-developed sensory organ any vertebrate has. The features that make it superior are the large size of the eye, its ability to control the light entering it, and the structure of the light-sensitive retina. These qualities give the eye the ability to see objects clearly under varied light conditions, to see in color, to judge the distance to objects, and all this in detail not realized by other vertebrates.

The external appearance of the bird's eyes reveals little about their true size, but in many species these structures are the largest organs in the head, weighing more than the brain. Most of the eye lies inside the bony sclerotic ring of the skull and the eyelids cover much of the eye outside this ring. The eye is enclosed by a tough fibrous coat, the sclera, and is filled with a clear fluid. Internally it is divided into two unequal chambers by the muscle and ligaments that suspend the lens. In the external chamber the sclera is transparent and is called the cornea. The shape of the cornea determines the different shapes of eyes found

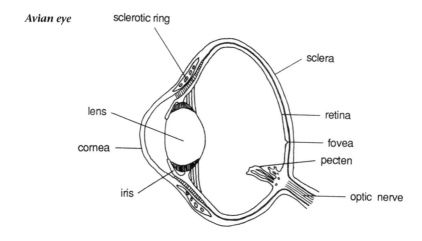

Avian eye

in birds. In most birds the cornea describes a very shallow arc, causing the external chamber to be small, and the eye is usually flattened horizontally. In nocturnal birds, among others, the surface of the cornea is increased, and with it the exterior chamber, by the cornea's bulging in the front, causing the eye to be elongated and to adopt a tubular shape.

Regardless of eye shape, the structure works in much the same way in all birds, in that the light that enters the cornea must pass through the lens to be projected onto the retina. On the forward-facing surface of the lens is the iris, which is made of pigmented circular muscle that, by its contraction and relaxation, changes the diameter of the pupil, through which light gains entry to the lens and to the internal chamber of the eye. In bright light the iris decreases the diameter of the pupil, and in dim light the pupil dilates.

Along with regulating the quantity of light passing through the eye, the cornea and lens project onto the back of the eye a sharp image of light. The amount that light needs to be refracted depends on how far the source of light is from the eye. To accommodate to the distance from the source, the elastic lens of the eye changes shape. When viewing a distant object the lens is stretched into a longer, thinner shape by contracting muscles in the eye. This shape refracts light less than when these muscles relax and the lens becomes more oval. Accommodation is critical for a fast-moving creature that must continually change its focus from distant to near objects. In hawks and other species the cornea also assists in accommodating to light. In these birds, muscular contractions change the shape of the cornea, and with it the amount that light will be refracted.

The cornea, iris, lens, and associated muscles prepare light to be seen. With its size and its ability to regulate and refract light, the avian eye produces images larger and sharper than those in animals of comparable size, and gives better vision in low light levels. These structures alone, however, do not account for the bird's visual acuity. The eagle's eye is of about the same size as the human eye, and the images produced by both these eyes would probably be equivalent. The real gain in the eagle's vision comes from the structure of the light-sensitive retina.

The retina is a sheet of nerve cells that covers the back of the eye. An embryological outgrowth of the brain, these nerve cells are extremely complex in structure and function. The commonest types of cells in the retina are the light-sensitive rod and cone cells. Rod cells generate electrical impulses in response to low levels of light, whereas cone cells respond to brighter light and to different colors of light. Rods, then, give the ability to see in black and white at night, and cones give color and detail vision during the day. The retina in birds is densely packed with these cells, with the greatest number concentrated in the fovea, a linear depression in the retina. The fovea of the European Buzzard, *Buteo buteo,* has 1,000,000 cone cells per square millimeter, whereas the human fovea has a mere 200,000 cells in the same surface area. Estimates of how superior a bird's vision is to ours range from as high as eight times to between two and three; the latter figure is more often accepted. But we must keep in mind that the human visual system is highly developed and that even a twofold increase in visual acuity is a substantial gain. This gain, however great, is in detail and not in magnification. An eagle perched on a lofty cliff would have the same retinal image as ours, but would "see" more in that image. The bird would pick up a rabbit moving in the valley below, but it would go unnoticed by our eyes.

Aside from such adaptations as sheer size and numbers of cells, avian vision is enhanced by subtler features. Associated with the light-sensitive cells in the retina are colored oil droplets. It is suspected these droplets act as filters reducing glare and causing some colors to stand out in the visual field. A tern hovering of the sea surface might be able to see through the water's glare, or an insect eater's preferred food might contrast more with its surroundings because of these oil droplets. Along with the rod and cone cells, the retina is made of cells that begin processing the image. Some of these cells are particularly sensitive to changes in the rods and cones and account for the bird's ability to detect movement in the visual field; others enhance the contrast in the image. The optic nerve, then, carries to the visual lobe of the brain not a "photocopy" of the image that is projected on the retina, but a picture equivalent to a computer-enhanced image.

Because the fovea is the most sensitive part of the retina, the eye, for detailed vision, must orient itself with an object in such a way that the image falls on this region of the eye. Unlike the human eye, which moves in its socket, the avian eye moves very little, and in owls the eye is immobile. For the best line of sight a bird must move its entire head, explaining the peculiar posture that hawks assume when scanning the sky. The fovea in these birds is on the upper portion of the retina giving them detailed vision in the downward direction, but to get a good view of the sky they must turn the head completely upside-down so that the incoming light focuses on the fovea.

For the visual system to judge distance accurately, it must sight an object from at least two angles. This binocular vision is readily achieved when both eyes are positioned at the front of the skull, as in our eyes, or those of birds of prey and owls. Here each eye sees an object from a slightly different position and the brain extrapolates the distance. Most birds, however, have a limited binocular field of view because their eyes are at the sides of the head. These species continually change the position of the head, and therefore of the eyes, to gain depth of field. The advantage in this monocular view of the world is that

The placement of the eyes on the skull of a bird determines the extent of both its field of view and its monocular and binocular vision. Seen here are the Short-eared Owl (left), the American Robin (upper right), and the American Woodcock (lower right).

these birds have a very large field of view. The woodcock, spending a good deal of time probing in the ground for food, has little need, and no ability, to see its prey under the surface, but while probing for food it must be on the lookout for predators. The placement of the eyes at the side and to the rear of the head gives this bird complete monocular vision laterally, and a binocular view behind and above.

The external surface of the eye must be kept moist and clean. In mammals the tear ducts and eyelids serve this purpose. In birds the muscles that control the eyelids contract more slowly than in mammals, making the avian blink take much too long to deprive the bird of sight, especially while flying. Birds, reptiles, and some mammals have a third eyelid, the *nictitating membrane,* which is transparent and moves quickly across the surface of the eye. Thus a bird in flight can clean and moisten its eye and still see.

HEARING

The sense of sight gives quick, detailed information about the environment, but the view provided is by no means complete. Light does not travel around objects and is at very low levels for twelve hours a day on average. These limitations, along with difficulty in altering visual signals of the feathers in communication, make sound a major stimulus and the sense of hearing essential for birds. Sound has some favorable qualities that light does not, for aside from traveling around obstacles, it can be produced at any time of day and can be generated and manipulated by any vibrating structure.

The avian ear is divided into three regions: the external ear, the middle ear, and the inner ear. Unlike terrestrial mammals, birds lack the external pinna, which collects and directs sound to the ear canal in the external ear. This entrance to the ear canal in birds is on the side of the head and is covered with contour feathers. The ear canal terminates at the eardrum, which vibrates when it is struck by sound waves. The eardrum changes sound energy to motion and causes the bone of the middle ear, the *columella,* to move in synchrony with the sound wave. The inner part of this bone taps against the fluid-filled, bony inner-ear structure, the *cochlea.* The ear, then, converts sound waves into mechanical energy, which is translated into fluid waves in the cochlea. As these fluid waves move through the cochlea they interact with sensory hairs running the length of this structure. The waves cause distortion in the sensory hairs, which project from nerve cells and generate electrical impulses. A sound is heard when these impulses reach the auditory regions of the brain via the auditory nerve. The two qualities of sound, amplitude (loudness) and frequency (pitch) are both decoded by the ear. Loud sounds generate larger waves in the cochlea, which distort the sensory hairs more and result in more impulses over a given amount of time. Different pitches result in different frequency waves in the cochlea and these interact with sensory hairs at different positions along its length. Nerve impulses generated at specific positions along the cochlea are interpreted by the brain as a particular frequency of sound.

Because most sounds that birds make are for communication, the frequency range that a bird can hear usually coincides with the frequencies of the species' vocalizations. Most small birds that produce high-frequency sounds are sensitive to these sounds and do not hear low-pitched sounds. Therefore the need for being silent when viewing birds probably does not matter too much because most small birds cannot hear normal human speech. But the bird's sensitivity to different frequencies is by no means uniform. Owls with their low-pitched voices are very sensitive to low frequencies; and during some species' lives sensitivity to sound changes. Chicks are most sensitive to low frequencies, in the range of the hen's vocalizations, whereas hens hear best the high-frequency sounds of a peeping chick.

Many avian vocalizations include very rapid changes in frequency and amplitude that are not heard by our ears. Only when the sound is tape-recorded and slowed are these sounds apparent to us. It is suspected that the bird's auditory system can discriminate among these rapid changes, which gives them, just as in vision, more detail in what they hear.

The most specialized ears among birds are those of the owls. Refinements in the owl's hearing result from adaptations in the ear and in the auditory lobe of the brain. Unlike those of other birds, the owl's outer ear canal is surrounded by a movable flap of skin that collects and concentrates sound. This flap is not apparent because it is covered by the contour feathers, which make up the bird's characteristic facial disk, and which also collect and focus sound on the ear canal. The external openings of the ear canal face forward and are asymmetric in the lateral plane. These features of the outer ear enable the owl not only to detect faint sounds, but to judge accurately the distance and direction of the sound source. The auditory centers in the brain are proportionally up to twice as large as those of day-flying species. This increased size apparently enables owls to better interpret differences in timing and intensity between electrical impulses arriving from each ear. When a perched owl hears a potential meal, it rotates its head to face the sound; when both ears hear the sound simultaneously (that is, when the arrival time of the impulses from both ears is equal), the bird has located the sound on the horizontal plane. The next adjustment depends on the intensity of the sound in both ears, and this is where the asymmetry of the outer ear counts. If the sound is louder to the higher ear, the head must be elevated until the sound is heard with equal loudness in both ears. Now the owl has placed the prey in its auditory cross-hairs. Other adaptations, such as silent flight and ability to hear low-frequency sound, like that of a mouse rustling on the forest floor, make owls extremely effective nocturnal predators. Experiments with the Common Barn Owl, *Tyto alba,* show that it can catch mice in complete darkness. Most nights have enough light for owls to locate prey by sight as well, for their eyes have superior light-gathering ability and a retina densely packed with rod cells. Yet even with these adaptations of eyes and ears, owls have no ability to locate silent objects in complete darkness; other birds can, however.

The Oilbird, *Steatornis caripensis,* of South America, is a nocturnal fruit eater. While flying and feeding at night it uses vision, but the birds nest in colonies in caves that are completely dark. Because obstacles in the cave emit no sound, the bird cannot passively listen and find its way; rather the oilbird, as it flies into the cave, makes short, frequent bursts of sound and listens for the echoes. The time difference of the echo return and its loudness give information on distance and direction of silent objects (Griffin, 1953). This *echo-location* is most highly developed in bats, which produce very high-pitched, loud vocalizations whose echo returns enable these mammals to locate not only obstacles, but flying insects as well. Although no bird has perfected this system as highly as bats have, the Oilbird and some species of cave-nesting swifts take advantage of the reflective qualities of sound to replace vision as the primary sense, at least in these unique habitats.

TOUCH, TASTE, AND SMELL

Sensory cells sensitive to pressure are located throughout the bird's body , but are most concentrated in unfeathered regions such as the feet, beak, and tongue. In feathered areas, touch receptors are located in follicles of the contour feathers, and are associated with bristle feathers that apparently send information to the brain on the location of the contour feather. The bird's feet, adapted for perching, walking, swimming, and catching prey, must be richly innervated with sensory cells that respond to pressure. The beak and oral cavity must also be so equipped. Bristle feathers surrounding the beak of flycatching species act as extensions of the sense of touch. The sensitivity to touch of the bird's mandibles depends greatly on the feeding habits of the species. Although most species locate their food by sight, those that probe or sift for food generally have many sensory endings on each mandible.

Taste and smell are closely related in that the nerve endings of both detect chemicals; these cells are then considered chemoreceptors. Birds as a group have reduced powers in both taste and smell. Most birds accept or reject food visually and therefore have fewer taste buds on the tongue and inside the beak. This preference has been shown in numerous observations of birds' accepting familiar-looking food even when it has been made very bitter.

Debate has been extensive on how well birds can detect airborne chemicals. Audubon observed how vision and odor helped the Turkey Vulture, *Cathartes aura,* locate carrion and concluded that vision was used exclusively. Subsequent observations have shown that the odor of rotting meat is a cue for these birds, but vision is the primary sensory modality. In the Turkey Vulture's brain the olfactory lobe is small compared to those of mammals and reptiles, but well developed compared to those of other birds (Bang and Cobb, 1968). Interestingly, in other vultures the olfactory lobe is reduced, suggesting that these birds, unlike the Turkey Vulture, do not rely on smell at all.

These observations by Bang and Cobb show that other species too have relatively well-developed olfactory lobes; smell might be a vital sense for them. The kiwi in New Zealand, evolving in an environment that had no mammals, in many ways has filled their niche. These nocturnal, flightless birds spend their days in underground burrows, thus having a reduced sense of sight, and seem to rely on smell to find food. The Procellariformes (albatross, shearwater, and petrels) have long been suspected of using smell to find food on the open ocean. Experiments by Grubb (1972,1973) confirm not only that a larger-than-expected number of these birds approached a cod-liver-oil bait from upwind, but that Leach's Storm-Petrel, *Oceanodroma leucorhoa,* used smell to locate its nesting burrow.

ENDOCRINE AND REPRODUCTIVE SYSTEMS

The sensory nerves, brain, and motor nerves gather information, integrate it, and control behavior, but the nervous system is not the only regulatory system in the body. The endocrine system alters the behavior of cells as it releases hormones from glands in the body, often complementing and enhancing the brain's effects. In fact many hormones are under direct nervous-system control. When danger approaches, a bird's nervous system must ready the body for flight; in part of this signaling, motor nerves stimulate the adrenal gland to release adrenalin, which increases heart and breathing rates and elevates the amount of sugar in the blood. As in human beings, blood sugar is regulated by insulin, which is produced and released by the pancreas. The brain also controls

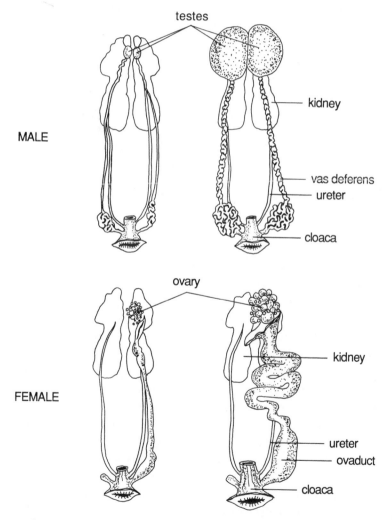

The reproductive systems in birds change dramatically from their nonbreeding condition (left) to their breeding condition (right).

other hormone-secreting glands that have long-term effects on the organism, such as the thyroid gland, which releases hormones that control the bird's growth and metabolism, and the parathyroid gland, which regulates the use of calcium and phosphorus, minerals vital to bone and muscle and also essential in egg development.

The complex interaction between nervous system and endocrine system in birds is best illustrated by their synergistic control of the reproductive system. In the Northern Hemisphere, most birds become sexually active in spring. Until then the sexual organs are much reduced in size, but they expand rapidly as the breeding season begins. This seasonal maturing of the gonads is controlled by hormones released by the pituitary gland. The pituitary hormones, however, are governed by a closely associated brain structure, the hypothalamus, which in turn is influenced by the *pineal gland*. The pineal gland, a midbrain structure directly under the skull, has sensory capabilities in that it becomes active as length of day increases. With lengthening daylight in spring the pineal gland acts on the hypothalamus, initiating a complex sequence of hormonally mediated changes, including increased size of the sexual organs, molt, migratory readiness, courtship, and territoriality.

Although all other physiological systems maintain the organism from day to day, the reproductive system is designed to assure the species of its place in the future. To this end, birds, like all other vertebrates, produce specialized cells in the gonads, which, by fertilization, develop into the next generation.

The two most notable features in the bird's reproductive system are the lack of external genitalia and the difference in size of the reproductive organs between breeding and nonbreeding seasons. Both of these features are adaptations for flight, the former maintaining a streamlined design and the latter reducing weight.

In male birds, the sperm develops in the paired testes, which are on the abdominal wall near the kidneys. As the breeding season opens, the testes increase in size more than one hundred times and begin to produce sperm in the complex tubular structure of these organs. The vas deferens carries sperm away from the testes and stores it before it leaves the body through the cloaca. Along with sperm the testes produce male hormones or androgens, which influence the male's behavior during the breeding season.

In females, the ovary produces eggs and hormones. Unlike most vertebrates, which have two functioning ovaries, most birds have only one functional ovary, usually the left. As in males, the mature products of the ovary are conducted away from it by a duct and the ovary secretes hormones that account for female breeding behavior. But the egg and sperm produced are quite different cells. Males produce millions of sperm cells during the breeding season and females make between one and twenty eggs, all many times larger than sperm. In fact, the mature product of the ovary is the yolk, by far the largest cell in the body.

Copulation transfers sperm from the cloaca of the male to that of the female. The sperm ascend the oviduct to fertilize the descending egg, which begins the complex work of forming the next generation. The first step is completed in the oviduct by wrapping the yolk with protein-rich fluids that will become the white of an egg and covering it with a hard shell before it is expelled from the body through the cloaca.

Suggested Reading

For anatomy, the classic work is *The Vertebrate Body*, by Romer, which gives the internal structure of birds and other vertebrates. Likewise, *Animal Physiology*, by Schmidt-Nielsen, describes the internal workings of animals. For birds, the two-volume text, *Biology and Comparative Physiology of Birds*, edited by Marshall, is a comprehensive work, as is *Avian Physiology*, edited by Sturkie. A less comprehensive but very complete description of the bird's anatomy and physiology can be found in Welty, *The Life of Birds*, chapters 4 to 8.

- 5 -

Behavior

THE SENSORY WORLD OF ANIMALS VARIES: bees see the ultraviolet patterns on flowers, some snakes locate their prey by heat waves, and sharks detect fish by electric fields. Most mammals live in a world permeated by odors of predator and prey, summoned or alarmed by chemical signals that few other animals can detect. Whether they are establishing a territory, tracking a victim, or attracting a mate, their lives are shrouded in these cryptic chemical signals. But birds are primarily seeing and hearing creatures, and so conduct their business very much out in the open. If they could not fly, total exposure would be risky business, but flight equalizes the eavesdroppers' advantages, reducing the potential predator to a mere observer. Human beings are similar to birds in that we too are creatures with vision and hearing, and over the ages we have looked at and listened to these other forms of light and sound, finding ourselves so intrigued by birds' varied behavioral repertoire that we have ascribed human, almost poetic qualities to the call of the loon on some misty northern lake, or the thrush song in the deep woods, but not to other animals' croaks, barks, and peeps. We also project into a line of ducklings swimming behind their mother the essence of childhood obedience and parental care, or into a redstart flitting in a white beech tree on a May morning the embodiment of energy and beauty. Although those who study animal behavior have striven to strike these human adjectives in describing birds' behavior, we know more about their behavior than about that of any other group of animals because of our sensory affinity with them and the human qualities they stir in us.

The scientific study of animal behavior is relatively new. Beginning in the 1920s with work by Konrad Lorenz, Niko Tinbergen, and Karl von Frisch, this discipline has set out to describe and understand the overt actions of organisms. It has employed many forms of research, from laboratory studies of sensory systems and learning to field observation and experimentation. Studying animals

83

in their natural habitat, or ethology, is one of the most fruitful endeavors in this science, for only in these natural settings do animals respond naturally to a world they are familiar with.

The ethological perspective is that animals' overt actions are adaptive. Although the behavior of organisms leaves no fossil record, these behaviors have evolved much like cells and bones and physiological systems. Any individual's behavior is determined by its anatomy and physiology, which are set by its genetic makeup; therefore any behvaior is designed to best fit it to the environment. In two broad but not mutually exclusive ways, however, an animal's physiology, and ultimately natural selection, control behavior: instinct and learning.

INSTINCT AND LEARNING

Instinctual or innate behavior consists of an organism's preprogrammed patterns of action. These actions are inborn and highly stereotyped in each species. Learned behavior is acquired by experience and thus shows extensive variability among members of a species. Innate and learned responses to the environment are different solutions to the same problem—staying alive. Innate behaviors, tested by time, are relatively safe and sure responses. In organisms with short life spans and little parental care, innate behaviors are absolutely essential for survival. The disadvantage in this type of fixed response is that if the environment changes rapidly, the organism's behavior can turn inappropriate and may take many generations to change, if it does at all. Such was the case with the Passenger Pigeon, *Ectopistes migratorius,* which would circle as a flock and return to the place where one bird had left the group to alight on the ground. This behavior must have had some adaptive value, perhaps in leading the flock to an individual that had broken away, having spotted food or a safe place to roost overlooked by the others. Such behavior, however, led directly to the mass slaughter of the species in the mid-1800s, for when the environment changed, bringing a new predator—man—and some members of the flock were shot from the sky, the entire flock returned to face the gunner's fire.

In learning, a behavior is altered by experience, eliminating maladaptive responses and adding successful ones. Unlike instinct, learned behaviors can change very quickly, but only if the inevitable mistakes are not too grave and are quickly corrected. Animals that have long life spans and extended parental care are more influenced by experience, and their behavior is formed more by learning than by instinct.

The role that instinct and learning play in species is illustrated in the migratory behavior of the Whooping Crane, *Grus americana,* and the Indigo Bunting, *Passerina cyanea.* Whooping cranes move seasonally from their winter range on the Gulf Coast to breed in central Canada. In late summer, when the chicks are fledged, the cranes fly south in families, making regular stops along the way. Although the fledglings instinctually feel the migratory urge and build up fat before the flight, the route south probably is learned from the parents. In spring the young birds again accompany the parents north. When Indigo Bunting chicks leave the nest, however, they remain with the parents for a relatively short time, after which the adult birds abandon the offspring and their temperate breeding grounds to begin the journey south. It is remarkable that the young birds find their way to the wintering grounds and return again in the spring, for the fall flight can cover well over 2,000 kilometers, traverses varied land forms and waterways, and takes place at night. This species gets no time for trial and error; the fledglings must do it right on the first try, which is primarily based on predetermined, inborn instructions.

Studies of the Indigo Bunting's seasonal behavior also point out how learning and instinct interact in a complex behavior like migration. For migration is not one behavior, but a sequence of related activities including molt, increased feeding to build up body fat, nocturnal restlessness, and orientation and navigation, among others. We might think the crane "learns" its migratory route and the bunting "knows" it, but this distinction is not so simple. For the bunting's nocturnal restlessness has been shown to be innate, but its ability to use the stars to orient itself southward is acquired by exposure to the night sky (Emlen, 1975).

Avian behavior is determined more by instinct than by learning. Lack of development in the bird's learning centers of the cerebral cortex suggests that instinct prevails; so too does the striking similarity in behavior among members of a species. Many behaviors such as food storage that seem "thoughtful" and show "planning" result from pure instinct. The Acorn Woodpecker, *Melanerpes formicivorus*, stores acorns in holes it drills in the surface of trees, but if the hole it drills leads into a larger cavity the bird will continue to try to fill the space, even though the food cache is now inaccessible; the seemingly thoughtful behavior is shown to be a simple drive to fill a space.

INSTINCTUAL BEHAVIOR IN BIRDS

When ethologists first went into the field to catalogue birds' behavior they were struck that actions engaged in by members of a species were similar. Whether the behavior they observed was nesting, courtship, or feeding and care of young, sequence and timing of every bird's movements were remarkably alike. All male Common Goldeneye ducks, *Bucephala clangula,* perform a characteristic "head throw" when courting a female; the timing of this behavior varies no more than one one-hundredth of a second among males (Dane and Van der Kloot, 1964). Courting male and female Western Grebes, *Aechmophorus occidentalis,* move together in a highly stereotyped and synchronous pattern that varies little among pairs. Observations such as these led Konrad Lorenz (1950) to propose that these behaviors are the result of innate, fixed action patterns.

Experiments show that these fixed action patterns were not in response to the entire range of stimuli in the environment, but were often released by

A male Common Goldeneye performs a "head throw."

exceedingly specific stimuli. For a male Euopean Robin, *Erithacus rubecula,* a tuft of red feathers will elicit the same aggressive response as an intruding male will, but a stuffed male with brown breast feathers will be tolerated on the territory (Lack, 1943). A male Northern Flicker, *Colaptes auratus,* will **drive** off his mate if the black mustache of a male is painted on her (Noble, 1936). And a female chicken will come to help upon hearing stressful sounds made by her chicks, but will ignore a chick in distress if it is only seen and not heard. These discrete signals that release a behavior are called sign stimuli.

In Lorenz's model of behavior, an organism has a motor pattern waiting and ready to go and the sign stimulus acts as a key that opens the innate releasing mechanism that allows the fixed action pattern to be expressed. Why one behavior is released and not another has to do with the organism's internal

A pair of Western Grebes courting

state, in that each fixed action pattern is stored discretely and builds up specific action-specific energy. This energy drives the fixed action pattern when the sign stimulus unlocks the innate releasing mechanism.

This interpretation has been extremely useful in explaining an organism's behavior, which we can now consider adaptive, but not necessarily purposeful. An adult Herring Gull, *Larus argentatus*, feeds its young because the sign stimulus of begging for food releases the adult's fixed feeding response; the sight of a clutch of eggs releases a hen's brooding behavior. The young are fed and the eggs warmed, but the adults do so to satisfy their internal drives; the young and the eggs only provide the correct stimulus. In fact, the behavior can be quite independent from the context in which it is given, as is readily seen in behavior by adults in a tern colony, where a chick outside the very small radius of the nesting territory elicits an aggressive response from the adult; if it evades the adult's pecks and enters the territory, though, it is likely to be fed.

This model of behavior is also useful in explaining actions that occur with no stimulus or are released by an inappropriate stimulus. Many birds have been observed going through the motions of nest building when deprived of nesting material, or adopting courtship postures when the opposite sex was not present, and more than one hundred published reports tell of birds feeding the young of other species during the breeding season (Shy, 1982), as well as an unusual report of a bird feeding goldfish in a backyard pond. The action-specific energy here has built up so strongly that the innate releasing mechanism cannot hold it back, and the fixed action pattern can be seen as breaking out more than as being released. Another consequence of this buildup of action-specific energy is that sign stimuli become more general as time goes on. When given a choice, male Mallards, *Anas platyrhynchos*, will court a female Mallard, for she has the appropriate shape and color to release this behavior, but if deprived of the female of this species, the male's behavior will be released by females of closely related species. The hybrids that have been observed between Mallards and American Black Ducks, *Anas rubripes*, or Mallards and Northern Pintails, *Anas acuta*, presumably result from this buildup of action-specific energy.

Surprisingly, artificial stimuli have been experimentally demonstrated to release a fixed action pattern more readily than the naturally occurring sign stimuli. The European Oystercatcher, *Haematopus ostralegus*, when given a choice between its own egg and a very large egg of similar color and pattern will invariably try to sit on the larger egg. Young Herring Gulls, *Larus argentatus*, will peck at a red spot on a yellow background, which is the color pattern of the adult beak, but an all-red beak model will elicit more pecks than that of the natural color pattern (Tinbergen, 1951).

Although this model of behavior is a widely accepted interpretation of animals' innate action, it does not escape criticism for two reasons. The first is that evidence is slight that the model's constructs of fixed action patterns, action-specific energies, and innate releasing mechanisms have any nervous-system counterparts. The brain does not seem to be organized in layers of very specific nerve cells that control motor patterns, each with a specific reservoir of action-specific energy and its releasing mechanism. Rather, the brain's structure is more complex, where motor patterns used in flying, for instance, are used again in display, but are altered by incorporation of other nervous-system pathways. This complex brain structure contributes to the second criticism of the model: this explanation of behavior is too simple. Animals are not robots; they have nervous systems that afford more flexibility in behavior than the model suggests. An example of a more flexible response in birds may be found in the territorial behavior of the male White-throated Sparrow, *Zonotrichia albicollis*. The male's aggressive response to a neighboring male's song decreases as the breeding season progresses. This pattern might result from a decrease in production of action-specific energy, and with it a decrease in aggressive response to the sign stimulus, which here is male song (Falls, 1969). But if a neighboring male is captured and in place of his song a tape-recording of another male's song is played, the response is as aggressive as it would have been at the beginning of the breeding season. The male's behavior is not consistent with, and is more complex than, the model of fixed action patterns, for if the song is a sign stimulus, the territorial male responds to it selectively.

Konrad Lorenz would probably concede that his interpretation of behavior is not free of problems, and that some innate behaviors do become more flexible during maturation and through learning. His theory, however, has survived, for it has generated much research, the results of which are mostly consistent with his ideas. This model is also important because it presents a unified view of behavior, joining such diverse actions as feeding, courtship, and song, in the same conceptual framework.

IMPRINTING

If innate behaviors are set in animals' genes and learned behaviors become incorporated into their nervous system, behaviors that result from imprinting share characteristics of both instinct and learning. For imprinting, once it occurs, resists change through an organism's lifetime but is modifiable during stages in the animal's development. Some authorities therefore have treated imprinting as either a special case of innate behavior or a primitive form of learning. Whatever its position, imprinting is a valuable adaptation that influences recognition of species, sexual behavior, preferences for food, and selection of habitat.

In imprinting, some behavior becomes associated with a specific stimulus. This procedure is widespread in animals and most pronounced in avian species with young that can run soon after birth, such as chickens and ducks. The first type of imprinting occurs soon after birth, when the young will follow almost any moving object. This bond between the young and an object develops very rapidly during the "critical" period, which in chickens and ducks lasts only twenty-four hours. If the young birds are deprived of any object to imprint on during this time, and then exposed to, say, their natural mother, they will not follow her.

A line of downy chicks following a hen is a natural result of imprinting, but these birds would have followed a rolling ball or a stuffed fox, if they were exposed to these objects during the first twenty-four hours of life. For many species, imprinting seems to depend on visual stimuli alone, where the object need only be of an appropriate size, but in species that breed in a habitat with visual barriers, such as a wood or marsh, sound is an important stimulus as well. For these species, if the ball does not quack, it will not be followed. Sound is also required in Wood Ducks, *Aix sponsa,* which nest in tree cavities where the young do not get a view of their mother until after they leave the nest.

Termination of the critical imprinting period coincides with development of the fear response in the young. On the first day of life an object that will elicit a following response will, to a bird held in isolation, be responded to by fear on the second day of life. The discreteness in the critical period of imprinting in the young of species that can run at birth must be one vital factor that has led these birds to hatch all their eggs at the same time. In species whose young are born helpless and remain in the nest for a long time, imprinting lacks this well-defined critical period.

After imprinting on an object to follow, the young become successively imprinted on the habitat in which they live, on food, and finally on the object to which they will direct their sexual behavior.

In most ducks and geese, imprinting on habitat and food occurs after the second day of life. This type of imprinting explains why the young of these species, especially the migratory ones, return to the same type of habitat, often to the same area, the next spring. This attachment to a site caused by imprinting also isolates species and can form subspecies. In Mallards, *Anas platyrhynchos,* birds that were raised on saltwater marshes will return to that habitat in the spring, but those born on inland ponds will seek a freshwater habitat on which to breed. In the Bald Eagle, *Haliaeetus leucocephalus,* imprinting on the habitat occurs only after the young have left the nest. Knowing this timing has been useful in reestablishing these birds in areas where they formerly nested, for young birds taken from Alaska can be released at a new site just before fledging, and the birds will attempt nesting in the latter areas when they are ready to breed.

Sexual imprinting occurs later in life—in ducks it is between the thirtieth and sixtieth day. After this type of imprinting the young will direct their sexual overtures to the imprinted object when they reach sexual maturity. That sexual imprinting comes later can be demonstrated by isolating a duck after it is naturally imprinted on its mother, and then exposing it to an inappropriate object. When this bird reaches sexual maturity it will attempt to court this object and not a member of its species. In species where the sexes look alike, such as most geese, both male and female goslings imprint equally on the opposite sex. But in many sexually dimorphic species the dull-colored female alone raises the young. In these species only the male young sexually imprint; the female young retain an innate response to the adult male. This difference is interesting considering the framework of sign stimuli and fixed action patterns. Here the male "learns" the correct sign stimuli that will release his fixed courtship patterns, whereas the female apparently is born with the correct innate releasing mechanism that will elicit her courtship behavior when she sees the brightly colored male in the next breeding season.

LEARNING

Although not known for their cognitive ability, all birds learn. Broadly defined, learning is a change in behavior through experience. Just what causes these changes in behavior is still open to question, for although learning is the mark of human behavior, as a process it is not well understood. The idea that each experience forges individual neural circuits in the brain has been discarded for the view that experience is stored diffusely in the brain, which makes recall and memory more complex than formerly thought. The different types of learning in birds generally entail modification of instinctual behavior. In describing the different types of learning, we will follow Thorpe (1963).

Probably the simplest form of learning is habituation. It is simple because a new or modified behavior is not acquired, but responses to some stimuli are lost. A flock of ground-feeding sparrows will take wing when the wind kicks up leaves, but after repeated exposure to windblown leaves, the birds will continue feeding on the ground; because the leaves' movements present no threat or reward, the birds habituate to them. This type of learning has obvious adaptive value in that it saves energy. Colonial nesting birds act aggressive toward their neighbors as the breeding season begins, but as time progresses this behavior wanes, allowing them to spend more time raising a family.

Habituation may be more complex than once thought because often the stimulus is ignored only when it is presented in a familiar context. A cat making its normal rounds may not elicit an alarm call from a jay, but if the cat appears on another part of the jay's territory, the bird will noisily mark its presence.

The most common form of learning in birds occurs when a stimulus has punishment or reward value. This type of learning is called associative learning. In associative learning, behaviors that result in pain are not repeated and stimuli associated with the unpleasant experience are avoided, whereas behaviors or stimuli that result in a reward are repeated or become attractive.

This type of learning is particularly necessary for choosing food in species that eat many kinds of food. Experiments on the Blue Jay, *Cyanocitta cristata*, show that a naive jay will consume Monarch butterflies readily. These butterflies, being poisonous, cause the jay to vomit soon after, and the unpleasant experience causes the bird to avoid them in the future. Interestingly, the jay will also avoid the Viceroy butterfly, similar to the Monarch in color and pattern, but not poisonous, showing that the stimulus associated with the unpleasant experience becomes generalized (Brower, 1969). This stimulus generalization is a vital part of learning, for objects with similar shapes and colors often yield similar rewards or punishments. In external appearance the Viceroy butterfly denies jays a palatable meal, but stimulus generalization allows them to look for food in similar places or in similar ways. Hummingbirds generalize on the color red, choosing red flowers or red objects to explore as a possible source of food, and birds at a seed feeder will try foods that they would otherwise never have been exposed to.

A unique example of avian learning was reported from England in the 1950s. Here several species of birds learned that a fresh supply of food was delivered every morning to their neighborhoods by the local milkman. After the bottles of milk were left at the doorsteps, the birds would remove the cardboard cap to get at the cream. They even raided milk bottles on the delivery truck while it made its rounds.

When scientists surveyed the neighborhoods to determine incidence of this thievery, they found that at least seven species were involved and that the crimes were local but widespread. They came to believe that the source of food was discovered by at least one individual in each locale and that other birds learned the trick by imitation (Fisher and Hinde, 1957).

Learning by imitation is a very effective way of acquiring information about the environment, especially in species that are social, for an individual need not directly experience the consequences of a behavior or stimulus, but may base its avoidance or acceptance of an object on actions by others.

Use of tools is probably another form that associative learning takes. Tool use was once considered an exclusively human characteristic, but it has been found in many animal species, including some thirty species of birds. In birds, tool use ranges from employing cactus spines to probe for insects in trees by the Woodpecker Finch, *Camarhynchus pallidus,* to herons dropping bait in the water to attract and catch fish (Higuchi, 1987). The Egyptian Vulture, *Neophron percnopterus,* drops stones on Ostrich, *Struthio camelus,* eggs to crack them open. This vulture regularly eats eggs, but the Ostrich egg is too hard and large for it to pick up and drop. Close observation of the bird's use of stones shows that the behavior probably results from associative learning and not insight. When a vulture first locates an Ostrich nest, it will repeatedly try to pick the eggs up. Failing to do so and probably out of frustration, the bird will pick up and drop stones in the vicinity as if they were eggs. If by chance the stone falls on an egg and cracks it open, yielding a reward, the Vulture will repeat this behavior sequence, refining it with repetition and giving the appearance that the bird is seeking a tool with which to open the eggs (Alcock, 1970).

Although a reward or punishment is essential for associative learning to take place, learning also occurs when these reinforcements are absent. In latent learning an animal will explore and gain information about its surroundings for no apparent reason except to have a look. Hawks and gulls will soar high above their territories or breeding grounds, and chickadees will move through the forest, simply to explore. This rather nonspecific type of behavior has adaptive value, for animals that have had time to explore the environment have a better chance than newcomers of surviving stress. Many experiments show that being familiar with a habitat increases an animal's chances of evading a predator by quickly finding a hiding place; but, to differentiate latent learning from associa-

This Green-backed Heron has learned, as have other herons, to drop bait into the water to attract fish.

tive learning, these hiding places have no value until the predator appears. Similarly, knowing a constant source of water, an abundant supply of food, or a protected roost well before drought or winter set in is another consequence of latent learning.

Play has always been considered an activity restricted to more intelligent animals. Although difficult to define, play most often involves incomplete behavior patterns performed out of context and from sheer exuberance. Play is useful in that it coordinates motor patterns and is practice for events to come. Though it was once considered exclusively a mammalian behavior, many species of birds have been observed at play. Crows and ravens, among others, have been seen playing in the wind. Crows have been known to fly in strong winds performing fantastic maneuvers for no apparent reason, and ravens will fly into the wind that blows across a ridgetop only to circle and do it again. Northern Fulmars, *Fulmarus glacialis*, have been observed flying repeatedly across the bow of a ship, their only apparent object being to get as close to the bow as possible without touching it, much as dolphins do. It is reported that eider ducks will shoot down a rapid section of a stream to calm water, where they will get out and walk back above the rapids to ride down again (Roberts, 1934). Many species of birds have been observed in mock attacks on objects such as sticks and leaves, grabbing the object as if it were a snake or mouse, playing with it, and letting it drop.

Observations of play, imitation learning, and tool use in birds give us some insight into cognitive development in the avian brain, showing that birds are not like their ancestral relatives, the reptiles. The latter strike us as mechanical and humorless, but birds are more akin to mammals in their ability to comprehend more complex relationships and possibly derive some pleasure out of life. It might be interesting, then, to look at what is known about the upper limit of learning in birds.

Insight learning deals with solving problems by understanding relationships between variables; that is, learning by concept and not by rote. In laboratory studies, Canaries, *Serinus canarius,* demonstrated that they could grasp the concept of uniqueness. When presented with a set of objects, one of which was different, the bird learned that under the unique object food was located. In subsequent trials, with different sets of objects, the canaries showed no hesitation in choosing the unique object to gain a reward. Birds have also demonstrated that they have at least limited ability to comprehend numbers. In the lab they have been trained to recognize and respond correctly to a number whether it is presented as a group of shapes, flashes of light, or sounds (Koehler, 1951). They have shown too that they can obtain food suspended on a string by pulling on the string with the beak, then holding it with the feet, while they reach down again to pull with the beak. This type of behavior has also been demonstrated in the field by crows, which have learned to rob ice fishermen of their catch. When the flag at a fishing hole goes up indicating a catch, a crow will fly in and begin to pull the line out by walking backward; some distance from the hole he will let go of the line and walk back to the hole, all the time stepping on the line so as not to let it slip back into the water. After repeated pulls the crow will have its reward (Welty, 1975).

SOCIAL BEHAVIOR

The male and female of a species come together to breed during the time when food is most abundant in the environment. At this time birds exhibit the greatest amount of social interaction and their most varied behavior, for during the breeding season they must establish and defend a territory, communicate their willingness to breed, build a nest, and care for and feed their young. These activities are quite complex and vary widely from species to species; because of this complexity we will deal with social behavior among birds during the breeding season in subsequent chapters; here we discuss their social behavior during the nonbreeding season.

In the nonbreeding season the food supply is generally low and birds' behavior is directed toward survival and not reproduction. At this time birds lead simpler lives and social interaction among members of a species is reduced. At this time of year social arrangement is determined mainly by the food supply and by predation.

The solitary animal has the simplest social arrangement during the nonbreeding season. Solitary birds are something of a rarity, occurring regularly only among hummingbirds, woodpeckers, and birds of prey. Their lack of social interaction is probably predicated by the type and location of their food in this season.

Hummingbirds depend on nectar in flowering plants, a source of food that is clumped and patchily distributed in the environment. Individual humming-birds defend these resources, limiting their interaction to driving off competi-tors at these sites. Because the flower bed or flower tree is a short-lived source, hummingbirds must continue to shift their territories throughout the season.

During the winter woodpeckers feed mostly on insect grubs and seeds, food that is more evenly spread through the environment. After the breeding season, woodpeckers stake out territories large enough to support only one individual. Woodpeckers seem intolerant of members of their own species and have been reported to squabble continually with their mates during the breeding season; this solitary existence in winter seems to suit their nature. Lewis' Woodpecker, *Melanerpes lewis,* is an exception; this species feeds on flying insects that are locally abundant when available, and thus is more gregarious than others.

Raptors are often loners for much the same reason as woodpeckers. Their food is evenly distributed, and they must hunt over a large area to support themselves. The day-flying hawks are seen in loose flocks during migration, but these concentrations are held together by locally favorable soaring conditions and the flocks disband when they reach the wintering ranges. Among owls, species such as the Long-eared Owl, *Asio otus,* are found roosting together in trees at times during the nonbreeding season, but only in habitats with limited daytime roosts, such as islands of trees in an extensive coastal marsh. The birds are solitary hunters at night, tolerating the neighbors' presence only as they sleep during the day.

Vultures also congregate in specific areas to sleep. After flying alone all day, these birds regularly return to roosting sites shared by other vultures. The roosts are favorable because they are close to physical features that develop thermals early in the day. Roosting here means they can start the next day's flying early and with little effort. Unlike the hawks, vultures do not defend areas and are more tolerant of one another. Again, their food source is a factor: vultures depend on food that is randomly distributed, but when it appears, is in large quantity. While looking for food, these birds distribute themselves evenly over the habitat, but always keep an eye on the neighbor. When one bird spots food and descends, adjacent birds are attracted, starting a chain reaction, drawing in birds from long distances to the source of food. Some species of eagles also con-gregate in specific areas during the nonbreeding season. Large groups of Bald Eagles, *Haliaeetus leucocephalus,* can be found along some rivers when fish kills occur, but these birds remain together only as long as the food persists.

Although solitary species remain intolerant toward members of their species after nesting, most birds show decided wariness about being alone through the winter, and this uneasiness leads them to form the *flock,* the most familiar and characteristic social arrangement of birds during the nonbreeding season. The flock is any aggregation of birds, but it varies widely in size, composition, and social structure. The size of a flock depends on the species and the habitat in which they are found, ranging from a handful to groups in the millions. A species such as the Cedar Waxwing, *Bombycilla cedrorum,* is the "bird of a feather," in that it rarely associates with other birds, but many flocks include a number of species. The advantage to the individual in associating with other birds in a flock is greater feeding success and better protection from predators than if they were alone.

The flock's many eyes and ears increase feeding success for the members in several ways. Species that gather nightly in roosts and disperse widely during the day to feed can transmit information on quality of the environment. Birds that have had a successful day feeding leave the roost early and fly directly to the feeding area next morning; it is thought that other members of the flock key in on this behavior and follow, especially if they have had little success the day before. On the open ocean, a diving tern or gannet is a sure sign of food and will attract scattered members of the group. In other species, not only does the group help in locating food, but they can concentrate it as well. Surface-feeding American White Pelicans, *Pelecanus erythrorhynchos,* gather in a line when they locate a school of fish and then drive the fish into shallow water, where they can be caught more easily. Although this is probably an innate behavior, the group's action seems intentional as they splash and raise their wings, finally cutting off escape for the school by enclosing them in a semicircle near the shore. Cormorants, avocets, and stilts have been observed in similar food-concentrating maneuvers. Flocks of ground-feeding blackbirds perform a terrestrial version of a food drive: while feeding in a field, they form a moving line a few individuals thick. The group behavior stirs up insects on the leading edge of the line, making them easy prey. While birds in the front of the line stop and feed, those at the back fly to the front, making the whole group appear to "roll" across the field. In forests, particularly in the tropics, flocks of mixed species move together while feeding. Again, this group behavior is thought to improve the individual's success in feeding by stirring up insects and making them easier to catch. Although seed-eating birds have no need for collective behavior in surrounding or concentrating their food, having other birds present increases feeding success for these species as well. A lone pigeon feeding on the ground spends much time on the lookout for danger; having other birds around decreases the time any one bird needs to watch, lengthening the feeding time.

If the group improves chances of finding a meal, it also reduces the probability that an individual will become a meal for a predator. Again, the flock's multiple eyes and ears make detection of predators more efficient, and often the group's behavior deters the predator.

When a member of a flock locates a predator it gives an alarm call. If the predator is on the ground or perched in a tree, the call takes the form of a harsh, easy-to-locate "chink" sound. This call shows strong convergence among species and is therefore understood and recognized by all members of a mixed flock. The group's response to the alarm varies. The call may simply alert other members and locate the potential predator, but the group may also proceed to harass or mob the predator. This mobbing behavior usually distracts the predator or ousts the raptor from its perch, but flocks of birds sometimes drive predators to their death. An unusual report relates how a flock of Common Loons, *Gavia immer*, caused the death of a swimming coyote by continually harassing it until it was disoriented and exhausted; then it drowned (Barklow et al, 1984).

When the predator is a flying, bird-eating falcon or accipiter hawk, the alarm call given by a member of the flock is quite different from the "chink" call. Often described as a "seeet" sound, its structure is high and thin in frequency, with a gradual beginning and end. This sound is difficult to locate, allowing the caller to alert the group to the danger without giving away its position to the predator.

These starlings group together in a tight flock to thwart the dive of a hunting falcon.

When a flock of birds encounters a falcon while flying, they respond by gathering tightly together. This flight formation is thought to discourage the predator from striking an individual in the group, because the hawk might injure itself by hitting another bird besides its intended victim. This idea is bolstered by observations of groups of blackbirds repeatedly thwarting a falcon's dive by forming a tight cluster at the last instant before the falcon struck (Mohr, 1960).

All flocks of birds exhibit these types of collective behavior in varying degrees in responding to food and predators, but most large flocks lack social organization. Members of these large groups act as individuals, simply taking advantage of the others' presence. The flock has no leader and no followers, and members are free to leave and join other groups. Only in species that live more or less permanently in smaller flocks do the elements of a social system begin to exhibit themselves. In a flock of domestic chickens, groups of ten or fewer birds form stable and orderly social relations, each member getting along on its own rung of the social ladder. When the group is increased to more than ten birds, its stable behavior often breaks down (Collias and Collias, 1967). This orderly social arrangement is maintained by a dominance hierarchy, commonly referred to as *peck order.*

The dominance hierarchy is quite common in flocks of birds, and although the expression peck order suggests internal conflict, that order reduces conflict. The dominant individuals always get uncontested first access to resources when they are limited, such as food or a favored perch. Only when the group becomes large and each bird's place in the social order is open to some question does some squabbling occur. These social species, in which the dominance hierarchy depends on individual recognition, often form closed groups, not allowing other individuals to enter the flock; new flocks form by splintering off from the group. As we shall see, that these groups do not allow outsiders to enter has important ramifications, for these groups are composed of family members, and what a bird will do for its neighbor is quite different from what it will do for its kin.

In species that re-form into flocks after the breeding season, each individual's social status is established at that time, and in subsequent years the individual's relative position changes because of experience gained during the breeding season. In birds that remain in a flock throughout the year the dominance hierarchy forms early in life, and, in species such as geese and chickens, status of the young is determined very much by the rank held by parents or mother. A high-ranking mother usually conveys her rank to her offspring. Thereafter, the individual's relative social position remains fixed for life. Many species have separate peck orders for each sex, like chickens, among which a low-ranking male is always dominant over the highest-ranking female. The social position is maintained by social signaling, and only when the dominant individual grows old or weak does the social order change; change is generally effected by having every member of the flock move up the social ladder at once.

The advantage in this type of social system is that it eliminates unncessary competition over resources, leaving more time for feeding, mating, and resting. In environments with plentiful and evenly spread resources, the dominance hierarchy is difficult to detect: a flock of chickadees foraging in the trees seems to have no dominant or submissive individuals; only when access to food is limited, as at a seed feeder, does it become apparent that some members of the group feed when they please and others must wait.

The species of birds that exhibit most social structure belong to the family Corvidae, the crows, jays, and magpies. Some species in this family remain together for the entire year, the flock being composed of related individuals; but these birds differ from other flocking birds in that they exhibit not only collective behavior, but cooperative behavior as well. We can see the distinction between collective and cooperative behavior by contrasting behavior of a group of blackbirds feeding in a field to that of a flock of crows. When approached, the first feeding blackbird to spot the intruder sounds an alarm call and the entire flock heads for the trees. A flock of crows feeding on the ground inevitably has a lookout perched in the trees close by. An approaching predator is first sighted by the lookout and its alarm call sends the ground feeders to a

Crows commonly post a "sentry" while feeding on the ground.

safe perch. That this social group posts a lookout suggests that individuals have roles and that their behavior benefits other members of the group. These roles probably are loosely defined, in that the job of lookout or scout is not always assigned to one individual, but rotates through members of the flock.

Not much is known about how extensive social interaction is in avian societies, nor is it known just how many species exhibit cooperative behavior. It has been assumed that the most advanced societies belong to species of crows and jays, but even about these species little is known because of the difficulty in studying a fast-moving and highly mobile group of birds.

One species that has been studied for a relatively long time is the Scrub Jay, *Aphelocoma coerulescens,* in Florida. The Jay's range is restricted to the scrub forests at the center of the state and this population is discontinuous with that of the Scrub Jay in the western states. The Florida Jays are sedentary, occupying the same territory all year. Apparently because the prime habitat is limited, the young do not leave the parents' territory to establish their own breeding area, but remain with the parents. The social grouping of these Jays, then, is a flock comprised of family members that collectively defend their territory. Younger birds are less dominant than older ones, and the adult male and female, the parents, are the most dominant and the only breeders. Behavior among these young birds during the breeding season points to the group's cooperative activity, for not only do they help defend the nest from predators, they also help

A pair of Florida Scrub Jays enlist the aid of a helper (left) at the nest.

their parents by feeding the young (Woolfenden, 1975). Nonbreeding nest helpers have been observed in other species, such as the Arabian Babbler, *Turdoides squamicips,* the Superb Blue Wren, *Malurus cyaneus,* and possibly some species of anis and New World cuckoos, suggesting that the social order in these species is also complex.

The study of animal behavior, then, has revealed much about overt actions among organisms other than ourselves. The principles underlying innate behaviors have been described, as have the effects of imprinting, and we have come a long way in understanding animals' cognitive abilities and social organization. Nevertheless, we know in detail about behavior in only a handful of bird species, and we know next to nothing about the lives of most species. Studying animal behavior has also given us a perspective from which to consider ourselves, and although human beings as a species show little instinctual behavior, some of our actions are surprisingly similar to those of birds. The effects of experience in early life on our later behavior are much like avian imprinting, and rights given a land owner are similar to territorial arrangements in avian species. In learning and social behavior, I think we have come to see that our superior cognitive ability differs only in degree from that of other organisms with which we share the planet, and that our social organization and behavior are governed by the same forces that shape interactions in other species.

Suggested Reading

Marler and Hamilton's *Mechanisms of Animal Behavior* is an extensive work on studies of animal behavior with many references to birds. *Animal Behavior: Its Development, Ecology, and Evolution,* by Wallace, is similar, but this author has more of an evolutionary approach to the subject. To gain some understanding about how a species behavior is studied, no book is better than Niko Tinbergen's *A Herring Gull's World;* close behind is Lack's *The Life of the Robin* and *Shearwater,* by Lockley.

Projects

Some simple experiments can be done at a feeder. Among the easiest is this one on food preferences of different species. Set out two or three feeders, each filled with a different type of food, such as sunflower, thistle, and mixed seed, and record the bird's choices by the species and the number of each alighting on each feeder. Because chickadees show a preference for sunflower seeds, I once presented them with a choice between shelled and unshelled seeds after offering them unshelled for most of the winter. Initially they chose the familiar seed, but then they gradually habituated to the fast-food variety.

Once you see which type of food is preferred, you can try more sophisticated experiments. Set out three identical feeders so that the food in each cannot be seen, and attach cards or flags that are identical for the nonpreferred food and a different one for the preferred food. I have used index cards, drawing black circles with an X in the middle for the nonpreferred feeders and red circles with a red X for the preferred one. The markers are possible cues to let the birds know which feeder contains the desired food. After a couple of days of training, start the test by changing the position of the feeders every ten minutes and record the number of birds that alight on each feeder. If the birds follow the preferential feeder it is because they have learned to associate the cue with that food. The same type of experiment can be done with hummingbirds at a nectar feeder by covering all but one port of the feeder and marking all ports in the same way except for the one from which food can be drawn, and then recording the bird's first preference when it arrives to feed. In these experiments you are testing not only the birds' ability to learn by association, but their ability to discriminate between different symbols and colors. Because this type of test works best with individual birds in a laboratory, where conditions can be controlled, don't be discouraged if the birds fail the test, for some birds might not have been present during the training, and on a cold winter's morning some individuals might choose a nonpreferred food rather than compete at a crowded feeder.

- 6 -

Migration

THE EARTH, TILTED ON ITS AXIS AS IT ORBITS THE SUN, exposes its surface to different intensities of radiation, causing uneven heating of the surface. The rays of the sun strike earth directly only between the Tropics of Cancer and Capricorn, transferring its energy more or less evenly there. At middle and high latitudes, energy from the sun always comes in at an angle. Here occur the most pronounced changes in temperature and length of day. These changes are called seasons.

Seasons significantly affect the life forms that inhabit the surface. The chemical process that creates the food base for the earth is photosynthesis. This largest chemical reaction on the planet depends on sunlight. Water in its liquid state is the stuff from which life is made. A human being is 70 percent water and the cell more than 90 percent. It has been said that life is a play of water. When the middle and high latitudes receive the sun's rays more directly, the energy for photosynthesis is abundant, water flows, and life flourishes. But when the sun's energy strikes earth more obliquely, photosynthesis is greatly diminished, water freezes, and life struggles.

Organisms that live in these boom-and-bust areas must adapt accordingly. Those that are rooted in the ground become dormant either in seed or adult form. Others endure and live on the ever-diminishing autumnal fat. The last group is our subject in this chapter. They are the migrants. They exploit the boom conditions, then flee, only to return, spending their lives in two regions of earth.

Many species migrate: insects, fish, amphibians, reptiles, and mammals. The only requirements seem to be a benign habitat that is close enough and the ability to get there. Whereas in other classes of animals some individual species are migratory, among the birds the facts of migration are overwhelming. Of the species of birds breeding in the middle and high latitudes, most are migratory.

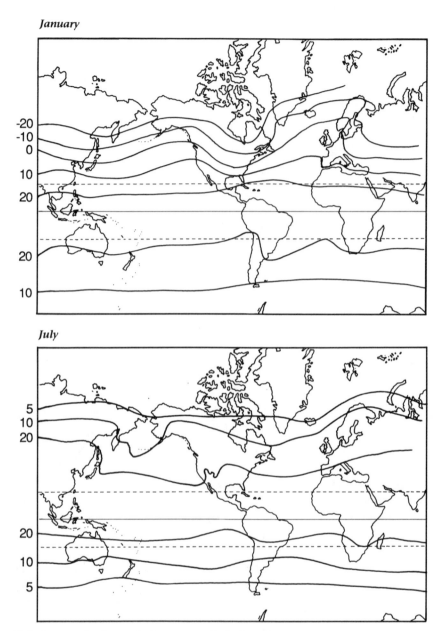

January

July

Global average isotherms for January and July (in Celsius).

Among the approximately 384 species that breed in Canada, about 329, or 80 percent, are migratory.

GEOGRAPHY OF MIGRATION

Just as the sun's energy is unequally distributed on earth's surface, so too is solid land. North of the equator, especially in the temperate zone, is an almost continuous land surface, interrupted by the Pacific Ocean and surrounding a polar sea. In the Southern Hemisphere above 40° latitude is almost continuous ocean, interrupted by South America, and these oceans surround a polar land mass. Add to these geographic facts that birds are best adapted to land (of 8,700 species, only 290 are marine); therefore migration of birds is predominantly a Northern Hemisphere phenomenon. Of the 215 species occurring in Michigan, only twenty are nonmigratory, whereas in southern Africa only twenty species are migratory.

But it would be misleading to suggest that migration is strictly a Northern-Hemisphere event. Most marine species in the southern oceans are migratory. Wilson's Storm-Petrel, *Oceanites oceanicus,* is a typical example. It breeds on the islands in the South Atlantic, but before winter it leaves on a circumnavigation of the Atlantic to return in the following spring. Likewise in the tropical regions birds do migrate. The Pennant-winged Nightjar, *Semeiophors vexillanius,* breeding

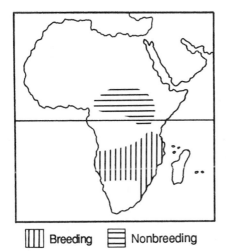

The migration of the Pennant-winged Nightjar coincided with the onset of the rainy season in different parts of Africa.

⦀ Breeding ⊟ Nonbreeding

in southern Africa during the rainy season, moves north of the equator to enjoy the insect-rich rainy season in the Sudan (Stresemann, 1927). But it is in the northern temperate and Arctic regions that bird migration reaches proportions so spectacular that even the most casual observer notices the event. Who has not rejoiced at the first robin of spring or wondered where the swallows spend their winter?

ADVANTAGES OF MIGRATION

Anyone who has endured a northern winter recognizes why birds migrate: conditions are just too severe to support large populations of animals. On the other hand, northern summers, even in arctic regions, are surprisingly mild. A large insect population at the end of the migratory journey also makes breeding conditions ideal for fulfilling the demands of a growing family. Other, subtler advantages accrue to the migrants. Vast expanses of northern land reduce the population pressures common in the tropics. Predators, denied a year-long food supply, are fewer up north than in the tropics, and the longer hours of daylight increase the time that can be devoted to rearing the young. At latitude 69°N, American Robins, *Turdus migratorius,* feed their brood for about twenty-one hours a day (Karplus, 1952). These conditions explain why migratory species generally have large populations.

With such advantages awaiting them, the wonder is that all avian species don't seek warmer climes as winter sets in. Some do remain sedentary though, probably because the migratory act exacts a high price in energy. It has been estimated that a small bird loses between 20 and 40 percent of its body weight during a long flight (Nesbet, 1963). And large numbers of birds are killed by vagaries of weather during migration. In 1907 in Minnesota as many as 750,000 Lapland Longspurs, *Calcarius lapponicus,* were found dead on a small lake after a late-winter snowstorm (Roberts, 1907).

Over evolutionary time, however, weighing advantages and disadvantages of migration, sheer numbers prove that for birds migration is an adaptive solution to the unavoidable seasonal changes on earth.

ORIGINS OF MIGRATION

If we seek a simple cause and date for the origin of migration, we will be disappointed, for we have few clues suggesting how the behavior began, and its history is clouded. Some authorities suggest that migratory behavior originated with the ice ages, and yet it was probably well established long before. Others speculate that it began as the continents separated in the Southern Hemisphere and that the general southerly movement in the fall is the birds' attempt to return to their ancestral homeland. Continental movement, however, probably was completed long before the species migrating today evolved.

Migratory behavior probably had multiple origins at different times in earth's history, responding to climatic changes. Evidence says, though, that this behavior is still evolving and that migratory movements have a strong genetic component that is determined by the environment.

Two basic drives, influenced by natural selection, may account for migration, a theory that seems to have validity. We might express the first drive as attachment to a specific place, to an ancestral homeland. This drive can be coupled with birds' need to live in optimal conditions. As a group, marine species show strong attachment to the island on which they were born, but after breeding they may follow conditions such as temperature, sunlight, and movements of preferred food. If two populations adopt different methods of living, one following these conditions and the other staying with their breeding islands, then in successive breeding seasons differential survival by the two groups could establish in the offspring either wandering or sedentary traits respectively. Similarly, species with large breeding ranges might be sedentary in the southern portion of their range and yet have a highly migratory northern population. In fact, specific routes away from and back to the breeding grounds may be reestablished genetically every year. A short-cut such as crossing the Gulf of Mexico may prove highly successful for a number of generations, but a change in climate devastating to that population might shift the migratory path to a longer but safer land route between traditional breeding and wintering sites.

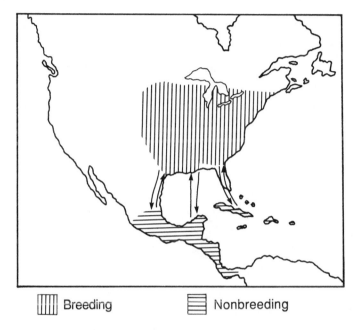

|||| Breeding   ☰ Nonbreeding

Migrations of populations of Indigo Buntings follow either the longer land or land-sea routes along the Gulf of Mexico and the islands of the Caribbean or a direct route across the Gulf.

Such speculations are borne out by changes in the migratory status of species that have taken place in the last century. The Serin, *Serinus canarius,* or wild canary of the Mediterranean region was formerly a sedentary species, but in the past one hundred years it has extended its range north into the more temperate zones in Europe. Individual populations that remain in the southern regions are still sedentary, but those which breed in Germany retreat in fall to their ancestral ranges (Dorst,1962). On the other hand, a population of Norwegian Fieldfares, *Turdus pilaris,* established itself in Greenland in 1937. These birds have remained sedentary, but the European population is migratory (Salomonsen, 1951).

This innate behavior probably evolved in different species at different times for various reasons. The examples we have cited show how quickly migration can become established in a population, probably demonstrating that no one event in avian history led to the behavior. But migration evolved as a way to resolve a homing drive and the bird's ability and need to seek optimal year-round conditions.

METHODS OF STUDY

Until the 1920s the study of migration was haphazard and chaotic. Although accurate dates were known for arrivals by some breeding species in the Northern Hemisphere, the mechanics of migration were little understood, and interpretations of what happened to these species in winter resembled leaps of faith. The common belief was that swallows and swifts spent their winter underwater, and because flocks of birds could be seen in the fall silhouetted against the full moon, people once concluded they flew to that heavenly body.

Not until birds were individually tagged with numbered bands could scientific study of migration proceed. In the 1920s, R. M. Lockley became interested in the comings and goings of the Manx Shearwater, *Puffinus puffinus*, on his island home, Skokolm, in the Irish Sea. In his delightful book *Shearwaters,* Lockley describes how he received his first set of bands (called rings in Britain): "I did not realize that in accepting the offer I was completely revolutionizing my haphazard method of studying birds, which was that of the average observer who writes in

his notebook 'March 25th, first chiffchaff heard. April 12th, cuckoo and swallow here' and leaves it at that. Only by the use of the rings is it possible to become a close student of the individual bird and to know it year after year."

With banding studies, then, scientists could follow migration closely. Recapturing a banded individual indicates something about the bird and about the species to which it belongs. From these studies the bird's movements through the year can be described. Scientists could begin to answer such questions as Where does the bird spend the winter? How faithful is it to its breeding and wintering sites? What is its migratory route?

In North America more than one million birds are banded each year. Although the data flow in steadily, answers to questions about migration have not come quickly. Banding studies, attractive because of their simplicity, nevertheless yield minimal results because the rate at which banded birds are recovered is low. Of the 11,718 Horned Larks, *Eremophila alpestris,* banded in the United States between 1945 and 1981, only eighty-seven, or less than 1 percent, have been recovered. Of these, most were recaptured in succeeding years at the original banding sites (Clapp et al, 1983). In other species, such as game birds, the recovery rate is higher.

Banding studies hold the potential for increasing our understanding of the individual bird as time goes on, but more sophisticated methods are being employed to speed the proceedings.

Radar operators have long been plagued by the nighttime "angels" that regularly appear on their screens in fall and spring. Once thought to be anomalies, they are now recognized as flocks of migratory birds. Using airport surveillance radar and long-range weather radar, observers can easily track the direction, altitude, and speed of these birds. With more powerful and accurate radar, an experienced operator can get some idea about size of the flock and even type of bird from these angels. This information can be correlated with weather conditions to reveal how cloud cover and winds at different altitudes affect migrating flocks.

Another method for studying migration is radiotelemetry. By affixing a tiny radio transmitter to a captured bird's back one can follow the signal either by truck or by plane for long distances after the bird is released. One can follow a bird during a little-understood portion of its migratory route, or for the entire route from wintering to breeding grounds. The technique has been applied to the Whooping Crane, *Grus americana.*

Laboratory studies have also revealed much about the migrant's ability to orient. The advantage here is that conditions can be held under rigid control and the birds' behavior carefully observed. Captive nocturnal migrants can be presented with a planetarium sky representing either a normal sky or some altered view.

With these varied methods of study, questions about migration have started yielding answers. Migratory routes are known for most species, at least in general. The speed, direction, and altitude at which some species fly have been determined, and some of the directional cues are beginning to be understood. But migratory behavior among birds and other species is still described, especially by experts, as a mystery that will probably remain so for many years. With that doubt in mind, let us see what is known and what waits to be discovered about migration.

MIGRATION: ROUTES AND DISTANCES

In late summer, before the chill of autumn winds begin to blow, the Arctic Tern, *Sterna paradisaea,* leaves its breeding grounds in the North Atlantic. Over the next nine months it will follow a path that twice crosses the Atlantic and the equator. During this time the tern will feed in the rich waters of the Antarctic Ocean and probably see more sunlight than any other species on earth. By late spring it will return to its traditional breeding grounds, a round-trip journey of 36,000 kilometers. The Arctic Tern is the premier long-distance traveler among migrants. Even so, the tern's behavior is not atypical among oceanic birds.

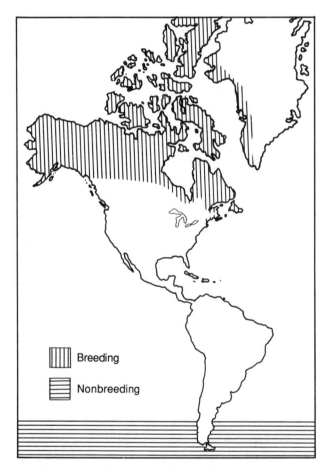

The Arctic Tern probably flies more kilometers in a year than any other species.

As a group the oceanic or pelagic birds are the global wanderers. Coming ashore only to breed, they show decided wariness of land. The Short-tailed Shearwater, *Puffinus tenuirostris,* migrates on a huge clockwise route around the Pacific Ocean after breeding on islands south of Australia. It travels as far north as Alaska and may be beyond sight of land for the entire trip, but returns with uncanny regularity next spring to the islands on which it was born.

Many pelagic species, unlike these two examples, do not cross the equator but winter in the hemisphere of their birth, for the tropical seas are a barrier. The clarity and warmth of these waters, so prized by human migrants in winter, carry few plankton upon which to feed: the water's very warmth decreases the oxygen it can hold. And so in the great southern oceans many migrating species move east to west, following the prevailing winds. In doing so they circumnavigate the globe at the same latitude, and in a year's time return to their breeding islands. In the Northern Hemisphere, presented with more confined flying space to the east and west, oceanic birds generally migrate south of their breeding grounds and winter at distances ranging from a few hundred to many thousands of kilometers from home.

Land birds can be divided into three categories according to whether they move in daylight or darkness. Those that migrate only during the day are considered diurnal. Nocturnal migrants usually fly between sunset and sunrise, and others apparently fly indifferent to daylight or darkness.

The diurnal migrants are the herons, hawks, eagles, storks, crows, humming-birds, swifts, and swallows. The larger species fly only in daylight for reasons that seem clear: they use the sun-heated surface to provide lift. These birds avoid moving over open spans of water where they find no thermal updrafts, and they use the updrafts caused by prevailing winds striking the ridges of mountain ranges. As a consequence, they concentrate or narrow their migratory route around land formations. The Bosporus and the Straits of Gibralter concentrate all such southbound traffic from Europe to points south. The Isthmus of Panama shows a similar concentration, as do the narrow water connections between the Great Lakes. Probably the best-known site for witnessing passage by birds of prey is Hawk Mountain in the Kittatinny range in eastern Pennsylvania. Here observers have counted as many as 22,000 hawks moving by in a season. The spring weather patterns are less favorable in concentrating these soaring species than those in the fall; large numbers of individuals are observed only in the latter season.

Nocturnal migrants are nearly all passerines. They are exclusively diurnal at times other than migration, but in spring and fall they are active and moving between sunset and sunrise.

One nocturnal migrant is the Blackpoll Warbler, *Dendroica striata*, which breeds in coniferous forests in the United States and Canada. In early fall the birds move at night south and east and concentrate in large numbers along the New England and Maritime coast. Here they increase their body fat until a strong cold front passes, and in the morning they are gone. Their next landfall might as well be the moon as South America, for these landlubbers fly three or four days nonstop—4,000 kilometers over open ocean—to mangrove swamps in Venezuela, quite a feat for a twenty-gram bird thirteen centimeters long.

The Blackpoll's long, nonstop oceanic flight is not characteristic of passer-ines, for most small birds follow safer land routes between wintering and sum-

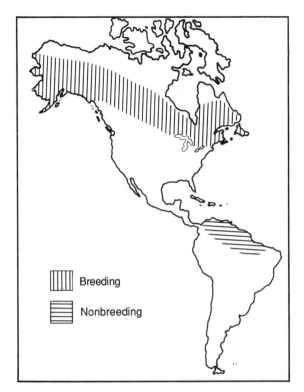

The Blackpole Warbler flies directly over the eastern Atlantic Ocean from its North American breeding grounds to winter in South America.

Breeding

Nonbreeding

mering ranges. But like the Blackpoll, many do cover long distances. The Indigo Bunting, *Passerina cyanea*, breeds in the eastern United States and winters as far south as Panama. The Bobolink, *Dolichonyx oryzivorus*, breeds in hayfields across the northern United States and southern Canada and winters in a similar habitat in central and southern South America. And, although many of these nocturnal migrants avoid crossing large bodies of water by island hopping or following the shore, others fly by a more direct route across such lesser bodies of water as the Gulf of Mexico and the Mediterranean Sea.

Unlike their day-flying cousins, nocturnal migrants are much less affected by topography and therefore show little concentration at particular land forms. They advance and retreat with the seasons on broad fronts determined by prevailing winds and food supply. In general, however, North American migrants are pushed east in fall by prevailing winds and do concentrate on the Atlantic coast as they move to wintering areas. Here again, because of prevailing winds and food supply, the spring return does not always follow the fall pattern.

The adaptive significance in migrating at night seems to be threefold. First, these migrants are small birds that do not soar, and although helped by tail winds, they probably do not benefit from the lift provided by rising columns of heated air. Second, these species are generally well protected in thick vegetation but rarely fly above the canopy of trees. If they were to move during the day they would be highly vulnerable to diurnal birds of prey. And last, by flying at night they can both rest and feed during daylight hours. If they flew during the day they could rest at night, but on an empty stomach, and would have to

110

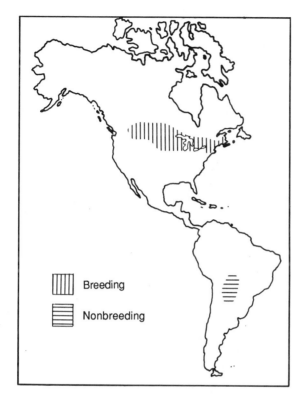

The Bobolink breeds in the hayfields of North America and winters in the grasslands of South America.

Breeding

Nonbreeding

spend part of the next day feeding before resuming their journey (Pettingill, 1970).

The last group of migrants we consider fly by day or night: loons, ducks, geese, and shorebirds. As a group they are large and powerful flyers. Their migration seems to have an urgency, and they have the physical ability to make long nonstop transits. These species are, as a group, the premier long-distance land migrants.

Like many other birds, shorebirds usually winter in habitats similar to their breeding range. Because many shorebirds breed along the cold northern ocean shores, their wintering grounds are in similar habitats in the Southern Hemisphere. Species such as the Lesser Golden-Plover, *Pluvialis dominica,* the Pectoral Sandpiper, *Calidris melanotos,* and the Hudsonian Godwit, *Limosa haemastica,* divide their year between extremities of the Americas. Like the Blackpoll Warbler they take advantage of the prevailing winds to make long nonstop flights over vast expanses of water.

Ducks and geese also have the ability to fly long distances. One documented instance was reported by Bellrose (1957). A huge exodus of geese and ducks was observed on the Canadian plains on October 31. By November 1, the flock was reported to be crossing the Dakotas, and by November 3, the vanguard was landing in Louisiana, totaling 3,000 or 4,000 kilometers.

It would be misleading, though, to suggest that all migratory species, whether nocturnal, diurnal, or both fly long distances over complex routes. For many mountain species the winter range is in sight of their lofty nests. The

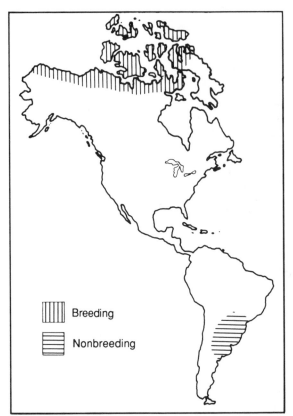

The long migration of the Pectoral Sandpiper is typical of many shorebirds.

Breeding

Nonbreeding

population of Dark-eyed Juncos, *Junco hyemalis*, which breeds in the Great Smoky Mountains, apparently moves only as far as the valleys in the winter. And the Mountain Quail, *Oreortyx pictus*, migrates in fall only about 1,500 meters downward—on foot! And although most species in northern climates move south in winter, some birds migrate due east or west to find milder marine climates after breeding in the interior. In fact, some albatross species move poleward in fall, and the Blue Grouse, *Dendragapus obscurus*, ascends the mountains before winter.

WEATHER AND MIGRATION

Although the popular belief is that spring migrants' arrival is exceedingly precise, vagaries in the weather affect arrival and departure dates. Even the swallows that return to Capistrano have been known to be a day or two late. But considering the enormous distances that some species travel and the trackless routes that some follow, the consistency in arrivals and departures ranges from uncanny to astounding. The Arctic Tern, *Sterna paradisaea*, returns to its northern breeding grounds during the same week late in spring each year, after traveling 36,000 kilometers in the intervening nine months. The famed swallows fly from central South America to California and usually do arrive on the same day each year. But other species show less precise patterns. How does the weather affect these events?

A long-term study in the northeastern United States correlated arrival dates for spring migrants with the average temperature, with results that might have been expected: later arrivals when weather was colder and earlier ones in mild springs (Saunders, 1959). But closer analysis of the data shows greatest variation in arrivals among the early spring species such as blackbirds, and less variation for those arriving late, such as warblers. In a similar study in Montana, because of severer and less predictable conditions, the variation was greater but the results were similar (Wedemyer, 1973).

Birds that can eat seed usually migrate earlier in spring and later in fall and show highest variability in arrival and departure dates. For these species the weather seems influential. Migrants that depend on insects arrive later and leave earlier, and their timing depends less on the weather. Two closely related species, the Red-winged Blackbird, *Agelaius phoeniceus,* and the Bobolink, *Dolichonyx oryzivorus,* illustrate this. In the United States and Canada the red-wing, a seed-eating bird in winter, is one of the earliest spring migrants, but its arrival can be delayed as much as two weeks by colder than normal conditions and snow cover. In the same area the Bobolink, more dependent on insects, arrives consistently in the first week of May.

Birds have been observed migrating in almost any weather. But most data show that they are weather-wise. They fly most often in calm air or with a tail wind. In autumn great waves of birds fly after a cold front passes. With such help their effective ground speed can be as much as doubled. Experiments on pigeons show that they can detect very slight changes in barometric pressure (Keeton, 1974). Probably all birds can, and thus they can anticipate the extent of the high-pressure system following a cold front, hence the strength and duration of the subsequent favorable winds. The Blackpoll, then, as it waits on the northeast coast, may depart early or late depending on arrival of winds that are critical to its short-cut to South America. Likewise in spring, waves of birds follow the warm fronts north. When the fronts stall, the birds settle down and wait for another surge of air from the south. This delay is most clearly seen along the Gulf coast. Here birds will continue to fly north after crossing the Gulf of Mexico if southerly winds persist. But if a cold front approaches as they near the coast, the birds swamp the coastal beaches and marshes.

SPEEDS AND ALTITUDES

The speed at which a bird flies is greatly affected by the rate and direction taken by the medium through which it travels. In calm air most passerines fly at ground speeds of between thirty-five and fifty kilometers per hour. When the wind is blowing, however, the speed at which a bird covers ground can be reduced to zero or doubled depending on direction of wind and bird. Birds on long flights, of course, wait for favorable tail winds to increase their speed. Also, some birds fly at altitudes where winds blow faster and with less turbulence than near the surface.

Radar observations of ground speeds indicate that most migrants fly between thirty and seventy kilometers per hour. But some are exceptions. Shorebirds are among the fastest: McCabe (1942), flying in an airplane at 150 kilometers an hour, was overtaken by a flock of sandpipers estimated to be going at 180 kilometers an hour. The Hudsonian Godwit, *Limosa haemastica*, a large shorebird, probably flies nonstop the 8,000 kilometers from Canada to southern South America in fall. With consistent and favorable tail winds this species might proceed faster than seventy kilometers an hour.

Other methods are used to determine the speed at which birds migrate: one is to divide distance traveled on long flights by estimated time in the air. The Blackpoll Warbler has been estimated to have fat reserves to fly continuously for 120 hours (Nesbet and Drury, 1967). For it to fly the 4,000 kilometers to South America, it must average at least thirty-three kilometers an hour and cover nearly 800 kilometers a day. Average speed can also be determined if a bird is captured and banded en route, and then recaptured farther along on its migration or on its breeding ground. The speed is calculated by dividing the distance between the two points by the time interval. For the relatively rare migrations so tracked, the rates of travel are lower than the 800 kilometers a day for the Blackpoll. A Mallard, *Anas platyrhynchos*, covered 890 kilometers in two days, and a Yellow-rumped Warbler, *Dendroica coronata*, 725 kilometers in two days (Welty, 1975). These data do not represent maximum rates of travel, for no one knows that the banded birds resumed flight immediately upon release, were recaptured immediately after arrival, or flew in a straight line.

Average speeds, and thus distances covered, generally are greater in spring than in fall. Apparently the drive is stronger to reach the breeding grounds than the wintering areas.

Radar observations indicate that birds generally migrate at altitudes below 1,500 meters. Lack (1963) observed that diurnal migrants on the average fly lower over land than water, whereas nocturnal migrants fly over land and water at the same altitude. When cloud cover is greater at night, birds attempt to climb above the clouds, apparently to get a clear view of the sky. If the cloud tops are too high, flocks will descend to fly beneath the cover at relatively low altitudes. Although these and other studies show that most migratory flight is done at altitudes below 3,000 meters (Nesbet, 1963), Lack (1960) has observed birds above 5,000 meters in the fall, and others have observed birds at altitudes above 6,400 meters. These observations clearly show how superior the avian respiratory system is, for at these altitudes human beings would need supplementary oxygen. The advantage in this type of high-altitude migration is that the birds increase their speed by flying in the jet stream, which blows consistently in broad bands at speeds greater than 180 kilometers per hour. But studies show that although birds make corrections for lateral wind drift at low altitudes, no such corrections are made at high altitudes (Alerstam and Ulfstrand, 1972). Flying high can increase speed, but birds run the risk of being blown off course.

ORIENTATION AND NAVIGATION

If the routes, distances, speeds, and altitudes of migration are a wonder of nature, in the mechanisms of migration we can appreciate nature's true complexity. Migratory birds carry within them an array of clocks, compasses, and maps that would put a ship's navigator to shame.

Migration is serious business; it must be anticipated and planned for. Well before the departure date, the old flight feathers must be molted and new ones grown, and body fat must be accumulated. Timing for these events is independent of the weather. The length of daylight, the photoperiod, does strongly influence these preparatory events, but birds kept in unnatural laboratory photoperiods will still molt and lay down body fat before their natural periods of migration (Gwinner, 1960). Birds and many other organisms have a yearly biological clock that alerts them to coming events. These clocks are especially needed by species that winter in the tropics, where cues for the changes in season are subtler (Pengelley and Asmundson, 1971).

As for finding their way, birds rely on physical cues to determine a compass direction. Nocturnal migrants seem to have the simplest orientation system. The Indigo Bunting, *Passerina cyanea,* uses the stars. In ingenious experiments, Emlen (1975) placed captive buntings in a test cage consisting of a blotter-paper funnel surrounding an ink-pad floor. When the birds were exposed to the fall night sky they hopped from the ink pad to the blotter in an apparent attempt to initiate flight. When the pads were analyzed they showed that the birds hopped consistently south. Under overcast conditions, the birds' nighttime patterns on the paper were random. Bringing this apparatus into a planetarium, Emlen was able to show conclusively that the birds were orienting by the fixed pattern of circumpolar stars and that their orientation north in spring and south in fall was controlled by their state of breeding readiness. In some species additional compass information is gained by the sun's position at setting and rising.

Being able to orient, or align oneself with physical cues, undoubtedly is essential to migrants. The Indigo Bunting uses the fixed northern stars to align its flight north and south. But this behavior by no means explains how the bunting proceeds from North to South America. Banding studies show that although the species moves north and south, individuals move much more precisely. A bird's wintering and breeding territories are within the same square kilometer year after year. A compass alone does not give information to make this type of precise movement. Also, birds at times are undoubtedly displaced by strong winds and therefore must make course corrections en route. Maintaining the same compass heading could lead to missing the breeding ground or continuing the flight over open water. Birds must have true ability to navigate, which means they must be able to keep referring to their goal as they proceed. For now, if we ask how nocturnal migrants make these very precise movements and compensate for lateral displacement, we come up with a simple answer: we do not know.

Quite a bit more is understood about orientation in day-flying birds, partly thanks to a species that is beleaguered, incredibly successful, and emphatically nonmigratory. The Rock Dove, *Columba livia,* or common pigeon, for all its faults is a remarkable species. Those bred for racing can maintain a land speed of between eighty and ninety kilometers per hour for twelve hours, flying nonstop for up to 1,000 kilometers a day. They also have strong homing ability. Pigeons can be displaced long distances in any direction from the home loft and return, a behavior that looks much like long migratory flight. But the advantage to the researcher in studying orientation and navigation in the pigeon rather than a migratory species is that pigeons will home not only in the spring and fall but every day of the year.

How does a pigeon find its way? It uses the sun as a compass. A pigeon displaced due south of the loft chooses its homeward bearing—north—from the sun. But the sun's apparent movement makes this choice more complicated than that of the Indigo Bunting, for the Bunting uses the fixed star groups around the North Star. At any time of night these cues are in the north. The sun, though, rises in the east, is in the south at its noon, and sets in the west. Its position is predictable as it moves through an angle of 15° per hour. To use the sun as a compass the pigeon must know what time it is!

A daily biological clock has been experimentally demonstrated in many animals, including human beings. If the pigeon in the example was released at 9:00 A.M., three hours after sunrise, it would have to fly at an initial angle of 135° counterclockwise from the sun. But during a three-hour flight the bird would have to correct its angle to the sun by 15° per hour as it flew, and as it approached home at 12:00 it would have to be flying directly away from the sun to maintain the northerly heading. It sounds unbelievable, but this type of orientation has been demonstrated in a number of day-flying birds and is probably a widespread method of orientation.

Proof that the sun compass with its clock is real comes from experiments in which the bird's internal sense of time has been artificially shifted. Pigeons kept in isolation will shift their time sense to match the photoperiod. Therefore, if a bird is isolated and a light comes on at 9:00 A.M. instead of natural sunrise at, say, 6:00 A.M., the bird over a few days will adjust to the new "sunrise" conditions. The same sort of adjustment happens to a person who flies to and remains in another time zone for a week. Jet lag is the first feeling, as the traveler experiences the effects of the new time. After a couple of days a feeling of adjustment comes; the biological clock is now synchronized with local time.

If the clock-shifted pigeon is released due south at 9:00 A.M. local time, the bird will feel it to be only 6:00 A.M. or sunrise. Because home is due north, it must fly at an initial angle of 90° counterclockwise to the sun to get home, whereas control birds fly at 135° counterclockwise. The clock-shifted birds make a 45°, or 15° per hour mistake, which is consistent with the sun-compass hypothesis.

The curious thing in experiments on clock-shifted birds is that if they are released with control birds as in the example, but on an overcast day, both con-

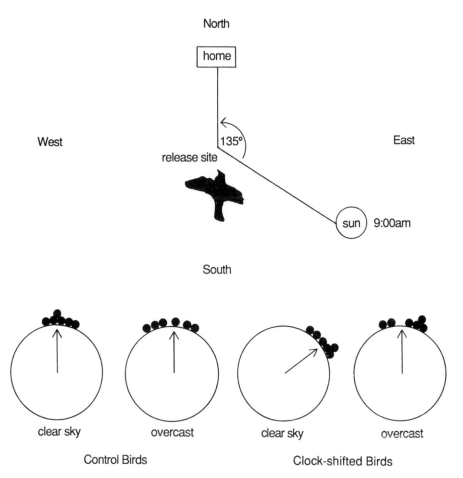

The top diagram shows a pigeon's position when released at 9:00 A.M. due south of home; from there, it must initially fly at an angle of 135 degrees counterclockwise from the sun to go north. The bottom diagrams show typical data when the experiment is conducted with control and clock-shifted birds under both clear and overcast conditions. The control birds in both conditions fly directly north. The clock-shifted birds in sunlight made the predicted 45-degree-clockwise error, suggesting the existence of a sun compass. The clock-shifted birds in overcast fly north, suggesting a magnetic compass. Each dot represents the direction of a bird when it flies out of sight; the arrows represent the average direction of all the birds released.

trol and clock-shifted birds will orient to the same northerly, or homeward direction. These results immediately suggest that they can use some other compass if the primary one is not available. And, because clock-shifted birds are not affected in overcast weather, this back-up compass must be fixed. The strong suggestion is that this secondary orientation system is based on the earth's magnetic field. When pigeons are released in overcast conditions wearing bar magnets, or when a magnetic field is induced around their heads, their ability to home is reduced to random searching (Walcott and Green, 1974). Pigeons, then, have two compasses, the primary sun compass and a backup magnetic compass.

We might ask if the abilities shown in pigeons are restricted to that species, or if we can generalize and include wild birds.

Many displacement experiments performed on wild birds indicate that the birds have strong homing ability. In the 1930s, Lockley displaced many of his banded Manx Shearwaters, *Puffinus puffinus,* from their nests as far away as the Mediterranean Sea and found their homing ability to be superb. Similar ability has been shown in herons, gulls, and swifts.

The sun compass seems widespread in the animal kingdom. Many experiments on birds show that they can use the sun to choose a compass heading. The sun compass has also been found in tortoises, lizards, frogs, and even bees. The magnetic compass has been demonstrated in Ring-billed Gulls, *Larus delawarensis;* European Robins, *Erithacus rubecula;* and other species.

Other similarities have been found between pigeons' homing behavior and that of other birds. Young or inexperienced pigeons do not home nearly as accurately as adults, and the same seems to apply to migratory birds. Perdeck (1958) banded 11,000 European Starlings, *Sturnus vulgaris,* in the Netherlands and released them in Switzerland during their fall migration. The recoveries later in that winter showed that the adults compensated for the displacement and wintered in the traditional wintering grounds, but the juvenile birds apparently maintained the original compass bearing and wintered in a completely different area.

Birds show strong ability to home and are able to choose a compass direction, but how do they know which direction to pick? It has been postulated that birds have some sense of where they are in relation to their goal; in other words, they have an internal map. Although intensive research has been done since the 1960s, very little is known about what this map is like or how it works. In his 1974 *Scientific American* article, William Keeton, an expert on avian navigation, described the pigeon's sense of knowing which way is home as if "before we release each pigeon we whisper in its ear 'home is north.' " As with the Indigo Bunting, our knowledge of how the day-flying birds navigate is really quite primitive.

Speculation on birds' maplike sense has ranged from their memorizing every twist and turn in the outward journey and reversing the trail to home, to their being able to detect and interpret the earth's centripetal force and thereby gauge the direction of their displacement. More substantial theories have come from researchers who feel that the olfactory sense could be involved. According to them, a bird learns to associate different smells with different wind directions. When displaced, the bird smells the area, remembers which way this smell came from, concludes home must be in that direction, and then uses its sun or magnetic compass to fly home. Improbable as it sounds, especially for a class of organisms whose sense of smell is far from acute, experimental evidence supports this theory (Papi, et al 1972). Other researchers have concentrated on earth's magnetic field. Here the small changes in the field strength or direction might cue the bird to the direction in which it is displaced. Pieces of inferential evidence suggest that magnetic cues contribute to the maplike sense in birds: pigeons homing poorly in sunny weather at times of magnetic storms; pigeons' homing sense failing them when released in areas where earth's magnetic field is distorted. They do have tiny magnetic crystals in the head between skull and brain (Walcott, et al 1979), but exactly how earth's magnetic field affects the bird's knowing where it is relative to where it wants to go is not understood.

You may wonder why in this discussion of orientation and navigation so little is said about landmarks. Because they are sure signposts, landmarks can clearly indicate direction without the complex mechanisms suggested above. No scientist involved in avian navigation would discount a species' opportunistic use of familiar land formations to find their way. Just as the skilled ship's navigator does not refer to a chart or read a compass along a familiar route, so too many species of birds probably use landmarks on routes they often fly. We would especially expect this technique in species that fly their migration routes as families, or follow prominent features such as rivers, to and from the breeding grounds. Experiments show that when displaced from breeding grounds in two successive seasons, Herring Gulls, *Larus argentatus*, return much more quickly the second time, apparently because of strong topographic memory (Griffin, 1943). Often, keen observers could at least guess their position using physical cues alone, for cues such as wind direction, cloud formations, temperature, type of habitat, sound, and physical landmarks may indicate the direction in which they are displaced, if not too far from home. But, like the navigator who, unsure of the ship's position, reaches for map, watch, and compass, birds unable to sight familiar cues must depend on a more reliable navigation system as yet mysterious to us.

Suggested Reading

Dorst's *Migration of Birds* is a complete review of the subject. In the more recent *Bird Migration*, Mead explains many developments in orientation and navigation and presents breeding, wintering, and migratory routes for many of the world species.

Projects

Record in your notebook arrival and departure dates for species in your area. Such data, carefully gathered year after year, can be correlated with monthly temperature and rainfall averages from the National Weather Service, to see how weather affects migration, and can yield valuable information such as a profile demonstrating migratory patterns of a species.

A more ambitious project would be an early morning census before, during, and after peak migration periods. Design the walk to cover two or three kilometers and go through as many habitats as possible. Record each species seen and tally numbers of each. Repeat the census as often as possible during a four-week period. At the end of the migration period, analyze the data for each species to see which are moving during this time: those that increase in number during the study are birds migrating into the area, those decreasing are birds migrating out, and those whose numbers stay the same are the sedentary populations. Check your findings with the migratory statistics in any field guide.

At times of full moon in September and October, and again in April and May, use a telescope to observe migrating flocks silhouetted against the face of the moon. Repeat these observations every hour to spot peak periods of movement. Also record weather conditions on the ground, such as temperature and wind direction. It is difficult to determine the birds' actual direction by this method because of the angle at which you observe, but approximate north and south headings can be determined.

To get in on the ground floor of research on migration and other avian studies, see if you can work with a bird bander. Banders are most active in spring and fall, and many welcome interested birdwatchers who wish to observe and even help. Much can be learned in banding studies, for banders are experts in identifying and aging species, and are rich in information on seasonal movements of species and patterns of species molts. Call the local Audubon Society office for banders active in your area, or write to Bird Banding Laboratory, U.S. Fish and Wildlife Service, Laurel, MD 20811 for names of banding organizations.

- 7 -

Vocal Communication

COMMUNICATION IS THE TRANSFER OF INFORMATION by means of common signals. It is an organism's only way of relating its internal state to others. Communication involves the sender of a message, the medium through which it travels, and one or more receivers. The medium used in communication affects the distance and the speed with which the message can travel; it also affects the quantity of information that can be transferred. Messages that are transmitted tactiley must obviously be given at close range, and the information content is generally low. Communication by chemical signals travels slowly, is subject to wind direction, and rapidly disperses as the signal spreads from its source; the signaler also is limited in the number of signals that can be sent by the number of odors the organism can produce. Visual signals can convey information more than a kilometer, but most often are used at close range. This speediest mode of information transfer is limited to the line of sight and can be used only in adequate light, with the receiver of the message facing the sender. The quantity of information carried in visual signals is variable; an animal's appearance relates its species and sometimes its age and sex along with its individual identity. More information can be sent when the organism assumes postures that relate its internal state. The Stellar's Jay, *Cyanocitta stelleri,* changes the angle of its crest to communicate different levels of aggression. The fully erect crest conveys its greatest agonistic (combative) state (Brown, 1964). Birds being visual creatures, this type of communication is a vital mode of information transfer for them, but the medium of communication that characterizes birds is sound.

Sound, as a medium for transferring information, is superior in many ways to tactile, chemical, and light signals, in that it travels quickly in all directions,

121

goes around obstacles, and can be produced in any environmental condition. Sound waves are set up by almost any disturbance; producing them requires relatively little energy, and very different sounds can be formed by the same structure. The two major characteristics of sound, frequency and amplitude, are readily manipulated by any sound-producing device. Not by accident is the human

A Scarlet Tanager in song

language mediated by sound, for no other medium (except possibly visual signals in written language) can convey so much information so quickly. With all these favorable characteristics, we may wonder why auditory communication is not more common in the animal kingdom. The reason seems to be that sound signals are easily intercepted. In communication, the sender of the message intends the signal for specified receivers, but using sound signals reveals the sender's location, and sometimes the message goes not only to the intended receiver but to the eavesdropper as well. Therefore, creatures that use sound as a primary mode of communication either fear no eavesdroppers or are well protected from them. Birds, being protected from the predator by their power of flight, have evolved from the relatively mute reptile to be, as a group, the most vocal creatures on earth.

SOUND PRODUCTION IN BIRDS

Birds produce sound in a number of ways. Many species make sound by moving their feathers; hummingbirds, and some ducks and doves, among others, use normal wing movements in flight to produce sounds that range from a hum to

The Ruffed Grouse creates a booming sound by rapidly vibrating its wings. This sound is amplified if produced while standing on a hollow log.

a whine. The woodcock and snipe make sound during their courtship flights with specialized sound-producing feathers. The Ruffed Grouse, *Bonasa umbellus,* vibrates its wings rapidly, emitting a powerful, low-pitched roll of sound; other birds shake their tail feathers, making a strange quivering sound. This type of sound production is discussed more thoroughly in Chapter 2, but these sounds are intended either to maintain contact among members of the groups, or are associated with breeding behavior.

Birds also use their feet and beaks to produce sound. Sage Grouse, *Centrocercus urophasianus,* stamp their feet on the ground during courtship displays, and many species of waterfowl splash with their feet. Owls and storks, among others, clap their mandibles together to make sound. Woodpeckers are well known for the drumming sounds they make by hammering on a hollow surface, including the side of a human habitation. These drummings are not necessarily related to feeding, for many woodpecker species produce unique tapping sequences, rendered most frequently at the beginning of the breeding season. This sound, then, is one method of communication (woodpeckers are also vocal birds) that is used to convey breeding information. So important are these drummings to their social interactions that in wooded areas that have been stripped of dead wood, but supplied with suitable nesting and roosting cavities, some species of woodpeckers will stay through the winter but leave them in spring, apparently because they lack proper resounding surfaces on which to drum.

These sounds produced by feathers, feet, and beak are only a small portion of the bird's acoustic ability, for most sounds birds make are achieved by air moving in and out of their mouths.

A small percentage of sounds produced in this way are made by pumping air through air sacs and the esophagus. Some grouse species make weird "plopping" and "booming" sounds by moving air in this way, and the American Bittern, *Botaurrus lentiginosus*, produces a hollow croaking sound by swallowing and releasing air in its esophagus. These rather crude sounds are made by only a few species. Most birds produce sound by moving air in the respiratory system.

As air passes from air sacs to mouth, it moves through the paired bronchi and into the trachea before leaving the body. The region where the bronchi and the trachea come together is the voice box in birds, the *syrinx*. Unlike the larynx in human beings and other mammals, which produces sound by vibrating vocal cords, the syrinx is a structure unique to birds. In normal breathing movements, the stream of air from both lungs passes unimpeded through the syrinx, but in sound production the syrinx muscles contract, decreasing the space through which air can pass, which builds up pressure in the bronchi, causing the *tympanic membrane* in the syrinx to vibrate. The motion of the tympanic membrane produces sound. The frequency and amplitude of the sound depend on the rate and force with which the tympanic membrane moves, but also on the length

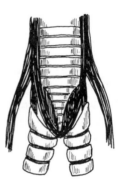

Syrinx of a songbird

and width of the trachea. The movement in the throat region that we see when a bird sings is caused by changes in length of the trachea, which produce changes in frequency and loudness of the sound. Unlike human beings, who modify the sound originating from vocal cords by tongue, teeth, and nasal cavity, the sounds birds produce are caused almost exclusively by the syrinx and trachea; therefore, birds can make essentially the same sound with mouth closed or open. This method of producing sound, however, somewhat limits the variety of sounds birds can make.

The structure, placement, and arrangement of the syrinx differs among families of birds. Owls and nightjars have two syringes, each located in the bronchi; in some birds the syrinx is in the trachea; but the usual placement for the syrinx is at the junction between bronchi and trachea. The Turkey Vulture, *Cathartes aura*, the Ostrich, *Struthio camelus*, storks, and some other species have either no syrinx or no muscle associated with the syrinx and thus produce little or no sound.

Songbirds are perching birds, Passeriformes, of the suborder Oscines, which are so classified because of the number of pairs of muscles that control the syrinx. Oscines have from five to nine pairs of muscles, but all other birds have but one or two pairs. These additional muscles give more precise control over the air flowing in this region and determine the more varied sounds these birds produce. The Oscines, more than half the world's species, are the most recently evolved group; therefore we assume that production of rich and varied sound must be favored by natural selection. It is interesting, though, that among this group of songbirds, with their complex vocal apparatus, are species whose vocal ability is ill developed. Notable among them is Henslow's Sparrow, *Ammodramus henslowii,* whose often-repeated song consists of an unmusical "tsi-lick," but many nonsongbirds, with much simpler voice boxes, make complex sounds. Loons are well known not only for their complex calls, but also for the varied sounds they make; gulls and some other shorebirds are just as versatile, and the lyrebirds are the consummate mimics.

In general, though, the songbirds are the divas in the avian world. As a group they create amazingly varied sounds, some of which have an especially full quality because of the syrinx's unique ability to produce two sounds simultaneously. The strange and haunting song of the Veery, *Catharus fuscescens,* is essentially two themes sung at once.

The frequency of the sound a bird produces very much depends on its size. Small birds make relatively high-pitched sounds and large birds usually have deeper voices. This relationship depends in part on the longer and wider trachea setting up longer sound waves with lower frequencies. Apparently to gain greater control over the sound, some species have evolved exceedingly long trachea by having the windpipe coil under the skin of the breast or fold back on itself in the sternum. The trachea of the Whooping Crane, *Grus americana,* is more than a meter and a half long, a good portion of it coiled on the sternum. The advantage in having this long tube is that its lower-pitched sounds carry farther than equally loud high-pitched sounds.

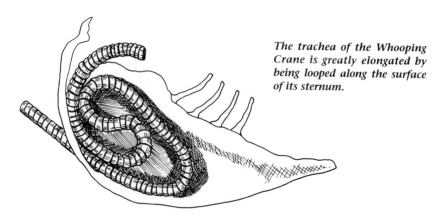

The trachea of the Whooping Crane is greatly elongated by being looped along the surface of its sternum.

That the avian voice is complex is clear from its ability to mimic other sounds. Human beings are the only other creatures with comparable ability. Although not all birds are mimics, the mimicry exercised by those which are suggests that the syrinx has enough flexibility to produce a greatly varied sound. The mockingbirds copy the sounds produced by other birds, and birds such as the Hill Mynah, *Gracula religiosa,* can mimic human speech. Many of these "talking" birds, like the mynah and parrots, do not however copy natural sounds in the wild as mockingbirds do.

With their extremely flexible voice, we find it surprising that the natural vocabulary of birds consists of fewer than forty signals. Comparing this capacity to the almost limitless human vocabulary, birds, it is thought, can make many types of sounds, but are limited in what they can say.

STUDYING BIRD SOUNDS

The sounds that birds make have been studied as long as birds have been observed. We have gained insight into the meaning of these vocalizations by studying the context in which sounds were used; bird song, it has been observed, is produced by the male during the breeding season and is therefore associated with attracting a mate. The sound that a member of the flock produces when a predator appears causing the flock to take flight was considered an alarm call. Until the 1950s, however, the study of avian communication was limited by the very impermanence of sound. Unlike the study of visual communication, in which response to an experimental model such as a tuft of feathers or painted beak could be tested, no one had devised an adequate way of studying or reproducing the sounds that birds make. This limitation disappeared when portable, high-quality recording equipment became available. Armed with a tape-recorder, the researcher no longer had to wonder if the song heard in the morning was the same as the one heard in the afternoon, or if different populations of species made the same sounds. Now tape-recordings preserved the sound and allowed direct comparison. Equally important, investigation into the meaning of these sounds could be subjected to experiment. Birds' reaction to a tape-recorded sound played back gives us deeper understanding of the signal's meaning. Along with sound-recording equipment came, at about the same time, the audiospectrograph. This machine visually represents sound in graphic form. The graph, or sonogram, precisely depicts the frequency of the sound, its temporal patterns, and its relative intensity. With this permanent record of sound we can study essential characteristics of the sounds birds make. Individual or population differences in these sounds are readily seen and measured, including their differences. Although the song of the White-throated Sparrow, *Zonotrichia albicollis,* loses some of its charm when converted from "O Sweet Canada-Canada-Canada" to horizontal lines on a graph, the audiospectrograph has been very important in understanding birds' vocalizations.

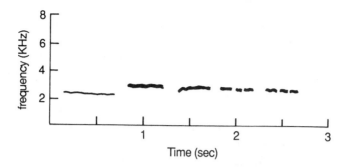

A sonogram is a visual representation of sound, with the frequency of the sound plotted against time. The clear, whistled song of the White-throated sparrow which seems to say "O-sweet-Canada-Canada-Canada," is represented by narrow, flat lines in the sonogram.

This technology brought the study of avian communication by sound into a new era. We now record and catalog the sounds that species make, and conduct experiments that present to birds sounds identical to their naturally occurring stimuli. This work has progressed so far that vocal communication is among the best-understood aspects of avian behavior.

CALLS AND SONGS

We divide the vocalizations that birds produce by structure and function into two types: calls and songs. Bird calls are usually simple sounds, commonly composed of one to four or five notes. They carry clear and unambiguous meanings. Calls are made by both male and female, as well as the young, and are produced all year long. Songs consist of more complex sounds, composed of notes sung in a relatively consistent pattern, making them recognizable and species specific. Most songs are expressed by the male during the breeding season, and they convey more information than do calls.

CALLS

Bird calls act as individual words that convey one meaning. Calls are used in two types of communication. The first is contact calls, which coordinate behavior of a flock, a mated pair, or a family group. The second type of call is used in aggressive encounters.

Contact calls, in one form or another, are common to almost every species of bird. One of their major functions is to locate the signaler. These calls usually share two acoustic features: they are broad in frequency, and the sound begins and ends abruptly. These sounds are harsh and sharp, giving them a clear difference in arrival time in each ear, making them easy to locate. Flocking birds use them to keep in contact. During migration many species of birds call continually in flight; the honking of geese is the familiar example, but these calls are also prevalent in loose flocks of nocturnally migrating birds, the call notes allowing them to remain in contact in darkness, at the same time preventing collisions. The Bobolink, *Dolichonyx oryzivorus,* renders a very distinctive "pink" note only while on its migratory flight. We rarely hear these contact calls issued by members of a migrating flock because these birds usually fly fairly high; but in the early morning, when the flock is descending, they can sometimes be heard.

Most flocking birds, especially those inhabiting areas with visual barriers, such as a wood, stay in contact with each other by calling. The familiar "chick-a-dee" call functions in this way. The American Robin, *Turdus migratorius,* and the Killdeer, *Charadrius vociferus,* among others, call when they take flight and land, apparently to inform others of their movement. Although contact calls usually give the location of members of the flock, in some species they also inform the flock that food or predators are present. When an individual in the flock increases its rate of calling, other members of the group are drawn to the signaler. In this way the temporal pattern of the call, not the call's structure, is used to give a different message; thus a simple contact call becomes an assembly call. Other species, such as the Herring Gull, *Larus argentatus,* are said to have unique calls that assemble the flock (Fringes et al, 1955).

Although the contact calls given by members of a flock during migration or while foraging do not reveal the caller's identity, other contact calls are specifically designed to identify the signaler as an individual. These calls are used to keep a mated pair, or parent and offspring, in touch. This type of signal is especially useful in reestablishing contact between mates in colonial nesting birds. The Northern Gannet, *Sula bassanus,* is one such species: one member of the pair gives a landing call as it nears the colony, and its mate responds to the call by an excited reaction, indicating the nest's exact location. A similar reaction from the mate is elicited when tape-recorded landing calls are played back in the colony; these calls are ignored by other birds (White, 1971). For the Gannet, these calls are useful not only for quickly establishing contact, but because landing on the wrong nest will elicit from other nesting birds vicious pecks that could cause severe injury. Calling between a mated pair is also essential in the breeding behavior of the Manx Shearwater, *Puffinus puffinus.* These shearwaters nest in underground burrows and exchange nesting duties at night. As they fly in from the sea at night their calls are answered by their mate, facilitating the task of locating the burrow as well as informing the mate of their return. In the Herring Gull, *Larus argentatus,* Tinbergen (1953) observed that a call by a bird returning to the colony would awaken only the mate. In birds that occupy larger territories than do colonial birds, vocal interaction between a mated pair is mediated by sounds simpler in structure that probably do not identify the individual by voice. Recognition of the mate is established by rapidly interchanged simple calls, in which location of the caller and the call's timing are the main clues to the mate's identity. This explanation undoubtedly fits the Northern Cardinal, *Cardinalis cardinalis,* whose sharp metallic sound is almost immediately answered by the mate.

Contact calls are also employed in communication between parents and young to ensure well-being of the offspring. Feeding calls given by the young attract the parents and stimulate them to feed the young. Like most contact calls, those of the young are harsh and easy to locate. In colonial nesting birds, the parents' call upon return with food causes the young to assemble and begin their begging calls, whereas in tree-nesting species calling is initiated by the young when the parent lands on the nest rim. After the young leave the tree nest, they vocalize when the parent comes into sight.

Other types of calls between parent and young include distress calls given by the young and alarm calls by the parents. In species whose young can run or swim at birth, calling is almost constant between young and parents. When one chick is separated from the rest, its calls become louder and more frequent, now communicating distress and causing the parent to approach. Adult birds also warn their brood of impending danger by issuing alarm calls. These calls often cause the young to group closely about the parent and follow it away from danger, and Bent (1965) reports that the hen of the Greater Prairie-Chicken, *Tympanuchus cupido,* renders a very specific command that causes her chicks to "freeze" when danger approaches.

The two types of alarm calls that flocking birds use (discussed in Chapter 5) may also be considered another class of contact calls. The easy-to-locate "chink" call, responding to approach by a ground predator, locates the predator and sometimes acts as an assembly call for mobbing behavior. The "seeet" call, given when a hawk appears, is unlike other contact calls in that it is difficult to locate, but it does coordinate the flock's activity.

Other calls that birds use are for announcing ownership in agonistic displays. These aggressive calls are usually given at close range and are accompanied by threatening postures. The calls establish and defend favorite or desirable feeding areas, establish or maintain dominance in a flock, or defend a territory during the breeding season. The latter function of calls is usually associated with song, but Oscines also use varied calls, as well as song, to declare their level of aggression.

Because bird calls are simple and birds raised in isolation develop calls, we can infer that ability to produce these vocalizations is mostly innate, although some calls do change with maturation and birds do learn to recognize meanings of other species' calls.

A bird's vocabulary consists of about fifteen to twenty-five calls, with the most social species having the greatest number of signals. This relatively limited repertoire of words generally agrees with the number of signals produced by other vertebrates and points to nature's simplicity: fifteen to twenty-five signals are all birds need to get by (Wilson, 1972).

SONGS

Song is not unique to songbirds or to birds in general; many insects, some fish, frogs, and whales produce sounds specifically associated with the breeding season. Bird song, however, is the most familiar to us, and, except for the sounds made by the Humpback Whale, is probably the most complex sound in the natural world. The richness and variety in song, combined with the fact that birds sing at the beginning of spring, give these sounds cheerful and pleasant associations. After a long winter, silent but for occasional calls, the robin's whistled caroling and the cardinal's sweet, slurred phrases are welcome relief and harbingers of better days to come. Bird song is an acoustic flower that blooms early in spring and lasts well into summer; but just as the flower's beauty seems to mask its essential function, which is reproduction, the robin's pleasant renderings that seem so cheerfully issued are primarily aggressive signals to other members of the species.

Bird song is familiar not only because birds are common daytime creatures; they are also persistent singers. Early in spring, many species spend more than half their waking hours in song. Passerines have been estimated to sing between 1,000 and 2,500 songs each day. A conservative calculation, based on a twelve-hour day, shows that birds sing more than one song a minute. The Grasshopper Sparrow, *Ammodramus savannarum*, has been observed to sing 220 songs in an hour (Smith, 1959); the Red-eyed Vireo, *Vireo olivaceus*, more than 22,000 times in a ten-hour period (de Kiriline, 1954). The feat is truly astounding for bird and observer alike. These high rates of production, coupled with usually quite high volume, make song a major energetic endeavor during the breeding season.

Unlike calls, songs are species-specific sounds. Anyone who has tried in vain to distinguish among the *Empidonax* flycatchers solely by their physical appearance knows, or should know, that these species are easily told apart once they sing. In fact, no two species that look alike have similar songs, and though the song of the American Robin, *Turdus migratorius*, and that of the Rose-breasted Grosbeak, *Pheucticus ludovicianus*, are quite similar, these birds are very different in appearance. Song, then, is a major factor in species isolation, ensuring, from a distance, a positive means for species recognition.

Birds' songs differ not only among species they also vary locally in different populations of a species, variations being called *dialects*. Song dialects result from genetic differences between separate populations, or, in some species, learning, and they probably accelerate formation of subspecies and new species. One hypothesis states that we have so many species of songbirds because song is so vital in species recognition and characteristics of song are modified so easily (Thielcke, 1972). For song, if it is a fixed action pattern, is not nearly as fixed as many visual displays; rather, it is subject to a good deal of variation in an individual bird. Male birds have been known to include new notes, alter the timing of their song, and drop out entire phrases, all increasing variability in their song. A male bird may sing as many as fifty versions of the species-typical song during the breeding season (Borror, 1959).

Unlike calls, which respond to specific situations, bird song is caused by the organism's internal state; birds in breeding condition can even be described as driven to sing. A male House Wren, *Troglodytes aedon*, flies to a favored perch in his territory and bursts into his energetic song not because another wren has

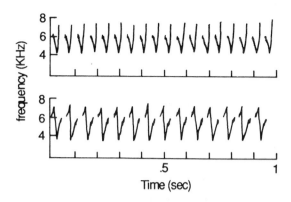

Even in the simple song of the Chipping Sparrow, no two individuals produce exactly the same sounds. These variations in song probably are a means of individual recognition in the species.

come in sight but apparently because he needs to release energy. When another wren does not appear or is heard, the male will sing, but often this song is elicited without a releaser (unless the territory itself is considered a releaser). Birds off their territory have also been observed to sing sometimes very softly; it is then called *whispered song*. Birds also sing during migration and infrequently will burst into full song in the winter. Before breeding season begins, some species sing an incomplete song composed of bits and pieces from the full species song; this type is called *subsong*. Some authorities believe singing is sometimes a form of play, and state that birds sing at times from sheer exuberance or for pleasure (Hartshorne, 1958).

Presence or absence of song is influenced by hormones. Injecting testosterone will bring a male bird, and in some species females also, into full song in the nonbreeding season (Nottebohm and Arnold, 1976). In nature, the changes in length of day that mark the end of winter are a major factor initiating these hormonal changes. Associated with song and hormonal changes is a general rise in intolerance for members of the same species, which leads to breakdowns in flocking behavior and to establishment of a territory. Species that sing all year, such as the Northern Cardinal, *Cardinalis cardinalis,* and the Northern Mockingbird, *Mimus polyglottis,* also defend a territory during the nonbreeding season. Maintaining a territory is one function of song. That song communicates ownership and warns competitors has been consistently shown in playback experiments. The species song was presented to territory holders, and the resident male approached the loudspeaker in an aggressive posture and sang back to the taped song, all the while looking for the intruder. In Red-winged Blackbirds, *Agelaius phoeniceus,* at least, the territorial male times his song responses to follow immediately after the taped song or a real intruder's song, leaving little doubt about his identity as singer of the song or his intentions (Smith and Norman, 1979).

Because song is closely tied to breeding behavior and territory, different

131

species begin their singing at different times of year. In some areas, male Red-winged Blackbirds arrive on the breeding grounds in February and March and begin singing in good weather, but the Yellow Warbler, *Dendroica petechia*, will not return to these areas from the tropics for two months; but by early May, the Great Horned Owl, *Bubo virginianus*, has already ceased singing, for its young are out of the nest and the adults' territorial behavior is beginning to decrease. For species that begin their singing early, weather significantly affects the rate of song production: high winds and precipitation may keep these birds off their singing perches for days, whereas, as spring approaches, birds settle into a regular pattern of singing each day.

Birds sing most often early in the morning, generally beginning before sunrise; as the day goes on song acitivity decreases, followed by a late-afternoon increase. Although this is the pattern for most diurnal birds, some are exceptions: the Red-eyed Vireo, *Vireo olivaceus*, and the House Wren, *Troglodytes aedon*, are relentless singers all through the day. Studies on the rate of singing in different species show that temperature and humidity do not affect rate of song, but wind and precipitation do put a damper on these vocalizations. These studies also show that song is initiated by increasing light levels in the morning, and that morning cloud cover often delays the time of first song. Singing is never as frequent at the end of the day as in the morning, and in many species the day's last song is sung an hour before sunset (Leopold and Eyman, 1961). Bright

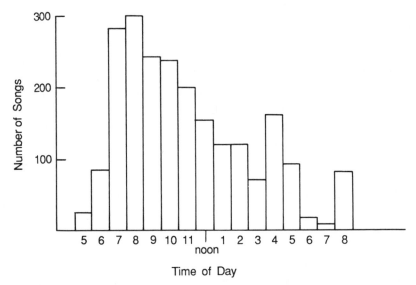

The graph shows the number of songs sung by a male Kirkland's Warbler at each hour of the day (Berger, 1961).

moonlight in a clear night sky stimulates some birds to sing after sunset; the Northern Mockingbird, *Mimus polyglottis*, is well known for its nocturnal singing, and bright moonlight early in the morning initiates some birds' first song earlier than usual. Singing by nocturnal species such as the Whip-poor-will, *Caprimulgus vociferus,* seems to be stimulated by decreasing light levels, and most of these nighttime singers are most vocal on the darkest nights.

Because song is a form of communication, birds must be able to broadcast their message at least past their territorial borders. Most birds seem to sing as loudly as they can and project their song as far as possible by singing from a high perch, where the sound is not absorbed by surrounding objects. In habitats with no perches, such as open fields, many species give their song in flight, like the Bobolink, *Dolichonyx oryzivorus.* Many forest-dwelling species that inhabit the lower story have low-pitched voices because these sounds travel around obstacles better than high-frequency songs. Species that live in very noisy environments, such as windswept prairies, have louder voices than those which live in quieter habitats. Birds seem aware that the sounds in loud environments drown out their message, for they sing most frequently in calm weather.

Birds sing most avidly in the prenesting portion of the breeding season. Once a mate is secured and the chores of building a nest and raising a family have begun, the rate of song production decreases. This falloff is not caused just by the singers' preoccupation with other activities; continued broadcasting the location of the vulnerable nest site would be maladaptive. Some birds are exceptions, however: the Warbling Vireo, *Vireo gilvus,* continues to sing after eggs are laid, and the male will even sing while sitting on the nest. When the young are fledged in midsummer, many species will again start to sing, either as a prelude to a second brood or simply to release energy. Other species, such as the Northern Oriole, *Icterus galbula,* which early in the summer sings frequently, will not sing again after the first nest is built.

Male song is an advertisement signal, announcing a warning to other males and alerting females that a potential mate is present. Females are attracted to the territory by the male's song. Once the female enters the territory, the male begins his courtship displays, which in some species include the territorial song and other types of vocalization, but also involve visual displays; his initial reaction to the female at times is hostile. The male Song Sparrow, *Melospiza melodia,* attacks the female when she first enters his territory, and males of other species chase the female as if to drive her away; but, if the female tolerates these initial aggressive overtures, the male's behavior abruptly changes and he begins his courtship displays.

At one time it was thought that if call notes acted as individual words, then the many notes in a species song acted as words in a sentence, and meaning was encoded in the sequence of sounds, different renditions of the song having different meanings. This hypothesis was tested in the Indigo Bunting, *Passerina cyanea,* by experimentally altering the position of notes in the male's song. Recordings of these scrambled songs were played back to territorial males with the idea that if they did not respond to the song it was because this "nonsense" string of sounds no longer conveyed meaning. The males' reaction to this altered song, however, was the same as if it had been normal song (Emlen, 1972). But other playback experiments show that phrases in the song do convey discrete bits of information. The Red-winged Blackbird, *Agelaius phoeniceus,* sings its familiar "conk-a-ree" song, which is composed of three phrases. The first two phrases do not elicit an aggressive response when played to territorial males, but reaction to the final trill is similar to the male's response to the entire song. These two experiments suggest that if song is not a sentence, neither is it a single word. Different components in the song have their own meaning, but the order of presentation does not change the meaning. For the Red-wing, the final phrase acts as a warning to males, and the first two phrases may convey the singer's identity. That a male's song individually identifies him to other members of the species has been demonstrated in many species. The male White-throated Sparrow, *Zonotrichia albicollis,* responds more vigorously to non-neighbors' songs than it does to a neighbor's song (Falls, 1969).

Information on a resident male's breeding status is probably not encoded in his song, for after the male is mated or the nest built, he does not change the song's structure to include this information; rather, the rate at which he sings may signal to others his progress in the breeding season.

The male song, then, identifies the individual's species and sex, signals ownership of a territory, attracts a female, identifies the individual, and relates his breeding status. For a purely functional purpose, the simple trill of the Chipping Sparrow, *Spizella passerina,* seems adequate to convey his intentions. This comparison leads to a question: Why have so many birds' songs evolved into such complex signals? This question applies not just to species that sing long and intricate songs, but also to those with rather simple songs sung in different renditions. The eighteen renditions of the Wood Thrush, *Hylocichla mustelina,* and more than fifty of the Lark Sparrow, *Chondestes grammacus,* (Borror, 1961) suggest that natural selection has favored extravagance in these vocalizations. This acoustic excess seems analogous to the elaborate plumage in many species, where the long showy feathers of a male do much more than communicate his sex, but apparently also impress other members of the species. Just so for the Lark Sparrow, in that the number of variations in his song may convey to others a subtler message about his genetic makeup. Observations of the Sledge Warbler, *Acrocephalus schoenobalnus,* show that males with more complex and varied songs secure a mate before those which sing with less variety (Catchpole, 1980). If this advantage is real, we can understand why some species incorporate in their songs phrases from other species, for although these phrases in themselves might be meaningless, they could attract a female or intimidate a male by relating the singer's age or experience. The Northern Mockingbird, *Mimus polyglottis,* sings a very long, complex song in which it repeats the phrases from as many as thirty other species (Forbush, 1925-1929).

As in the evolution of any sexual dimorphic characteristic, male song undoubtedly evolves by female selection, but just how she brings about these changes is still open to question. Darwin realized that the male's elaborate secondary sexual features came about either because they were attractive to the female, or because they gave the male an advantage in male-to-male competition; these males then were able to establish dominant positions, and to attract females that would choose to mate with these dominant creatures. We must ask about male song if its complexity charms the female or if it gives the male a competitive edge in establishing a territory. Because the male's song both attracts a female and wards off a male, the question is extremely difficult to answer experimentally, and perhaps the song's function is different for different species. Some evidence shows that in polygamous species the female chooses a mate primarily by the quality of the territory he is able to maintain, and not for his physical characteristics (Orians, 1969). Experimentally muted male Red-winged Blackbirds, *Agelaius phoeniceus,* which are still able to maintain their territories, attract females, and mate normally (Smith, 1979), suggesting that the male song is complex because of intrasexual competition. In other species, however, the female might be choosing between males more for the individual complexity of their song.

We have concentrated on male song, but the females in some species do sing. Female song has received much less attention than male song because females do not sing as frequently as males and are not as responsive as their mates to play-back experiments with taped song. In the Northern Cardinal, *Cardinalis cardinalis,* and the Rose-breasted Grosbeak, *Pheucticus ludovicianus,* the female sings the same song as the male. Females in many other species sing in some form during the breeding season. The female Red-winged Blackbird sings two songs during the breeding season, both different from the male song. In this species a number of females nest on a male's territory, and each defends a subterritory from other females. One song these females produce responds to the male's song, and apparently informs the male of her location and identity; the other song is

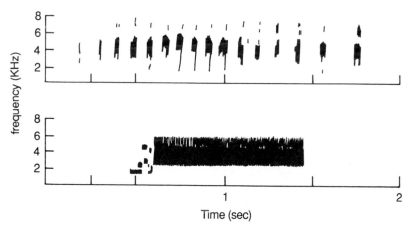

Time (sec)

Both male and female Red-winged Blackbirds sing. The female song (top) is given only during the prenesting portion of the breeding season, while the male song (bottom) is sung throughout the entire breeding season.

directed as a warning to other females, and therefore communicates ownership of a territory. This female behavior is rather short-lived, for it occurs only during the prenesting portion of the breeding season; once the female builds a nest and lays eggs, her vocalizations cease (Belesky and Corral, 1979).

In a number of species, female vocalizations respond to the male's calls, producing a *duet*. This mutual song is weakly developed in North American birds, being found in some quail species and the Brown-headed Cowbird, *Molothrus ater* (Brackbill, 1961). In a number of tropical species, however, notable among them African shrikes and tropical wrens, duetting has reached surprising com-

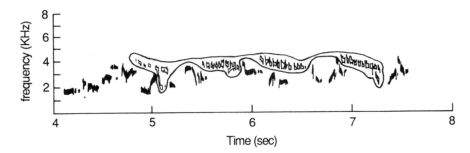

In some species the male and female sing together, producing a duet. In the White-browed Robin Chat, Cossypha heuglini, *the male sings for as long as five seconds before the female adds her notes (circled) to finish the song in a crescendo (Thorpe, 1973).*

plexity, the songs produced by the male and female each providing alternating notes. This vocal exchange is very rapid, and unless the observer is between the two birds, it is difficult to detect that more than one bird is singing. Duetting occurs in species of which male and female live together all year and mutually defend a territory. In the African Boubou Shrike, *Laniarius aethiopicus*, each pair sings a duet different from those of other pairs, for the mates "work out" the duet as they mature, establishing new combinations of notes. This mutual song is therefore unique to the pair and ensures that the two birds recognize each other with certainty. In this way the duet acts very much like contact calls between members of a mated pair, but this type of vocalization is generally considered a song because of its complex structure and because it is used in territorial defense (Wickler, 1972).

ACQUIRING AND CONTROLLING SONG

As with other avian behaviors, bird song is instinctual in some species and learned in others. In species with limited vocal ability, such as doves and quail, all vocalizations are innate. The young of these species raised in isolation or by foster parents develop species-typical sounds at the appropriate age. Birds with more complex voices learn their songs, but how much learning takes place varies with the species.

The White-crowned Sparrow, *Zonotrichia leucophrys*, has been extensively studied for its ability to learn song. This species has a large breeding range in North America and many local song dialects have been described. If young birds are taken from the nest before they are ten days old, and are reared in complete acoustic isolation, they will sing a much simplified version of the adult song in the next spring. If between day ten and day fifty, however, they listen to recordings of White-crowned song, they will sing a typical species song when they mature, and their dialect will be that of the recording and not necessarily that of their parents. But if these young birds are exposed to songs of other species during their isolation, their song when adult will be similar to that of birds raised in complete isolation (Marler, 1970).

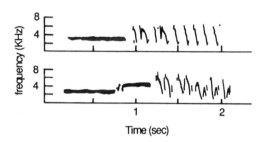

Along with individual differences in song, isolated populations of birds show variability in their songs, with each population singing a dialect of the species-specific song. The sonograms show the dialects of two populations of White-crowned Sparrows.

This study shows clearly that song is learned, and the critical learning period suggests that this type of learning is similar to imprinting, except that acquisition of sounds is restricted to vocalizations produced by the bird's own species. The study also shows how song dialects develop, the innate component of song ensuring that the young will learn only the species song, but learning determines the song's exact structure and pattern. It is also interesting that these birds learn their song months before they can sing.

The European Chaffinch, *Frigilla coelebs*, acquires song as the White-crowned Sparrow does, except that this species has two widely separated learning periods. The Chaffinch's first sensitive period comes early in life, like that of the White-crowned; but in the following spring, as these yearlings begin to sing the species song they learned months before, the song is modified as they listen to other Chaffinch songs. In about two weeks the young birds complete this learning, their song crystallizes, and thereafter it does not change (Thorpe, 1969).

The songs of other species, especially those which are not highly territorial, are thought to be influenced more by learning, for many of these birds change their song from year to year. This sequence applies in the Canary, *Serinus canarius*, which develops a new song as each breeding season begins by improvising and by imitating other males.

These studies of Canary song have led to attempts to understand changes in the nervous system that account for the learning and control of song. In Canaries, only the males sing; comparative studies of male and female brains show marked differences between sexes in size of the two *telencephalic nuclei*. This area of the brain controls the song produced by the species. In this study it was also found that the left telencephalic nucleus was larger than the right in both sexes. These observations are significant because they document the first sexual dimorphism in the brain of any vertebrate, and demonstrate that, unlike most motor patterns, which are thought to be diffusely located in the brain, control of bird song is centralized. The study also shows that control of this activity in Canaries apparently is dominated by one side of the brain, like many human activities, such as writing and artistic ability (Nottebohm and Arnold, 1976).

Although these findings help us understand how the avian nervous system is organized and how control of a motor pattern is effected, later studies of song learning in the Canary reveal some remarkable facts that may have ramifications outside the field of song acquisition.

The male Canary sings only during the breeding season and abstains from song for the rest of the year. Comparing the size of the telencephalic nuclei in breeding and nonbreeding birds shows that this area increases up to 20 percent when the male is in song. Nottebohm (1981) hypothesizes that these changes in the brain are made by new nervous system connections formed as a new song is learned, and when the breeding season ends, this cellular "wiring" is shed, accounting for the brain's reverting to its original size.

If this interpretation proves correct, it will add much weight to the long-suspected belief that changes in behavior result from corresponding changes in the brain. These cellular changes have been very elusive, but these results on Canary song learning seem quite consistent with that contention. This study's deepest implication may be the influence that hormones have in learning, in that testosterone, either directly or indirectly, not only initiates physical changes in the brain of these birds, but seasonally rejuvenates this region of the brain. If this rejuvenation occurs in the brains of some birds, it might be possible in human brains as well.

Suggested Reading

You will find extensive reviews on the entire subject of songs and calls in *Bird Vocalization*, edited by Hinde, and *Acoustic Communication in Birds*, edited by Kroodsma and Miller. Chapter 11 in Welty's *The Lives of Birds* is a good outline of songs, calls, and other avian sounds.

Projects

For those of us with limited memory for bird song, perhaps just beginning by

July to tell the difference between the song of a Chipping Sparrow and a Junco and then having to wait for reinforcement till next year, very good albums and tapes are now available in stores and catalogs. They will keep your musical memory sharp and bring a pleasant reminder of spring in the middle of winter.

Although many studies of bird song require expensive sound-recording equipment, other projects on song can be done with pencil and notebook. One of the simplest is to keep a calendar on the first and last song you hear from a species each year. A more time-consuming project is to study the song rate of a specific male of a species throughout a day or during the whole breeding season. You can trace the rate more easily for species that are highly visible in their territory, such as Red-winged Blackbirds, House Wrens, or Song Sparrows. The song rate can be determined by tallying the number of songs the male sings in an hour; make the count for each hour on a specified day in spring, or for a specified hour (record time after sunrise, not clock time) each day throughout the breeding season. During these observations, be sure to record factors that might influence song rate, such as weather, appearance of an intruding male or prospective mate, and stage in the breeding season. This project might get you labeled something of an eccentric, but such close observations on a species give far greater insight into birds' lives than simply identifying and listing species.

- 8 -

Mating Systems, Courtship, and Territory

PHILOSOPHERS DEBATE THE PURPOSE OF LIFE, but for creatures other than ourselves the reason is clear; they must leave behind as many copies of themselves as possible. Success or failure is measured in the number of viable offspring organisms can produce. They attempt to achieve immortality by passing on their traits to successive generations and, because any trait is an expression of the chemical deoxyribonucleic acid (DNA), which forms the genes, it is ultimately the DNA that seeks immortality by assuming the various forms of life that we see around us. This striving has led the prominent evolutionary biologist E. O. Wilson to update Samuel Butler's aphorism, "The chicken is only an egg's way of making another egg," to "The organism is only DNA's way of making more DNA."

From this perspective on life, it is fascinating to see how different creatures have evolved to make more DNA. The first bacterium-like organism probably replicated its DNA and simply split in half, producing two identical cells. This method is extremely efficient, for it can make millions of copies of DNA in a short time—so efficient that we wonder why asexual reproduction has been abandoned in complex organisms in favor of sexual reproduction. For sex presents difficulties in the drive for immortality: not only must an organism find a member of the opposite sex in order to reproduce, but sex dilutes the amount of each partner's DNA in the offspring by half, compared to asexual offspring. By this time-consuming method, then, an organism must produce two offspring for every one produced asexually in order to send the same amount of genetic material into the future, the only advantage being that progeny of the sexual union are different from the parents and each other. At face value this advantage may not seem overwhelming. In fact, in a constant environment asexual reproduction would be favored; but environments are rarely constant, and a change detrimental to one bacterium would equally affect all, whereas some off-spring of a sexual creature might not merely survive a change, but actually thrive on it. Without sex the only variability in the young would result from random changes in a rather sturdily built double helix of atoms, whereas sexual reproduction offers a consistent method for mixing new combinations of DNA, from which nature selects the best adapted.

If sex offers an advantage, it also presents to an organism something of a dilemma. Just as the lonely bacterium strives to make as many replicas of itself as possible, so too does the complex vertebrate. But to do so these creatures must compromise their selfish nature to cooperate with another creature just as selfish. This compromise between male and female takes form as a pair bond.

At its simplest, a pair bond might be considered an equal partnership between a male and a female, in which each sex contributes an equal share of energy and DNA, and both reap the benefits as their young mature and pass their genes on to the grandchildren. For the union between male sperm and female egg to take place, however, some distance must be traversed, and for the egg to mature, it must be supplied with food until the young can obtain food on its own. For this reason, males produce sex cells that are small and mobile, but female cells are large and sessile (fixed). Therefore, though equal amounts of genetic material are contributed by each partner, the amount of energy invested is much higher for the female than the male, for her eggs are many times larger than the male sperm. In birds, one egg may weigh 15 percent as much as the female's body weight, and an entire clutch may equal her weight, whereas the male's contribution is exceedingly small. This partnership, which has an equal evolutionary payoff for both male and female, is invested in differentially by each. And their initial investment in the endeavor is only seed money; subsequent expenditures also most often fall more heavily on the female. This imbalance is particularly evident in mammals, where the female must not only provide the anatomical site for fertilization, but must care for the developing fetus, must risk her life in birth, and then must nurture the offspring alone until they reach independence. In birds, however, the female's commitment is more flexible because the egg, once it leaves her body, can be cared for by either sex.

These biological differences between the sexes in parental investment have made the male and female of a species very different creatures. The male is often less discriminating in his choice of a mate, as if playing his cards where they fall, but the female loses much more if her clutch of eggs fails because of an inferior male. The evolutionary consequence of these differences is that mate selection is very much up to the female. The question now becomes: How does she make her choice? She cannot see the quality of the male's genetic makeup and therefore must base her decision on the male's external appearance, his behavior, the quality of his territory, or all these features. These factors become extremely important as the breeding season opens, when the male must convince the female by his courtship behavior that he is a worthy partner.

With these ideas about evolution of sex in mind, we will consider how avian species reproduce. We seek some understanding of how biology and environment of a species modify the selfish nature of the individual in developing different mating systems, courtship behaviors, and territorial requirements.

MATING SYSTEMS

The type of bond an organism can establish during the breeding season is limited because there are only two sexes. Therefore an organism may bond exclusively with one mate, forming a monogamous pair bond, or may have more than one mate and be polygamous. If a male mates with two or more females, the polygamous mating system is called polygyny, whereas a female's mating with two or more males is called polyandry. Monogamy is the most common mating system in birds, more than 90 percent of the species forming this type of bond (Lack, 1968). Our understanding about why these different mating systems have evolved has been advanced by Verner and Wilson (1966) and Orians (1969), and it is primarily on these works that this description is based.

For birds to produce viable offspring, the eggs and young must be cared for until they reach independence. This is no trivial task, for a young titmouse may require as many as 1,000 feedings a day (Royama, 1970), and a nestful of four to eight young demands almost constant attention. Because the male can care for and feed the young as well as the female can, the number of offspring that birds can produce is increased by the male's presence throughout the breeding season. Apparently for this reason, movement to a polygamous system has been limited in birds, for if one member of the pair left to seek another mate early in the breeding season, mortality among the nestlings would increase from starvation and from being left unprotected while the only parent was off finding food.

Although monogamy is by far the most common mating system in birds, the character and duration of the pair bond vary extensively among species. In species with long life spans, such as geese, albatrosses, birds of prey, and large shorebirds, the pair bond is usually lasting. These species are exceptionally faithful to their partners and for some species the bond lasts for the individual's life. Pairs of Royal Albatross, *Diomedea epomophora*, remained together all during a fifteen-year study of their breeding biology (Richdale, 1952). Captive flocks of swans and geese also exhibit this quality, and it is suspected that the lifelong pair bond is the rule for these species in the wild. Terns and gulls also are thought to form lifetime pair bonds.

Birds of prey, storks, cranes, and petrels also establish long-lasting pair bonds, but in these species, attachment to the shared breeding territory or nest site draws them together year after year. Geese and swans differ, apparently forming very personal attachments that have led to observations of a male goose remaining with his wounded mate as she attempted to walk the migratory route to the breeding grounds (Hudson, 1901).

The advantage in mating with the same partner year after year probably is that the pair can make the transition to the breeding season more smoothly and quickly; the two individuals are familiar with each other and their surroundings. This advantage has been demonstrated in the Black-legged Kittiwake, *Rissa tridactyle:* previously mated pairs bred earlier and with greater success than birds that were pair bonding for the first time (Coulson, 1966). Lifelong monogamous pair bonds are also suspected in species with shorter life spans than those mentioned. Species in which a mated pair mutually defends a territory all year, such as the Florida Scrub Jay, *Aphelocoma coerulescens,* as well as some tropical duetting species, probably mate for life. In other short-lived species, the pair bond has been observed lasting up to four years in some species, but most passerine species probably do not mate with the same partner from one breeding season to the next. Long-term studies of the Song Sparrow, *Melospiza melodia,* show that only 4 percent of pairs mated again in the next year (Nice, 1943).

One consequence of a monogamous mating system is that it does not encourage evolution of sexual dimorphism as much as polygamous systems do. The equal sex ratio in monogamy ensures that each will have a mate, discouraging the intense sexual selection that occurs in polygamous species. Even though males of some passerine families are often brighter in color than the females, among most long-lived birds the sexes are identical in physical appearance, probably because the female chooses a mate more by his behavior than by his external appearance. Males of monogamous species also handle many domestic duties, and so their appearance must not give away the location of the nest.

Although monogamy is the prevalent mating system among birds, nature is not nearly so neat as the categories we impose on her. We know about many instances of infidelity in a member of a mated pair during the breeding season. This wandering is most often observed in males, but the tendency is also seen in females. In some species of bluebirds and swallows, the female has been observed deserting her mate as the young fledge from the nest, leaving him to care for the offspring until they are completely independent while she seeks another mate.

These lapses into polygamy are consistent with the birds' selfish nature, for they have evolved not to be faithful to their mate, but to maximize their own genetic output. Monogamous species, however, generally maintain an exclusive pair bond because of family life's demands; only in species whose families demand less parental investment does polygamy become a common trait.

Polygamy has evolved in response to a number of conditions that allow only one parent to successfully raise the young. Polygamy is most prevalent in species that had *precocial* young; that is, young that can run and feed themselves at birth. In species whose young are born *altricial*, or naked and helpless, polygamy is not common, but does occur in some species that live in environments where food is particularly abundant.

Because polygyny is far more common and better understood than polyandry, let us first consider it in species that have precocial young. Remember, though, that not all precocial species are polygynous: geese are well developed when they leave their eggs, but for reasons not understood they are monogamous. Polygyny is most frequent in species of chickenlike birds of the order Galliformes; in these birds the precocial condition of the young has emancipated one of the parents, the male here, from almost all parental duties except contributing his genes. He is therefore free during the breeding season to mate with as many females as possible. The problem he now confronts is that other males are just as free and have the same intentions. The potential conflicts between males are much lessened, however, by the rigid dominance hierarchy in these species, whereby the dominant male gains greater access to females than the subordinate. Dominance is established by social signaling, which has led to extreme sexual dimorphism in these groups. Males are larger and have more elaborate plumage than females. During the breeding season the males erect their feathers, and in some species inflate air sacs on the neck and chest, while assuming some of the most outlandish postures in the avian world, all to inform others of their social status. The female, confronted by the prospect of no domestic help, chooses to mate with the most dominant male. As one might expect, the bond between male and female in these species is not strong. The males in some species associate loosely with females while they are nesting and raising the young, but in other species the bond between mates is very short, even measured in minutes, as in the Sage Grouse, *Centrocercus urophasianus.* Because of such brief pair bonding, the mating system in this and similar species has been called *promiscuous,* implying that choice of a mate is indiscriminate. This description may fit the male of the species, but it does not apply to the female. As we shall see in this chapter, these birds have evolved courtship displays that present the female with a clear choice of a mate.

In species that have altricial young, polygyny is confined to species that

Polygyny tends to encourage sexual dimorphism, which is pronounced in these Sage Grouse.

breed in exceptionally productive habitats, where food is abundant enough for one adult to feed the young alone. The key to understanding why polygyny evolved in these species is that productivity in any large area is not uniform; as highly productive marshes may be unevenly distributed in a poor environment. The abundance of food in these habitats makes it possible for the female to raise the young by herself. Her evolutionary choice has been to mate monogamously with a male on a poor territory, or to choose an already mated male on a highly productive one. The numbers of offspring raised on these two territories have favored polygyny, for a female alone can feed her young better with no help from the male in a marsh than the monogamous pair can in a weedy field.

In North America only fourteen species are both polygynous and altricial; of these, thirteen breed in habitats with standing water. Two of the best-known species are the Red-winged Blackbird, *Agelaius phoeniceus,* and the Yellow-headed Blackbird, *Xanthocephalus xanthocephalus*. Both these species, like other polygynous birds, are sexually dimorphic, the male being larger and more brightly colored than the female. This sexual difference undoubtedly comes from intense competition among males for territories in favored habitats. Unlike the gallinaceous birds, males of these altricial species do maintain a bond with the female throughout the breeding season, and although they do not help feed the young, they are active in protecting nest sites from predators such as crows and hawks.

Polyandry is very rare in birds, occurring regularly in fewer than 1 percent of species. How this mating system evolved is not well understood, for the female is in the unusual position of contributing less energy during the breeding season than the male, leaving him with most of the parental investment after the eggs are hatched. This condition occurs in species with precocial young that live in habitats where food is abundant. After the female lays a clutch of eggs, she seeks another mate, leaving the first mate holding the bag. The habitat's richness in food counts heavily not only for the young, but also for the female, who must be able to quickly muster enough energy to lay another clutch of eggs.

Polyandry occurs in rheas, tinamous, jacanas, and in some species of sandpipers. Because the female adopts a male breeding strategy in polyandry, role reversal is also seen in courtship behavior in these species: the female is more active in establishing the pair bond than the male. Phalaropes have long been thought to be the typical polyandrous species because the female is not only more aggressive on the breeding grounds than the male, with the male brooding the eggs and caring for the young, but she is also more brightly colored than the male. Phalaropes, however, are probably polyandrous only in specific environments and have been shown to be monogamous in others: the female leaves the male after she lays the eggs, not for another mate but for safer feeding areas (Hohn, 1969). The role reversal in this species is, then, probably a consequence more of female dominance during breeding than of widespread polyandry.

Studies of the Northern Jacana, *Jacana spinosa,* show this species to be truly polyandrous. In these birds, females maintain a large territory along a pond that is covered with floating vegetation. Up to four males set up smaller territories inside her territory and build floating nests. The female then mates with each male and lays eggs in his nest. Thereafter she does not visit the nests again, but does maintain a bond with each male, assisting him in driving away other males and predators (Jenni and Collier, 1972).

Surprisingly, homosexual behavior has been observed many times in captive birds, though rarely in nature. A unisexual pair of Black-crowned Night Herons, *Nycticorax nycticorax,* remained together throughout the breeding season, with one male acting as the subordinate to the territorial male (Armstrong, 1942). In Ring-billed Gulls, *Larus delawarensis,* pairs of females have been observed nesting together, each laying eggs in the nest, and, though most of these eggs were infertile, some did hatch, undoubtedly from prior copulation with a male (Conover et al, 1979). And in a park population of geese, a male Canada Goose, *Branta canadensis,* and a male Snow Goose, *Chen caerulescens,* formed a close relationship, remaining together during the day and roosting close to each other at night. Interestingly, the much larger Canada adopted the subordinate role to the Snow Goose (Starkly, 1972).

COURTSHIP

Most birds come into breeding readiness only once a year, and because this is their one opportunity to raise young, the breeding season is filled with intense activity. As the season begins, before mating, such activity comes to a climax as birds seek and secure mates. As in other species the behavior that leads to reproduction is called courtship, and in birds, courtship accounts for some of the most intriguing and spectacular behavior, along with some of the most bizarre activities found in the animal kingdom.

The functions served by courtship behavior include a method for species and sexual recognition, attracting a mate and signaling an individual's social status and intentions. It also stimulates and synchronizes the breeding behavior by members of the species. Courtship begins sometime before mating and generally ends with copulation; in some species, it is a prelude to a lasting relationship, but in others it is the only interaction between the sexes.

Courtship behavior initiates the breeding season, even for old "married"pairs that have spent the winter together. In most species, timing of courtship coincides with establishment of a territory. Some species, however, begin courting well before this step: many species of ducks court in winter and fly to the breeding grounds as mated pairs, and Whooping Cranes, *Grus americana,* court on stopovers during the migratory flights north. Such early courtship activities usually occur in species whose breeding season is short or its beginning unpredictable; where a pair must raise their young quickly, and some must molt and migrate south before the food supply gives out. Arriving on the breeding grounds paired and in breeding readiness allows more time for these other reproductive activities.

In most species of birds, the male initiates courtship and is most active at this time of year singing and displaying, but in a few species such as phalaropes,

A pair of Northern Gannets courting

females more actively court the male. In some species, however, and particularly among the long-lived ones that mate for life, courtship behavior is shared equally by male and female. In many species of large pelagic birds such as gannets and albatrosses, the male and female face each other with wings spread, point their beaks skyward, bow, and then rapidly strike their mandibles together. The mutual display in other species takes the form of a synchronized "dance." These dances occur on water among some ducks and grebes, and on land among cranes. This type of display is often highly intricate and strengthens the pair bond as well as mutually stimulating the pair.

In species in which the male is more active in courtship than the female, his behavior is designed to accentuate his fine external appearance. The Blue-footed Booby, *Sula nebouxii,* lands on the breeding grounds in such a way as to show off his conspicuous blue feet, and then high-steps around a prospective mate. During their display, many species of ducks point with their bills to the brilliantly colored secondary feathers on their wing, and other species erect and display patches of feathers, or vividly colored bare skin—some even while hanging upside down—all to attract a mate. These displays range from an enormous patch of red skin inflated by the male Magnificent Frigatebird, *Fregata magnificens,* to the spectacular plumes of the birds of paradise, but include the rather modest patch of red head feathers of the Ruby-crowned Kinglet, *Regulus calendula.*

Flight display is another aspect of courtship common to many species; in hawks and eagles, the male in many species performs aerial acrobatics, and in the Bateleur Eagle, *Terothopius ecaudatus,* the pair executes flying maneuvers, including tumbling with locked talons toward the ground. Less spectacular but no less impressive are the courtship flights of the woodcock, snipe, nighthawk, and some hummingbird species, which produce sound in their power-dives and loops. In passerine and other species, song is one obvious method for attracting a mate, but when the female enters the territory, males begin more intimate vocalizations, accompanying visual displays. In some species such as Budgerigars, *Melopsittacus undulatus,* courtship includes mutual preening as a behavior vital to forming a pair bond.

Courtship behavior also includes many symbolic breeding and nesting activities that are used to attract a female or cement the pair bond. Probably the most common behavior of this type is courtship-feeding by the male. Among many species of birds, the male brings food to the female as part of the courtship display. In gulls and other species this behavior is strikingly similar to that of feeding the nestlings; the female gull takes a begging posture and even pecks at her mate's beak, causing him to disgorge the contents of his crop. Such feeding apparently has little to do with hunger, for it has been observed in pairs in which the female has just returned from foraging and the male has not eaten for hours. In many species, courtship-feeding is a prelude to copulation; but in the European Starling, *Sternus vulgaris,* feeding also occurs after copulation takes place. In many of these species the male continues to feed the female after the eggs are laid, but this behavior is more functional because it allows the female to remain on the nest longer. In button quail, however, the female feeds the male in courtship, and it is he who primarily broods and cares for the young.

Food is used in courtship by many species, but other species include nesting material in their displays. The male Adelie Penguin, *Pygoscelis adeliae,* presents stones to the female before mating; in the dance by the Western Grebe, *Aechmophorus occidentalis,* the male and female dive together, rise, and present to each other bits of nesting material; and the Roseate Spoonbill, *Ajaia ajaja,* presents to a prospective mate a twig during courtship. In the courtship display of the male House Wren, *Troglodytes aedon,* nesting material is used less symbolically, in that he excitedly presents to the female partially built nests he has constructed, and if the female chooses him as a mate she will finish the job of nest building in the cavity she finds most desirable.

Courtship behavior is usually an intimate affair between the male and female, but some species display in groups. Typically, the males of these species gather and begin displaying, which attracts nearby females, who then choose and mate with the males. The species that mate in these social arenas, or *leks,* are polygynous and sexually dimorphic. The lek is the mating area where the males display; these are then considered lek species. This type of courtship behavior occurs in several orders of birds, including some shorebirds, many species of grouse and pheasant, some hummingbirds, and some tropical New- and Old-World passerines. The leks are traditional areas, used year after year, and whether they are particular perches in a forest clearing or a section of open prairie, the males establish mating territories and display the breeding plumage as in the Sage Grouse, *Centrocercus urophasianus,* and the Ruff, *philomachus pugnax,* or by adopting striking poses, as among the birds of paradise, or by flight displays, as among tropical manakins and hummingbirds. In any species,

A male Ruff possesses elaborate breeding plumage.

females are confronted with a dizzying array of sights and sounds that are thought to stimulate them into breeding readiness. The lek is built around a traditional mating center, where most of the copulation takes place, and males compete for territories close to the center. When the females approach, the male display intensifies, but the females ignore peripheral males and proceed to the center of the lek, where only the most dominant males catch the females' attention. Among Sage Grouse, fewer than 10 percent of the males account for more than 75 percent of the copulation (Wiley, 1973).

Our description of courtship behavior would not be complete unless we mentioned the mating activities of the birds of paradise and the bowerbirds. Related to crows, the birds of paradise are a group of forty-three species that inhabit New Guinea, northern Australia, and associated islands. These birds are not qualitatively different in mating habits from other birds, for some species are monogamous and others are polygamous, some of them displaying in leks, but they are the evolutionary extreme in birds' courtship displays. Males of the polygamous species sport every hue and color of the rainbow, with feathers creating fantastic cape and bib shapes, surrounding their bodies with a cloud of

The mutual display area, or lek, of the Long-tailed Manakin, Chiroxiphia linearis, *is a limb of a tree. Here two males are displaying in front of a female.*

soft color. I hope you will get some idea about this phantasmagoria from these descriptions based on studies by Ripley (1950).

The Twelve-wired Bird of Paradise, *Seleucides ignotus,* is named for the twelve wirelike feather shafts that extend from along its flanks. Its glossy black and purple upper body contrasts with soft yellow side and belly feathers; the throat and breast are black, fringed with green. During courtship the bird raises its wings and fluffs up its yellow feathers with the black-shafted wires pointing forward, at the same time erecting breast and throat feathers, which form a circular black bib bordered with green that completely covers its face, with only the beak protruding. The Six-plumed Birds of Paradise are similar-looking species that have six long feather shafts arising from the back of the head, each shaft tipped with barbs that form a tiny racketlike structure. The male birds are mostly dark in color, with iridescent feathers on head and throat. In courtship display the breast feathers form a soft black bib that accentuates the throat's iridescence, and the six head plumes are directed forward across the face. The Lesser Superb Bird of Paradise, *Lophorina superba,* is a rather nondescript starling-sized black bird until it erects an enormous feather cape that frames its head in a curtain of black, and a triangular bib of glossy green feathers extends from the throat, both of which direct attention to the bird's lime-green open mouth. The Blue Bird of Paradise, *Paradisaea rudolphi,* hangs upside down from a limb, swaying sideways, allowing its soft blue contour feathers to flow, transforming the bird into a wash of blue as two long feather shafts arch gracefully from its tail.

If the birds of paradise have taken visual courtship displays to the limit, their cousins, the bowerbirds, have pretty much cornered the market on courtship-related paraphernalia. For, unlike the birds of paradise, the bowerbirds are rather dull-colored, but their physical appearance is enhanced by the elaborate constructions they build and decorate. These structures are called *bowers,* and the less colorful the bowerbird, the more elaborate the bower. The design of the bower is species-specific, most them built as a variation on two parallel walls of sticks and twigs, lined with grass, leaving a display avenue down the middle. Other species build a tall bower with sticks around a sapling, piling them up to two meters high, and in the broad base of the bower the birds cut out a display area, which sometimes forms a hut. Whatever the design, the bowers are decorated with colored stones, flowers, leaves, and berries; some species even smear

A male Satin Bowerbird decorates his avenue bower.

the sticks composing the bower with colored berry juice, and the Satin Bowerbird, *Ptilonorhynchus violaceus,* uses a piece of bark as a brush to apply the "paint."After the bower is built, the male clears the display area and decorates it with objects. Some species are very particular about the type and color of the object used: the Satin Bowerbird uses primarily blue objects; the Spotted Bowerbird, *Chlamydera maculata,* accumulates shiny ones; and other species decorate with fresh-picked flowers, leaves, and berries. The reason for all this activity is that the bower is essential for attracting a female, who is drawn to the male not just by the bower, but also seems particularly interested in his ability at exterior decorating, the more dominant males having the most elaborately decorated bowers. When she appears, the male frantically begins to display by pointing at objects in the display area, even picking them up and throwing them about. If the female continues to watch this display, which may last up to twenty minutes, the male approaches her and they mate. Afterward she will leave to build a nest and raise the young alone, while the male replaces and rearranges the objects in the display area, anticipating another female.

Another remarkable feature of the avenue bowers is their compass orientation: Satin Bowerbirds orient the avenue north and south, but avenues made by the Yellow-breasted Bowerbird, *Chlamydera cerviniventris,* lie in an east—west direction (Marshal, 1954).

TERRITORY

Important though courtship behavior is in reproduction, a territory too is essential for birds to see reproduction through to its conclusion. A territory is defined as any defended area. During the breeding season birds establish and defend a space from their most feared competitors, members of their own kind. In this way territory is an isolating mechanism, giving the pair some protection for mating and raising a family. Although this isolation is considered the most important function for a territory, other advantages accrue to the territory holder. The territory helps spread a species over a habitat, discouraging overpopulation and conserving the food supply, and also possibly keeping infectious diseases from spreading. Territory holders also have a chance to intimately learn physical features in the defended area, an advantage in adverse conditions. A territory also gives the resident a psychological edge over competitors, for even a low-ranking member of a flock acts dominant inside its territorial boundaries. The size, quality, and, in some species, the relative position of the territory are physical extensions of a bird's personality, signaling its ability to compete with members of its own kind. Although not all these territorial functions apply to any one species, the importance of territory in the avian world is evident from its almost universal presence in this class of animals. Not all birds, however, maintain the same type of territory, for the breeding habitat strongly determines the type of territory a species will establish.

The commonest type of avian territory is one in which all breeding activities take place.This all-purpose area is generally established by the male at the beginning of the breeding season; from here he attracts and courts a mate, and thereafter the pair will raise a family here. The mated birds will rarely venture outside this space until the breeding season ends. This all-inclusive territory is larger than other types, for it must include enough resources not only for the adult birds, but for the young while they still depend on the parents for food. This is the typical territory of the passerines and also occurs in woodpeckers and some birds of prey.

The second type of territory is defended primarily for mating and nesting, but most of the feeding is done away from the territory. This type is found in some species of swans, hawks, shorebirds, and swallows; among songbirds the Red-winged Blackbird, *Agelaius phoeniceus,* and the Yellow-headed Blackbird, *Xanthocephalus xanthocephalus,* establish this type of territory. Because these birds regularly leave to feed in neutral zones, the psychological edge any territory gives is illustrated nicely by comparing birds' behavior on and off the territory. While inside the invisible boundaries the male birds are clearly dominant and aggressively respond to approach by intruders, but as they cross their borders they become more tolerant and submissive. Male Red-wings can be observed at this time of year feeding close to other males just meters from their territories; their nonaggressiveness is signaled by their provocative red shoulders' being covered with black contour feathers.

These mating and nesting territories are not so large as the all-inclusive types. As a consequence, the territories of some species are tightly packed together, forming a semicolonial or neighborhood nesting arrangement. The marsh-nesting blackbirds and sometimes the Barn Swallow, *Hirundo rustica,* live in such conditions; these birds have evolved to take advantage of others' presence in that they mutually respond to predators by mobbing them. The mass attack is quite effective in driving away threats to their nests.

Species that defend only the nest site have the third type of territory. This condition is common in many seabirds and also occurs in swifts, swallows, herons, and some weaver finches, among others. A common feature among these species is their food, which is patchily distributed and unpredictable, but when present is enough to feed all; in short, their food is not defendable. These species, then, remain in flocks all year, benefiting by having others around to find food and detect predators, but establishing small, defended areas in which they raise their young during the breeding season. Individual territories in many of these colonial birds are no larger than the reach of the resident's beak while on the nest.

Colonies are traditional breeding areas used year after year and, because they are often quite conspicuous, they draw predators' attention. Apparently for this reason many colonial seabirds nest on isolated oceanic islands where land predators are a minimal threat, but even here many of the small species are threatened by predatory birds such as large gulls. Many species of petrels and auks therefore nest in burrows to protect their eggs and young and come and go at night so that they themselves will not be attacked. Gulls and terns, though, will nest in less isolated areas, but these aggressive birds will vigorously defend the entire colony from predators by communally mobbing any potential nest robbers. In these species, pairs of birds that hold territories on the colony's edge are more vulnerable to predators than those nesting toward the center; the territories away from the borders thus are more hotly competed for and are generally occupied by older, more experienced birds.

The last type of territory characteristic in the breeding season is defended only for mating. In lek species, males establish and defend mating territories, with the most dominant birds close to the mating center of the lek. Mating territories are also known in solitary species such as the Ruby-throated Hummingbird, *Archilochus colubris,* the Ruffed Grouse, *Bonasa umbellus,* and bowerbirds.

Most terns, like the Sooty Terns at right, nest colonially on the ground; yet the Black Noddy, Anous stolidus, *builds its nest in trees.*

Many studies show that when a male is removed from its territory during the breeding season, the area is quickly absorbed by adjacent males or taken over by a new individual. These results indicate continual pressure on the territory holder to defend his breeding rights. This defense usually consists of social signaling by song and display. These signals are generally sufficient to maintain the territory's integrity, but at times some species, especially those which have peppery dispositions or which breed close together, resort to physical combat.

Song is probably the most efficient and economical method of territorial defense because it warns others from a distance about the resident's location and breeding condition. If these signals are ignored and the intruder approaches the territory more closely, the territory holder will sing more frequently and meet the threat by heightening its display of species colors, meanwhile assuming the fighting posture typical of the species. If the encroacher flinches at this display, the territorial male will fly at him to drive him away, but if the intruder holds his ground, a fight may ensue. These encounters usually take place along the borders of the territory, and if the conflict is with a neighboring male at the beginning of the breeding season, the two birds signal aggressively back and forth. As one male leaves his territory to chase the neighbor away, however, he finds himself the interloper, confronting a male whose territory confers dominance upon him, and the episode ends with the invader quickly retreating. These border skirmishes usually end in a stalemate in which each bird learns not only to tolerate its neighbor, but to observe mutual territorial boundaries.

Although territories are defended against members of their own kind, many birds also act aggressively toward other species that enter the territory. Many species will attempt to exclude potential predators such as crows and hawks, as well as cats, dogs, and human beings from their breeding areas. Kingbirds are especially well known for the vigor with which they attack crows as these nest robbers fly over their territories; crows commonly change oft-used flyways to their feeding areas when the kingbirds arrive in spring, resorting again to their proverbially straight routes only after the pugnacious kingbirds leave at summer's end.

Size of territory varies with the species: pairs of colonial nesting birds occupy the smallest areas and solitary raptors the largest. In birds that maintain all-purpose territories, food requirements strongly determine the territory. An insect-eating House Wren, *Troglodytes aedon,* requires about 4,000 square meters (Kendeigh, 1941), and the Red-tailed Hawk, *Buteo jamaicensis,* which feeds on mammals, has been observed to require more than 1 million square meters (Fitch et al, 1946). Within a species, variation in the size of territory depends on availability of food, population pressure, and individual territorial experience probably being factors. In habitats where food is abundant, territory holders require smaller areas in which to raise their families. If the density of breeders is high, pressure from adjacent males also reduces the territory, whereas in poor habitats breeders need larger territories. Studies on the Song Sparrow, *Melospiza melodia,* breeding in the same habitat year after year, show that territory size remains pretty much constant regardless of the number of breeding males (Nice, 1943). ·

The territory's shape is influenced by the habitat's physical features. Highly productive areas along a river determine for many species that their territories follow the waterway, and thus are long and thin. Other species must shape their territory to include such features as suitable nest sites or singing posts. On the American Great Plains where the habitat is uniform, most birds establish territories that are roughly circular.

Suggested Reading

For the evolutionary significance of sex and mating systems, refer to chapters in Wallace's *Animal Behavior: Its Development, Ecology, and Evolution* and Wilson's *Sociobiology: A New Synthesis.* Courtship behavior is described completely in chapter 13 of *The Life of Birds* by Welty, and chapters in Burton's *Bird Behavior* have stunning photographs of birds in display as well as informative text. For more detailed information about the courtship behavior of a species or group of birds many fine books are available, such as *Birds of Paradise and Bower Birds,* by Gillard; *The Life of the Hummingbird,* by Skutch; and *The Owl Papers,* by Maslow.

Projects

Of all the avian behaviors, courtship, excluding song, is probably the most difficult to observe because it occurs for only a short period in the mating season,
often for only a small part of the day. To see these most interesting behaviors
one must be alert to the species' habits and must above all have patience. If you
hear the distinctive "peent"of a woodcock late in the evening in early spring it
may be the prelude to a courtship flight once it gets a little darker—sit down
and wait. Male flight display and territorial behavior in hummingbirds most
often occurs around flowering shrubs early in spring, and courtship in ducks
occurs in late winter, most often when the water is calm. Probably the easiest
species to observe in courtship are the gulls and terns, because many pairs come
together in spring and their colonies are out in the open. You can find no better
way to become a keen observer of birds than to bring along a camera and try to
capture birds' courtship or territorial behavior on film.

- 9 -

Nests, Eggs, and Young

A COMPLEX RELATIONSHIP CONNECTS THE PHYSICAL EVENTS that signal favorable breeding conditions with the internal physiological changes that direct an organism to arrive at breeding readiness at the proper time and place. For Northern Hemisphere birds, the sun's gradual return from the Tropic of Capricorn and increasing hours of daylight impel the brain to signal the body to prepare for reproduction. In birds this sequence culminates with egg laying, but is preceded by molting, migration, song, territorial behavior, courtship, and nest building. These behaviors, causing the birds to be in breeding condition, in optimal habitat with a mate, are mostly controlled by hormones secreted by the testes and ovaries. The primary function of these organs, though, is to produce sperm and egg so that genetic material can be combined.

Copulation in birds technically occurs only in the relatively few species in which the male's cloaca has sufficiently large erectile tissue to enter the female. Aside from these species of ducks and ratites, mating is accomplished by touching the outward-turned cloacal linings together in a kind of "kiss." By either method, mating is a rather unsteady affair, with the male climbing on the female's back, twisting and lowering his tail, while she raises and angles hers so that the undertail coverts press together and their cloacas meet. During this relatively short union, millions of sperm enter the female and begin their journey up the oviduct. Associated with mating is release by the female's ovary of a mature sex cell that begins to move down the oviduct; when the sperm and egg meet, fertilization can take place. These internal events are accompanied by physical activities as the birds prepare a suitable site for depositing the eggs. This site is the nest and, though the internal events of fertilization and egg development are similar in many ways among species, the physical places where the eggs will develop into young vary considerably.

NESTS

Nests are an extension of parental care that protects the shelled life forms and, in many species, facilitate their development. Among all the nests that species employ, a basic division differentiates species that use cavities for their nest sites from those that build their nests out in the open. This distinction is useful but not as clear-cut as it seems, for some species use both nest types, others build a cavity out in the open to nest in, and still others use an open-nest design, but build in a physical enclosure such as a cave or barn. With these exceptions in mind, let us look at some of the types of nests birds use.

Birds that nest in tree holes are the most common cavity nesters, the most familiar example being the woodpeckers. These birds are well designed to excavate a cavity in a tree, for their beak, skull, and body construction allows them to hammer away at hard surfaces. Chickadees and nuthatches also excavate their nesting cavities, but these species must do so in softer wood, or shape naturally occurring holes to their needs. Other species must rely almost exclusively on ready-made cavities, for hole nesters such as the Tree Swallow, *Tachycineta bicolor,* bluebirds, and many owls are ill-adapted for hollowing out a cavity. These species, then, must rely on abandoned cavity nests or on holes that occur naturally, both of which are more prevalent in dead wood. The human practice of "cleaning" woods of dead trees negatively affects these species, for as the number of holes decreases, competition for nest sites increases, and more aggressive species such as the European Starling, *Sturnus vulgaris,* and the House Wren, *Troglodytes aedon,* displace bluebirds and other species. Happily, this condition is being corrected in many places by manufactured nesting boxes, which are readily accepted by most cavity nesters. These boxes can be built to accommodate particularly hard-hit species by making the entrance hole small enough to allow only chosen species to enter, excluding larger species. Other birds that also nest in tree cavities are a number of species of ducks, the Wood Duck, *Aix sponsa,* being the most familiar.

Less familiar cavity-nesting species dig holes in sand or clay banks. Among these, the Belted Kingfisher, *Ceryle alcyon,* and the Rough-winged Swallow, *Stelgidopteryx serripennis,* excavate solitary holes by digging away at the bank with beak and feet, and the Bank Swallow, *Riparia riparia,* digs similarly, but is colonial in its nesting habit. Many seabirds, especially petrels and auks, make nesting burrows by digging out an entrance tunnel and then making an egg chamber, but they will also nest in natural rock crevices. On the prairie, the Burrowing Owl, *Athene cunicularia,* will excavate a nest underground, but more often uses burrows abandoned by prairie dogs and other mammals.

Cavity nests give both parents and eggs protection from predators not possible in nests built out in the open, for they are concealed places with limited access. Asian and African hornbills increase the site's protective value by sealing up the entrance to their tree nest with mud. After preparing the nest, these crow-sized birds seal off the entrance, the female working from the inside and the male from the outside, until the hole is just large enough for the male to pass food to the female, who remains imprisoned with eggs and young for almost the entire nesting season. Cavity nests are also subject to slighter temperature changes, are not affected by chill winds or the sun's scorching rays, and are generally immune to an early spring snow or summer downpour. All these qualities contribute to a lower mortality rate among offspring in cavity nests than those hatched in other types of nests (Nice, 1957). With these advantages we would expect the cavity to be the most common nest type, but one disadvantage in using cavities is that their number is limited, and the site of the cavity, not the organism using it, determines the nest's location; open-nesting species do not have these problems.

Species that nest out in the open choose as their nest site the most suitable place in the environment. Some species, though, build no nest at all. Most birds in this category lay their eggs on the ground, on cliff ledges, or in caves. Among these, nightjars lay their eggs on the forest floor, and the Common Nighthawk, *Chordeiles minor,* increasingly uses flat pebbly roofs on city buildings. A number of species of murres nest on cliff ledges, as does the Peregrine Falcon, *Falco peregrinus,* which has also been known to use ledges on city buildings. Turkey Vultures, *Cathartes aura,* and the California Condor, *Gymnogyps californianus,* commonly lay their eggs on cave floors.

Probably most remarkable among the species that make no nest is the White Tern, *Gygis alba,* of the tropical oceans. This elegant bird lays its single egg on a forked branch in a low tree or shrub. The parents very carefully incubate this egg, and when it hatches the young grasps the branch with its feet, an adaptation not found in ground-nesting terns. Unlike the White Tern, most terns prepare a site for their eggs by scraping out a depression in the sand. These *scrape nests* are also found among some species of ducks and sandpipers, which line these simple depressions with plant materials or down feathers, as do the Savanna Sparrow, *Passerculus sandwichensis,* and the Grasshopper Sparrow, *Ammodramus savannarum.* The nests of these ground nesters commonly become enclosed by grass growing around the scrape as the breeding season progresses.

The disadvantages in having no nest or a simple scrape nest are that the eggs are vulnerable to predators and that they are in direct contact with the ground, which can cool or heat them quickly. To insulate the eggs from the ground, many species, especially those nesting near water, pile up plant material or mud in a mound, on which they lay their eggs. Mound nests are found among grebes, gallinules, some pelicans, swans, and gulls. Flamingos, which nest in shallow water, build a mud cylinder that is cup-shaped at the top, to hold the eggs. Some species that usually nest in trees will build mound nests of sticks when breeding in treeless habitats, among them the Osprey, *Pandion haliaetus,* and the Bald Eagle, *Haliaeetus leucocephalus,* which nest in marshes.

Mound nests in themselves do not protect the eggs from predators, however, which has led some species, such as gulls, to vigorously defend the nest sites, whereas other species choose inaccessible places in which to build their nests. A number of these species build their nests in shallow water, where the mound becomes a floating raft that is anchored to the bottom by floating vegetation. This type of nest is common in some species of grebes, loons, jacanas, and swans. Supplying in a suitable lake an artifical floating platform will attract the Common Loon, *Gavia immer,* and the nest built here is far more successful than a nest at the edge of the lake (Klein, 1985).

The nests discussed so far are rather crude constructions, made by coarse body movements that scrape out or pile up materials. Most of the avian world, however, is much more adept at nest building, and its nests are more complex in design and made by combining materials. These nests are assembled with very fine movements, some of them the most complex structures found in nature.

The most typical and familiar of nests built in the open is the cup nest, for this is the type used by most tree-nesting passerines, as well as other species. In some of these species the nest rests on top of a limb, in others it is wedged into forked branches, and still other species suspend the nest from tree branches. These nests are generally made of plant fibers, with coarse material on the outside and finer material lining the interior cup. A number of species, such as the American Robin, *Turdus migratorius,* cement their nests together with mud, and hummingbirds bond their nests with spiders' webs and caterpillar silk. This cup nest is also characteristic of field-nesting species such as the Bobolink, *Dolichonyx oryzivorus,* which builds its nest on the ground, as do a number of forest-dwelling warblers. In marshes, species such as wrens attach their cup nests to tall grass stems. To further conceal or protect the nest some species build a dome or roof over the cup. This is the method used by the forest-dwelling Ovenbird, *Seiurus aurocapillus,* which builds its enclosed, oven-shaped nest on the forest floor. An enclosed design is also used by species of magpies, which build a dome over their nest with sticks.

Possibly the most extraordinary cup nest is that of the Long-tailed Tailorbird, *Orthotomus sutorius,* of southeast Asia, for, as its name implies, this bird uses plant fibers to sew its nest together. The birds choose as their nest site two large green leaves that grow close together. The bird then pierces the leaves with its beak and draws long stringy fibers through the adjacent holes and then pulls these tight, forming a pocket in which the cup nest is built.

The Barn Swallow, *Hirundo rustica,* also builds a cup nest, but instead of plant material, this species uses mud as its primary medium; some flycatchers, as well as other species, also use mud. In spring after a rainfall these birds can be seen on the ground gathering mud in their mouths. Each mouthful of mud is an individual brick for the nest, and as the mud dries it hardens into a firm nest. Because these structures are weakened by rain, many of these birds choose a protected site in which to build; for the Barn Swallow the nest site is almost invariably a human structure, and phoebes commonly nest on girders under bridges. The Rufous Ovenbird, *Furnarius rufus,* of South America builds a domed nest of mud out in the open, but these birds breed in a dry climate and their nests are built from soils that are much more resistant to rain than that available to the Barn Swallow. In North America, the Cliff Swallow, *Hirundo pyrrhonota,* builds an elegant domed structure of mud under a protective cliff or building eaves.

Many species of swifts build a nest similar to that of swallows, but instead of using mud these species cement their nests together with a sticky secretion of their salivary glands. The Chimney Swift, *Chaetura pelagica*, gathers sticks while in flight and binds them to the wall of a vertical structure with sticky saliva. Some swiftlets in southeast Asia make a shallow cup nest almost entirely of these secretions. As mentioned earlier, their nests are gathered by the thousands and exported to China, where they are used to make the broth for bird's-nest soup.

Sewing is a rare nest-building technique in birds, but weaving is a rather common method. Many types of cup nests are made of plant fibers looped around each other, a practice most highly developed in species that build hanging nests. Such nests are attached at the very tip of a branch or palm-frond at only one place, and thus are quite different from suspended-cup nests, which are woven to a branch in two or more places, like the nest of the Northern Oriole, *Icterus galbula*. Species that build hanging nests use plant fibers to attach their globe-shaped nests to ends of branches by winding the fibers around the point of attachment, then looping these under the turns, before finishing them with a knot. These fibers are added to until the long, woven piece is drawn into a loop, to which the rest of the nest is woven. The weaving that produces the nest exterior is impressively like that used to make baskets; in fact, it has been suggested that early human beings got the idea for making baskets and cloth from plant materials by watching these birds build their nests. Weaving individual nests to a tree produces a Christmas-ornament type of colony among the Village Weavers, *Textor cucullatus*, and other species of weaver birds build their nests so close together that the result is a coarsely woven structure consisting of many individual nests. The Social Weaver, *Philetarius socius*, of Africa builds a huge insectlike structure that may hold several hundred nesting pairs.

Most bird species are hardworking nest builders, but some are opportunistic, readily using nests built by other species. This is obviously the tactic applied by many cavity-nesting species that rely on abandoned woodpecker holes. Falcons and large owls will use abandoned crow nests instead of building their own, and anhingas commonly employ old heron nests. Such opportunistic habits undoubtedly led some species to lay their eggs in occupied nests as well. Although this behavior has been observed in many species, it is the only egg-laying method for a group of birds that are *nest* or *brood parasites*. Represented in North America only by the Brown-headed Cowbird, *Molothrus ater*, and the Bronzed Cowbird, *Molothrus aeneus*, brood parasitism is practiced by more than eighty species worldwide that neither build a nest nor care for their young, but rely on the foster parents' inability to recognize the parasites' eggs and young. How they manage this feat we will explore later in this chapter.

The oddest nests in the avian world are built by the megapodes of Australia. The ten species of megapodes are gallinaceous birds that apparently have retained, or more probably reverted to, the reptilian characteristic of burying their eggs underground. Because the avian egg must be kept warm for it to develop, these species choose nest sites that remain warm during the breeding

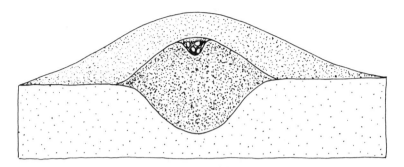

Megapodes bury their eggs, with some species filling the pit with organic material before laying, then covering the eggs with sandy soil. As the organic matter rots, it generates heat, which incubates the eggs.

season or sites that generate their own heat. Some species of megapodes nest only on black sand beaches or near hot springs, and others dig their nests but, before laying the eggs, they partially fill the pit with plant material and then cover the eggs with a mound of sandy soil. As the organic material decomposes it generates heat that warms the eggs (Frith, 1956). This seemingly simple method of nesting turns out to be complex, as we shall see.

Among birds the duty of constructing the nest generally falls primarily on the female. She either builds the nest alone or in some species is helped by the male, who brings nesting material. Among the many exceptions are House Wrens, *Troglodytes aedon;* the male builds the outer portion of the nest unassisted and the female finishes the work by adding fine material to line the cup. Among woodpeckers and swallows the nest is built by both sexes, each doing an equal share of the work. And among megapodes, many species of weaverbirds, and some polyandrous species, the male is the primary nest builder. The time it takes to build the nest varies widely; simple cup nests take from two to five days, and the more complex hanging nest can take up to two weeks. The eagles' huge stick nests may be eight weeks in construction.

Except when the male builds the nest alone, selecting a nest site is also the female's responsibility. The site is extremely important, for it must have adequate support and cover, beyond the reach of potential predators. For greater protection against predators, some species build their nests in close association with other species; in the tropics species such as the South American Cacique, *Cassicus cela,* nest close to nests of stinging bees and wasps. These insects do not bother the birds but will attack other organisms that approach too closely. Some cavity-using species actually nest inside bee, ant, and termite hives as a protective measure. Other nesting associations pair powerful birds of prey with smaller birds, where the risk in nesting near the raptor is outweighed by the benefits the predator confers by driving away snakes and egg-eating mammals. Kingbirds or grackles sometimes nest in the large stick structures made by Golden Eagles, *Aquila chrysaetos.* A number of species have also come to nest close to people, some of them benefiting by the increased food supply and others being more protected by nesting near human structures. The White Stork, *Ciconia ciconia*, of Eurasia is protected by the tradition that this species brings good luck to the village or to the house on which it nests.

EGGS

The parents' genetic material, united by fertilization, directs the fantastically complex development of an amorphous egg into a creature that is a marvel of design. First, however, the ovum must be prepared to live outside the female's body. As the ovum, which is the yolk of the egg, moves through different portions of the oviduct, it stimulates production of *albumen,* or egg white, and a hard shell. Albumen derives its name from the most abundant protein in the jellylike mass. The albumen protects the ovum and supplies it with some nutrients and water; it is made of three layers with different consistencies. The one closest to the yolk is thin and watery; surrounding this is a layer of thick albumen, which is encased by another thin layer. Albumen also forms a dense cord that runs lengthwise from either end of the yolk to the shell interior. This cord, the *chalaza,* keeps the yolk centered and also allows it to rotate as the egg changes position. In this way the developing fetus in the shell is always above with respect to gravity, and the heavier, food-containing portion of the yolk is always below.

At the terminal portion of the oviduct, the yolk and albumen stimulate production of membranes that surround the mass and finally the minerals, mostly calcium carbonate, which will harden into a shell. After the shell hardens, cells of the oviduct secrete pigments that form either blotchy marks on the shell or a uniform color, depending on the species. If no pigment is applied to the egg it will be white. The egg then is forced by muscular contraction into the cloaca and expelled from the body. When the egg leaves the body, its contents cool and shrink so that the membranes surrounding the albumen separate from the blunt end of the shell, forming an air space. The entire procedure is essentially the same for an unfertilized egg as for a fertilized one.

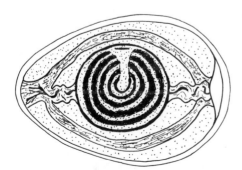 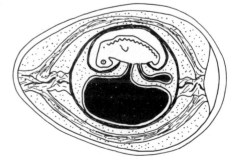

Avian egg at different stages of development

After copulation, the female, among chickens at least, is able to store the male's sperm as long as three weeks. This ability allows timing of copulation and ovulation to be rather casual, in that copulation may occur during courtship, before the nest is built, and the female still can produce fertilized eggs, timing her laying with completion of the nest. Nevertheless, it is not unusual to find an egg on the lawn in spring, dropped by a female in flight before the nest was ready.

Once the first egg is laid the others that will complete the clutch usually follow twenty-four hours apart in most birds, including most passerines, ducks, geese, woodpeckers, and small shore birds. Larger birds such as hawks and swans lay eggs at about two-day intervals, and some species lay eggs up to seven or eight days apart. Some species, especially those which lay eggs at intervals of more than one day, begin incubation when the first egg is laid, but most birds hold off incubation until the clutch is complete. The result of waiting until the last egg is laid is that all the eggs begin development at the same time and all the eggs hatch out on the same day; in hawks, cranes, owls, and others the first egg laid hatches first.

Although birds strive for maximal reproductive output, the means to this end is not the same for all species, in that some birds invariably lay only one egg during the breeding season, and at the other extreme some lay fifteen or more eggs. In fact the number of eggs a species lays seems to have little to do with the size of its population. The European Partridge, *Perdix perdix*, which has been known to lay as many as twenty-three eggs in its nest, is not nearly so numerous as the Wilson's Storm-Petrel, *Oceanites oceanicus*, which lays only one egg, and yet is considered one of the most abundant species in the world. The size of the clutch is adjusted by natural selection to maximize not the number of eggs the female can lay, but the number it can fledge. The list of factors that influence clutch size is long, including size of the bird and its longevity, population and predation pressures, type and availability of food, and so on. Some factors count more than others. Most species of penguins lay two eggs, but the larger species that breed in colder climates lay only one. Among these larger birds the body heat transferred during incubation probably precludes their attempting to raise another chick. Paradoxically, then, species like the Emperor Penguin, *Aptenodytes forsteri*, maximize their genetic output by reducing the number of eggs they lay. Albatrosses, petrels, and most auks also lay only one egg; the determining factor here is the long distance the parents must travel to find food, which for the chick means long intervals between feedings. Large doves and several species of swifts and nightjars also lay one egg; the amount of food available probably does much to determine that these species will rear only one chick at a time.

Two eggs is the normal clutch for kiwis, hummingbirds, cranes, loons, boobies, most penguins, and pigeons. For the kiwi, the enormous egg—up to 25 percent of the adult body weight—makes it impossible for the female to lay more than two eggs and still continue incubation, with its demands on energy.

Although cranes and boobies also lay two eggs, they rarely raise more than one chick. In these species it has been suggested that the second egg, laid two or more days after the first, is a reproductive option in case the first egg fails. These species begin incubation with the first egg and are more attentive to it when it hatches. Hawks and owls, which lay from two to eight eggs, depending on the species, are also more attentive to the older, more vigorous chicks in the nest, and, though they will fledge the entire brood when food is abundant, in lean years the later-hatched checks are fed last, and are sometimes even killed and eaten by their older siblings while the parents look on.

Terns and gulls generally lay three eggs, but in contrasting their clutch size with that of the albatross and petrel, we must remember that these birds are primarily inshore feeders and thus are able to return frequently to the nest to feed the young. Smaller shore birds, such as sandpipers and plovers, which are precocial, lay four eggs. In these species food is not a big factor in clutch size because the young can feed themselves at birth, but four eggs may be all the adults can incubate. Most passerines lay two to six eggs per clutch, with a tendency toward larger clutches in species that breed at higher latitudes, many tropical species laying only two eggs. A number of interacting factors account for these differences: northern breeding species are subject to more variable breeding conditions and suffer higher mortality during rigorous migration or during severe winters than do their southern counterparts. These birds then must compensate for years when the entire clutch is lost, or when the fledglings do not survive the winter, by producing a larger clutch of eggs. The larger clutches are permitted by long hours of daylight, abundant insect populations, and lack of competition during these northern summers. In the tropics, a climate more predictable but with greater competition encourages smaller clutches with lower mortality rates. The large clutches observed in ducks and gallinaceous birds probably result from the precocial condition of the young, coupled with the higher mortality rates in these species caused by predation.

The cue for the female to stop laying eggs when the species-specific number has been reached differs among species. In most birds egg production is arrested by some internal signal, and, if an egg is destroyed or removed from the nest, it will not be replaced. Birds that do not replace eggs are referred to as *determinate layers. Indeterminate layers,* among them ducks, chicklike birds, some woodpeckers, and a few passerines, will also stop laying when the nest is full of the species-specific number of eggs; in these species ovulation is thought to be inhibited when the sitting female feels the "correct" number of eggs. Removing eggs from the nest of these birds will usually cause the female to lay others to take their place. The domestic chicken is valuable to us partly because it is an indeterminate egg-layer, for by continually removing an egg after it is laid, one can cause a chicken to produce another, and so on, at a rate of more than 300 eggs a year.

The size of the egg varies predictably with the size of the species. The Ostrich, *Struthio camelus,* produces the largest eggs of any living bird, and hummingbird species the smallest. This measure is mainly reversed when we compare the weight of the egg with the bird's weight. The Ostrich's egg is only 1.7 percent of its body weight, whereas a small hummingbird's is more than 10 percent. In general, large birds lay eggs that are less than 5 percent of body weight, and smaller ones run to more than 10 percent. Because most smaller birds lay more eggs per clutch than do larger ones, egg laying is more demanding for small species.

Another factor that influences egg size is condition of the young at birth. Species that hatch precocial young lay larger eggs than do altricial species of the same size. The precocial species egg is larger because it must hold more food and water to allow the fetus to develop further so that it will hatch out with feathers and be able to move and feed itself.

Not all birds lay eggs of the same shape. The familiar shape of the chicken egg, pointed at one end and blunt at the other, is the commonest, but other shapes are found. Eggs laid by pigeons and nightjars are pointed at both ends, those of many cavity-nesting species are nearly spherical. Hummingbirds and swallows lay long, elliptical eggs. In some species egg shape has clear adaptive value: Common Murres, *Uria aalge,* lay their eggs on bare rock where wind or sudden movement by the parents could roll them off if it were not for their very exaggerated pointed shape, which causes them to roll in a tight circle (Johnson, 1941). Many small shore bird species arrange their eggs with the pointed end toward the center of the nest so that the four eggs fit tightly together, apparently for even distribution of heat when they are being incubated. Cavity nesters, with no danger of their eggs rolling out of the nest, lay them in the shape that accommodates greatest mass in smallest volume, a sphere.

Egg color also varies among species. Ground-nesting birds, more subject to predation, generally lay eggs that blend in color or pattern with the background. Most of these eggs are marked with splotchy blacks or browns that disrupt their shape. Some ground nesters, as well as tree-nesting species, lay eggs of uniform tint; the American Robin, *Turdus migratorius,* lays eggs that are blue and ducks of some species lay green eggs. White is probably the original egg color of the first-evolved bird species, because reptile eggs are white. Most cavity-nesting birds whose eggs are concealed in the nest lay white eggs. Other cavity nesters such as the Black-capped Chickadee, *Parus atricapillus,* and the Eastern Bluebird, *Sialia sialis,* lay spotted and colored eggs respectively; this characteristic, and their building a cup-shaped nest in the cavity, probably indicates that these species have recently evolved into cavity nesters.

Most species of birds do not recognize their eggs clearly enough to distinguish them from those of other birds, and many will accept almost any round object introduced into the nest. This inability to discriminate has been exploited by workers trying to increase the population of the endangered Whooping Crane, *Grus americana.* As we saw, cranes usually hatch two eggs but rarely raise both to fledging; ornithologists have transferred the second Whooper egg to the nest of the closely related Sandhill Crane, *Grus canadensis,* after its own eggs have been removed. The Sandhill foster parent seems perfectly willing to incubate the egg and raise the young (Drewien and Kuyt, 1979). But the Common Murre, *Uria aalge,* is able to pick out its own eggs when mixed with other murre eggs, probably from nesting on bare rock in a colony where strong winds could blow several eggs together. Individual egg recognition probably occurs in other colonial birds, such as some tern species, which nest close together and build nests that do not hold eggs well.

Cavity-nesting and cup-nesting species do not retrieve an egg if it is moved from the nest, even if the egg is moved just beyond the rim of the nest. Instinct tells these species that almost anything in the nest is to be incubated and anything outside ignored. Most ground nesters, however, will roll an egg, whether their own or that of another species, back into the nest.

BROOD PARASITISM

That most birds are not good at distinguishing their own eggs from others' has led some species to exploit this "weakness" by laying their eggs in nests belonging to other species and letting the foster parents incubate and care for their young. Of the eighty brood-parasite species, fifty are in the cuckoo family; the other thirty include one species of duck, a number of honey guides, weaverbirds, and blackbirds. In North America, the only true nest parasites are the Brown-headed Cowbird, *Molothrus ater,* and the Bronzed Cowbird, *Molothrus aeneus.*

The relationship between any parasite and its host is extremely interesting, for the parasite's intention is to exploit its host but not kill it, and the host strives to develop defenses against the parasite's actions. If the relationship is a long-term one, or subject to intense selection pressure, the measures that the host takes to thwart the parasite are countered by adaptations in the parasite, and an evolutionary chase is set in motion. The parasite then becomes less detrimental to the host and at the same time becomes more dependent on it. Brood parasitism in birds is particularly interesting because the species that practise this reproductive method can be identified at different stages in this slow chase through time.

The Redhead duck, *Aythya americana,* seems to be in the initial stages of brood parasitism. The female deserts her young at an earlier age than other ducks, or else lays its eggs in nests of other species. Weller (1959) estimates that in Redheads only 10 percent of the females are totally nonparasitic; the other 90 percent either build a nest and incubate some eggs, depositing other eggs in another nest, or spend the entire breeding season parasitizing nests of other aquatic species. The evolution of true, or obligate parasitism in this species rests on the relative success of the eggs laid by the females in these three categories. If the parasitic females are more successful, the Redhead may join the South American Black-headed Duck, *Heteronetta atricapilla,* as the second obligate parasite in the order Anseriformes.

The Brown-headed Cowbird, *Molothrus ater,* is the common obligate parasite in North America. This species is rather nonspecific in choosing a host species, in that it has been observed to lay its eggs in the nests of more than 200 species. The major parasitic adaptations in this species are that the incubation period for its young is a day or two shorter than those of most other passerines, and that its young beg aggressively for food. Unlike that of more advanced parasitic species, the Cowbird's egg does not necessarily mimic the host's eggs. Cowbird eggs are often found in the nests of the American Robin, *Turdus migratorius,* but the Robin ejects the white egg from its nest, apparently because it is so different from its own in size, shape, and color. Cowbirds are more successful with species such as Song Sparrow, *Melospiza melodia,* Yellow Warbler, *Dendroica petechia,* and Red-eyed Vireo, *Vireo olivaceus,* because these species cannot readily distinguish their eggs from the Cowbird's. If these species do react to having their nests disturbed by the Cowbird, they will not eject the egg, but rather abandon the nest entirely. The Yellow Warbler will often build a new nest on top of the abandoned one, only to have it parasitized again by the same Cowbird.

Although the lack of a specific host species, combined with lack of egg mimicry, seems to be a product of recent evolution, many cuckoo species ply their craft with more skill. The European Cuckoo, *Cuculus canorus,* is more selective in choosing a host, and its eggs mimic those of its host very closely. Although this species has been known to parasitize more than 125 species, local

A fledgling European Cuckoo continues to be fed by its foster parent (here a Redstart) even when the former is nearly twice the size of the adult.

populations concentrate on only a few host species. In Finland the Cuckoo lays speckled blue eggs closely resembling those of its major host, the Redstart, *Phoenicurus phoenicurus,* but in central Europe it lays greenish eggs like those of the Great Reed Warbler, *Acrocephalus arundinaceus.* In southwest Africa, the Black Cuckoo, *Cuculus clamosus,* has only one known host, the Crimson-breasted Shrike, *Laniarius atrococcineus,* whose egg it matches almost exactly in size, color, and pattern (Jensen and Clining, 1974). As with the Cowbird, the cuckoo egg develops more quickly than its host's, generally hatching first, but the young of most cuckoo species ensure that they will be the sole object of their foster parents' attention by pushing other eggs and chicks out of the nest. Some species of parasitic honey guides achieve the same result by biting its nestmates to death with uniquely designed hooked mandibles.

Apparently as a measure against brood parasitism, some waxbill species will not only eject eggs that do not match their own, but have evolved to feed only young that strongly resemble their own. This adaptation is matched by that of species of parasitic weaverbirds, the widowbirds and whydahs, whose eggs and young are very similar to those of the hosts. This mimicry presents the foster parents with alien young having almost identical mouth markings and begging calls. But, unlike the cuckoo's nestlings, these species do not eject their nestmates, for it is to their advantage to keep their hosts alive and at high population levels.

A unique but not totally unexpected result of the parasite-host relationship is the beneficial effect the Giant Cowbird, *Scaphidura oryzivora,* has on the breeding success of Wagner's Oropendola, *Zarhynchus wagleri,* and the Yellow-rumped Cacique, *Cacicus cela,* in Central America. In some breeding areas these two species of blackbirds lose 90 percent of their nestlings because of botfly infestations. But if the nest contains an egg of the Giant Cowbird, the mortality rate is much lower because the Cowbird nestlings pick off and eat the botfly eggs and larvae from their foster brothers and sisters, reducing the effects of the parasite (Smith, 1968). It is interesting to speculate on the possible future adaptation of the Cowbirds' hosts if these conditions continue, for the host species might actually advertise its whereabouts to the parasite, even competing for the right to have a parasitic egg in the nest.

NEST DEFENSE

How well birds defend their nests varies with the species and with the stage in the breeding season: species defend most vigorously from just before the eggs hatch until the young are fledged. Early in the breeding season many species will abandon their nests when a predator approaches, saving themselves to re-nest and lay another clutch of eggs. As the season progresses, however, they are increasingly reluctant to leave the nest, and in many species are very aggressive in its defense.

Large, powerful species like the Great Horned Owl, *Bubo virginianus,* and the Northern Goshawk, *Accipiter gentilis,* will attack any threat to the nest, even species many times larger than themselves. Smaller species will do the same, including the Common Tern, *Sterna hirundo,* and the Red-winged Blackbird, *Agelaius phoeniceus.* Species that are more timid, or those which are no physical match for the predator, resort to trickery to protect their offspring. The Killdeer, *Charadrius vociferus,* comes off its nest when a predator approaches, but instead of fleeing makes itself conspicuous, produces loud sounds, and feigns injury. It will flop on the ground with one or both wings spread, drawing the predator's attention. Just as the predator closes in on the adult, the Killdeer flies away. This broken-wing display is common among many ground-nesting species. The Purple Sandpiper, *Calidris maritima,* achieves the same result with a different display, the rodent run. These birds leave the nest quietly when they see a predator, and at some distance from the nest will begin to run rapidly away in a zigzag pattern, holding their head down with wings drooped, giving the impression of back legs, all the while producing mouselike squeaks (Duffy et al, 1950). A number of tree-nesting species distract the predator from the nest by feigning illness and acting disoriented. The Common Eider, *Somateria mollissima,* and the Northern Shoveler, *Anas clypeata,* thwart the predator by using a very different tactic. They excrete the contents of the cloaca on the eggs before leaving the nest. Though it has been shown that a predator such as a fox will normally eat eggs covered with excreta, the droppings during the breeding season render the eggs unpalatable to most predators (Swennen, 1968).

INCUBATION

For development to take place inside, the egg must be kept at a relatively high and constant temperature. All birds, except megapodes, warm their eggs by incubating them. The amount of heat transferred is significantly increased by the parent's developing a brood patch before completion of egg laying. The *brood patch* is formed by loss of down feathers, exposing the skin on the bird's underside. The hormones that cause this loss of feathers also thicken the skin and increase blood flow to this area (Bailey, 1952).

Depending on the species, either one or both sexes develop a brood patch. In polygynous species, usually the female alone incubates the eggs, and the male of these species does not form a brood patch. An exception is in tinamous, where the polygamous male alone incubates the clutch of eggs laid in a common nest by his harem of females. In many monogamous species, such as sparrows, crows, and jays, as well as some ducks, hawks, and owls, only the female develops a brood patch. Although the male of these species does sit on the eggs at times, this behavior does little more than cover the eggs, for the feather's superior insulation prevents much heat transfer. In other monogamous species, both sexes develop a brood patch and incubate the eggs. In polyandrous species, the male alone develops a brood patch.

Incubation is remarkably efficient at keeping the eggs at a constant temperature despite greatly varying environmental conditions. The Emperor Penguin, *Aptenodytes forsteri,* which incubates in the depths of the antarctic winter, maintains its egg as much as 90°C above the ambient temperature, and the eggs vary less than 7°C. With the Herring Gull, *Larus argentatus,* the eggs are kept at a steady 37°C, and most species maintain them at between 30 and 39°C. These constant temperatures are necessary because the cellular processes taking place in the egg occur most efficiently under such unvarying conditions. Despite this control, eggs are tolerant of temperature changes, especially at low temperatures; in fact some eggs can withstand a freeze and still hatch. Abnormally high temperatures are more detrimental: species that nest in places exposed to the sun's direct rays shade their eggs during the hottest part of the day, and some species even douse them with water. Because heat from the brood patch is not distributed evenly to the entire egg or clutch, birds periodically turn and rearrange the eggs in the nest.

Megapodes, as we saw, are exceptional in that they do not incubate their eggs; rather, they allow natural heat from the earth to speed their development. This seemingly carefree method of incubation is complicated by the need to keep the eggs at a constant temperature. To do so, the male of these species carefully monitors temperature in the mound of sandy soil above the eggs. When the temperature drops, the male builds the mound higher to increase the insulation between the cool air and the eggs, and as the ambient temperature rises the male opens up the nest to allow cooling. These birds detect temperature changes by sampling the soil with the beak; the behavior has earned them the name thermometer birds. In interesting observations on the Mallee Fowl, *Leipoa ocellata,* Frith (1956) placed a heating coil in the mound nest and discovered that the male's temperature-regulating behavior depended only on the temperature in the mound, and not air temperature, for on cool days males in the study would open up the experimentally heated mound, while other males piled them higher.

The incubation period for eggs ranges from ten to twelve days among some woodpeckers and cowbirds to eighty-one days for the Royal Albatross, *Diomedea epomophora.* Small passerine species incubate for about two weeks, larger ones, such as crows, three weeks. Larger hawks and vultures incubate their eggs for up to seven weeks. Large eggs usually require longer incubation than smaller ones; eggs of hole-nesting species develop more slowly than those of species that nest out in the open; and the eggs of precocial species take longer than those of equal-sized altricial ones. During the incubation period, cells on the upper surface of the yolk begin to divide rapidly, and it is here that the embryo forms, while the lower portion of the yolk provides food for the embryo. The albumen forms membranes that supply the fetus with some nutrients and water, and other membranes store the waste products of metabolism. As this amorphous mass consolidates into a chick, the egg's contents decrease in volume, which expands the air space at the blunt end of the egg. From this space the chick will take its first breath before beginning its struggle to break free of the shell.

YOUNG

The chick's hatching out of the shell is preceded by a number of developments. The young of almost all species form an *egg tooth* and *hatching muscle* sometime before emergence. The egg tooth is a hard growth at the tip of the bill, and the hatch muscle on the back of the neck controls movements of the head. For a chick to hatch it must first reorient itself lengthwise in the egg; in doing so the chick breaks through the membrane that separates it from the air space at the

A hatching, here an American Golden Plover

blunt end of the shell. The chick now begins to breathe, although most of its oxygen supply still comes from blood vessels in the egg itself. The new alignment also brings the egg tooth into contact with the inside of the shell, and contractions of the hatching muscle, along with a push of the feet, put pressure on the inside of the shell, which eventually cracks, or *pips,* at this place. Once this start is made the chick rotates slightly inside the shell and again the egg tooth pips the shell. Repeating this motion makes circular cracks at the blunt end of the shell and from here the chick will emerge when the shell is sufficiently weakened. With the head out, moving the body and feet will free the chick from its calcified womb.

The time between the chick's pipping and its emergence is only thirty minutes in the Northern Bobwhite, *Colinus virginianus,* (Johnson, 1969), but up to a day in most passerines and ducks and two or more days in albatrosses and petrels. The sounds and movements that come from the struggling chick inside the egg cause excited behavior in the parents, but they do not help the chick in hatching.

The fate of the young after hatching differs according to whether the species is precocial or altricial, for the well-developed young of the precocial birds require much less care than the naked, helpless offspring of altricial birds. To trace the development of avian young from hatching to independence, we look first at precocial species, then at altricial.

Unique in each phase of their nesting cycle, the young of the megapodes dig their way up through the sandy soil that has kept them warm. Upon reaching the surface, they run for cover and begin their life alone. Over the seven-week incubation period these birds have developed into completely independent

Hansen 89

Precocial young (left, a Great Black-backed Gull) are born feathered and able to run, while altricial young (right, an American White Pelican) are born naked and helpless.

creatures. They are able to control their body temperature, feed themselves, and even fly soon after they hatch.

Ducks, geese, and small shore birds are still physically tied to their parents, however, because they hatch with limited ability to control their body temperature. Although they are covered with an insulating layer of downy feathers, they still require the life-sustaining warmth that was critical for them in the egg. These young, then, follow their parents or parent from the nest soon after their downy feathers dry. They are able to feed themselves, choosing their food by trial and error, and acquiring the appropriate responses to the environment by imprinting, but when they begin to cool down, they run back to their parent to be brooded.

In chickenlike birds, parents more actively direct the young to food; the female in these species will lead her brood to food and even pick it up and drop it while the young look on.

Young grebes and loons follow their parents into the water soon after hatching much as ducks and geese do; but, because their food, mainly fish, requires more skill to catch, the young of these birds wait at the surface for the parents to bring them a meal. After a few days the young will begin to dive on their own. These species, along with other waterfowl, allow the young to ride on their backs to relieve them of the constant heat drain to the water. Young gulls, terns, and auks are also precocial, but are unable, until they gain the power of flight, to feed themselves. These young, although capable of moving, remain close to the nest, waiting for their parents to bring food.

In most precocial species the bond between parents and young begins to wane when the young develop *homeothermy,* or the power of flight. Flight develops in most terrestrial precocial species at between one and five weeks, depending on the species, though some quail species, which are poor runners, fly a week after hatching, and other gallinaceous birds fly by the time they are four weeks old. Shore birds can fly between two and five weeks after hatching, and acquiring flight takes aquatic species from four to twelve weeks. Although in most precocial species flight marks the end of the offspring's physical dependence on the parents, the young of others remain dependent on their parents for food, and still others remain socially dependent much longer. The Royal Tern, *Sterna maxima,* continues to feed its lone chick well into the winter when they are thousands of kilometers from the breeding grounds (Ashmole and Humberto, 1968), and some species of geese remain together as a family unit through the winter and into the next spring.

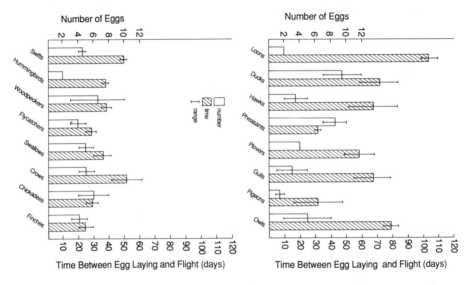

The average number of eggs and the time between egg laying and flight are shown for a number of families of birds. (Pettingill, 1970 Appendix H)

Paradoxically, the reproductive strategy of altricial species, which consists of hatching their young at an underdeveloped stage, is more advanced evolutionarily. The most recently evolved order of birds, the passerines, are all altricial, as are many other families. Unlike precocial species, they do not show vestiges of their reptilian ancestors, whose young hatch as miniatures of the adults. Numerical comparison of altricial to precocial species shows that altricial adaptation is more successful. For altricial species the basic strategy is parental intervention in development of the young by increasing their food supply as soon as the embryo can exist apart from the shell. This increased food supply speeds the offspring's development toward independence. Comparing altricial and precocial species of about the same size by measuring the time between egg laying and development of flight in the chicks shows that crows fly at about eight weeks, terns at ten, thrushes at only five, and phalaropes at nine.

The evolution of immobile young was probably paralleled by adaptation of the nest site to contain the chicks and prevent them from falling out during their longer stay there. And because as long as they are in the nest chicks remain as vulnerable as the eggs, the parents must continue to conceal their presence from predators. To do so, most species remove any foreign matter from the nest; this cleanup includes egg shells, which are carried away, eaten, or fed to the nestlings, depending on the species. In most species the waste produced by the young is also removed. This chore is efficient because the nestlings' excreta are surrounded by a membrane, forming the mass into tidy little fecal sacs, which are carried away in the parent's beak, or in some species, eaten. This behavior is not observed in predatory birds, or in species that nest in places inaccessible to predators; hence these nests become clearly marked by white droppings of the young as the breeding season progresses. So attentive are some parents to cleanliness in the nest that they have been observed trying to remove the silver bands placed on the tarsus of the young by banders, and so blind is their instinct that they have been known to break the chick's leg in the attempt, and even to drag the chick away to rid the nest of the band (Berger, 1961).

Although altricial young are born underdeveloped, they are well designed to grow quickly, for their digestive system is efficient at processing food. Shortly after hatching, these neophytes begin to practice their only coordinated movements: raising their heads, opening their mouths, passing food through the digestive system, and eliminating waste. The mouths of most altricial chicks are brightly colored, the edge of the beak being yellow or white, and the interior mouth lining a contrasting bright color or pattern. These bright markings, which are not found in precocial young, stimulate the parents to feed their offspring; such markings also provide a target for the food. Adult hawks do not place food in the mouth of their young, but tear the food into small pieces and present it in front of the nestling's beak. Adult pigeons, pelicans, and others open their mouths wide, allowing the young to plunge the head inside and take food from the contents of the crop. After a day or two in the nest, the young further stimulate the parents to feed by incorporating calls in their begging behavior. Begging behavior is released in the young of most species by mechanical stimulation of the nest, which usually indicates that an adult has landed; simply tapping on the edge of nest causes the young to pop their heads up and gape for food. In the Bank Swallow, *Riparia riparia,* and other species, the returning parent gives a feeding call that arouses the young and releases begging behavior. The food the parents feed to their young is high in protein, most passerines feeding their young invertebrate creatures even if the adults are primarily seed eaters. Distribution of food to the young is equalized by change in a chick's behavior once it has eaten its fill, for satiated chicks no longer beg, which allows the parents to concentrate on the other hungry nestlings; feeding stops completely only when all the young are quiet. In this way the parents' feeding behavior is controlled by the offspring, in that the parents will continue to bring food in response to visual and auditory signals from the young. As the young grow and demand more food, the parents work harder to provide it. For small species that feed their young insects, the number of feeding visits made by the parents commonly rises to more than 300 a day before the young fledge.

The sequence of events in the early life of a Song Sparrow, *Melospiza melodia*, from hatching to independence, is described by Nice (1943) and here serves as an example of early life for most passerines. During the first four days of life outside the egg the young remain immobile in the nest, for they are unable to control their body temperature and need to be brooded. They initially beg for food simply by gaping, but by day two they begin to signal that they are hungry with calls as well. By day four, feathers start to develop. On days five and six feathers grow rapidly, as do the physiological systems: eyes open, control of body temperature begins, and the nestlings can now stand in the nest. Days seven through nine bring rapid increase in body weight, and by the end of this period the chicks have increased their weight by ten times. The nestlings are now flapping their wings in the nest, and by day ten they are changing from nestlings to fledglings. Although these fledglings can fly, they remain near the nest and are inactive until their parents come into view, whereupon they beg noisily for food. During the next ten days they gradually reach independence, and increasingly show the motor patterns of their species' feeding behaviors, but they will still beg for food and even chase their parents for it. By day seventeen they can feed and care for themselves.

The young of altricial cavity-nesting species generally remain in the nest longer than those of altricial open-nesting birds. In these species, the nest affords greater protection from predators, allowing the nestlings to spend the beginning of the Song Sparrow's fledgling period in the nest, and not out on a limb. Larger species follow the same pattern of development but each stage takes longer. Some larger birds of prey spend up to ten weeks in the nest, and at the end of this period seem very reluctant to leave. Adult Bald Eagles, *Haliaeetus leucocephalus,* begin to reduce the amount of food they bring to the grown nestlings and by ten weeks entice their young to leave by bringing food to a perch close to the nest.

The transition between leaving the nest and full independence, the fledgling period, is usually marked by the young bird's growing ability to find and capture food on its own. During this time the parents supplement the brood's diet as they develop the necessary skills. In many species this learning is facilitated by play, with the fledglings making mock attacks on inanimate objects. Peregrine Falcons, *Falco peregrinus,* hone skill in their young by dropping prey in midair, giving one of the fledglings a chance to make the kill.

With the young independent and off to face a very uncertain future, adults in many species now concentrate on increasing their body fat, molting, and otherwise preparing for winter. Other species, however, especially altricial ones, are already preparing for another round of nesting before the first brood reaches independence. This preparation generally includes an abbreviated second courtship and building a new nest that will hold a new clutch of eggs. The number of broods a pair of birds will attempt during the breeding season depends on the species and the latitude; more northerly breeding birds tend to raise only one brood per season, and more southerly birds generally raise more than one. In the United States the American Robin, *Turdus migratorius,* usually nests twice, the Song Sparrow, *Melospiza melodia,* three to four times, and the Mourning Dove, *Zenaida macroura,* four to five. The Orchard Oriole, *Icterus spurius,* which breeds at the same latitude as the species above, raises only one brood and migrates south late in July or early in August.

Even in the most persistent breeders, the reproductive fires eventually burn out as the days shorten with fall approaching. Accompanying these internal changes are significant changes in behavior beginning a new set of responses to a changing environment: birds that defended their territories so aggressively now allow members of their own kind to approach, and they no longer respond to calls and displays by their mates and offspring. They are now content to obey that other life force, survival, and in doing so they lose their special place and individual identity in the world, and begin to fall into ranks with others of their species to wait out the winter, temporarily suppressing the drive to reproduce.

Suggested Reading

For more information about the avian egg, see Sturkie's *Avian Physiology.* Each North American species Bent describes in *Life Histories of North American Birds* has information about nests and nesting behavior, as does *The Audubon Society Encyclopedia of North American Birds,* by Terres. More detailed information about nesting of birds around you can be found in books about birds in your state. *Birds of New York State,* by Bull, for example, gives data on location of nests, clutch size, hatching, and fledging dates, along with distribution of species in the state.

Projects

The breeding season offers many opportunities to increase your understanding of avian biology. The first task is to locate a nest, which for some species such as the Barn Swallow is rather easy; most species' nests are harder to find. Watch these birds early in the breeding season when they are carrying nesting material: they will bring you closer to the nest site. For orioles, setting out nest material such as yarn or cotton string will attract the nest builders and facilitate locating the nest. For cavity-nesting birds, build a nesting box to attract pairs of these species; you can get specifications by writing to the Massachusetts Audubon Society or your state's society. Once you locate the nest, record in your notebook such information as which sex does the building, the height of the nest, its location, and how long it took to complete.

During incubation, see which sex spends most time on the nest. Record frequency of feeding by the mate of the incubating bird on the nest and changes in pattern of incubation in different weather conditions.

A sure sign that the eggs have hatched is the parents' beginning to bring food to the nest. If you are starting late, this is a time when you can find the nest by following the bird carrying food in its beak. Monitor the number of trips the parents make during this phase of nesting while continuing to record their incubation behavior. Record the time between hatching and fledging and try to observe and record behavior of the parents and young birds after fledging until they reach independence, and be on the lookout for a second brood. Throughout these observations be careful not to disturb the nesting pair, for their business is more important than yours; all these observations can be done from a distance through binoculars. After the nesting season is over you can collect the nest to examine it in detail.

To become active in the breeding biology of birds you can get involved with the numerous research projects that are trying to map the breeding distribution of birds in the United States and Canada. Here are names and addresses for some of these projects.

Breeding Bird Atlas
North American Ornithological Atlas Committee
Chandler S. Robbins
Migratory Bird and Habitat Research Laboratory
U.S. Fish and Wildlife Service
Laurel, MD 20708

Breeding Bird Census
American Birds
National Audubon Society
950 Third Avenue
New York, NY 10022

The Colonial Bird Register
Cornell Laboratory of Ornithology
159 Sapsucker Woods Road
Ithaca, NY 14853

Being involved with this type of project gives the amateur a chance to share information with the scientific community, which is a tradition in ornithology.

- 10 -

Geography and Ecology of Birds

IN WINTER 1974, ON THE EXTENSIVE TIDAL FLATS that show where the Merrimack River mixes with the Atlantic Ocean, an unusual sighting was made. Among the thousands of Bonaparte's Gulls, *Larus philadelphia*, which regularly winter in this estuary was a Ross' Gull, *Rhodostethia rosea*, whose pigeonlike flight, wedgeshaped tail, and pink cast separated it from the others. The news of this bird spread quickly through the eastern Massachusetts bird world, and with it bird enthusiasts dropped everything and came to Newburyport. They had reason to be excited, for the Ross' Gull is rarely seen outside the Arctic Circle, and its stay here was a unique opportunity to see and list this species (Miliotis and Buckley, 1975). Sighting this pink piece of arctic life created ripples beyond the bird world—news of it spread to the general public as well. Regional and then national media picked up the story, and the Ross' Gull was featured on major television news programs.

As odd as it may sound, such "unusual" sightings happen all the time. A Yellow-nosed Albatross, *Diomedea chlororhynchos*, was sighted off Jones Beach, New York, on May 29, 1960, fully one hemisphere from home; for another, a Mottled Petrel, *Pterodroma inexpectata*, was found alive in a farmer's field in upstate New York in April, 1880, more than 20,000 kilometers from its breeding grounds in New Zealand (Bull, 1961).

Rare birds such as these have been sighted in every region of the country, and these sightings illustrate two aspects of the worldwide distribution of birds. The first is that birds are uniquely equipped by their power of flight to travel to almost every part of earth; but the second is that because these sightings are accidental, birds generally restrict their movement to one region.

RANGE

The geographic area in which a species is found is its *range*. Migratory species have two ranges, a summer breeding range and a winter nonbreeding one. Considering the long stretch of evolution and birds' ability to fly, surprisingly few species are found on every continent. These species with worldwide, or cosmopolitan, distribution are the Cattle Egret, *Bubulcus ibis,* the Barn Owl, *Tyto alba,* the Osprey, *Pandion haliaetus,* the Common Moorhen, *Gallinula chloropus,* and the Least Tern, *Sterna antillarum.* Exceptional too are cosmopolitan families of birds, for fewer than one third of the families of birds are found throughout the world. Most species and most families are geographically confined, some exceedingly so. The Kirtland's Warbler, *Dendroica kirtlandii,* breeds only in a 240-square-kilometer area in central Michigan and winters only in the Bahamas.

The geographic range of a species is not fixed but rather is in continual flux, and some species show rapid changes in their range over short periods. The Great Black-backed Gull, *Larus marinus,* has significantly expanded its range during this period. Formerly a North Atlantic species, this gull now commonly occurs as far south as Virginia. In the same period, the Northern Cardinal, *Cardinalis cardinalis,* has extended its range northward through temperate North America. We can infer alterations in range that have occurred in the past from

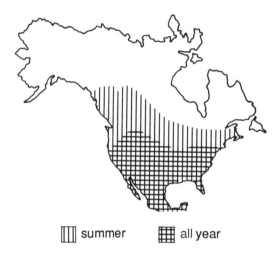

||||| summer   ⊞ all year

Red-winged Blackbirds are found in virtually all of North America.

the isolated remnants of populations left behind, far from the bulk of their species' present range. The Grey-cheeked Thrush, *Catharus minimus,* must have had a more extensive breeding range in North America some time ago when the climate was colder, for it is now restricted to Alaska and Canada, but isolated populations of this species still breed on the small, cold islandlike mountaintops in the northeastern United States.

Probably the most spectacular and swiftest expansion of range in the last fifty years is that of the Cattle Egret, *Bubulcus ibis*. Before the 1930s, this species was confined to Eurasia and Africa, but sometime during the 1930s a flock apparently flew across the Atlantic Ocean and appeared in northern South America. Descendants of these colonizers have spread through the New World, reaching Florida in the 1940s, California in the 1960s, and as far north as Newfoundland in the 1980s.

Underlying these changes in species' range is the stabler distribution of the world's birds. Studying the range not only of species but also of families and orders of birds in combination with geographic and climatic changes helps us understand how a group of birds originated and also track the changes that have occurred in these groups over these long periods.

ZOOLOGICAL REGIONS OF THE WORLD

The great convection currents flowing in molten rock in the bowels of the earth have continually rearranged our planet's surface. The ancient land mass called Pangaea formed 200 million years ago, then fragmented into the separate continents, which continue their slow drift. As continents moved, great mountain ranges have been vaulted skyward and others have eroded away; some basins have filled with water and others have been drained. During this time the energy on which all life depends has not been constant; changes in the rate of the sun's nuclear fires have cooled and warmed earth. These changes in the energy budget have had their effects on the life forms that inhabit earth, accelerating the formation of species here, causing mass extinctions there, and allowing species to expand their range at other times, only to cut these colonizing organisms off from their ancestral homelands. Although many species have been mixed and moved, and the paths they have taken have been obliterated, remnants revealing the origin, evolution, and travels of many species are still evident today. These living impressions of the great forces that govern our planet give geographic regions a distinct organic flavor. When naturalists began to survey earth's creatures, they quickly recognized this distinctiveness, and they divided the world, not by its land or water masses, but by its inhabitants' unique character. Thus we refer to zoological regions of the world, six of which have been recognized since the early 1900s: the Neotropical, the Australian, the Ethiopian, the Oriental, the Palearctic, and the Nearctic.

Of the six, the most distinctive for its avifauna is the Neotropical region, which includes all of South America, tropical Central America, and the Caribbean islands. The combination of a warm, wet climate, extreme diversity in land forms, and periods of geographic isolation have made the Neotropical the world's most prolific avian region. Although now attached to North America, the Central American land bridge has twice been covered with water in recent geological history, restricting movement by species in and out of this region. This isolation, combined with ideal conditions for species formation, has led the Neotropical to contain nearly one third of earth's species and more

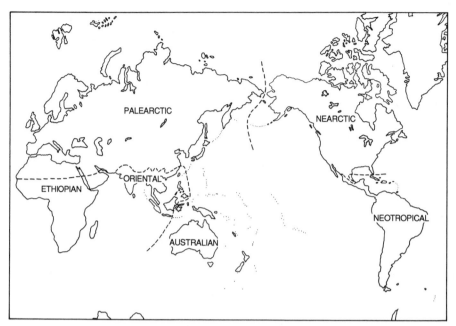

Zoological regions of the world

than one half of the world's families of birds. Because most of its species are sedentary and also geographically isolated, thirty-one of these families are found only here, including rheas, trumpeters, todies, toucans, manakins, and plant-cutters. When geological rebuilding of the Central American land bridge was completed, Neotropical families such as hummingbirds and flycatchers moved north into the temperate Nearctic, but by far the majority of the species shared between the Neotropical and Nearctic are the result of the southerly expansion in range by passerines (but relatively few songbirds), waterfowl, hawks, owls, and woodpeckers to the Neotropical region.

The Australian region, which includes Australia, New Guinea, and New Zealand, has endured geographic isolation longer than the Neotropical, and is second only to that region in number of endemic families, with thirteen. And although this region has a warm climate and parts that are well watered, most of it is arid and so has not encouraged species formation as the Neotropical region has. The Australian region has a few more than 900 species, classified in sixty-four families that include the Emu, *Dromaius novaehollandiae*, cassowaries, kiwis, lyrebirds, birds of paradise, and bowerbirds. Like the Neotropical, this region is not dominated by songbirds as are the other regions.

Unlike the two previously mentioned zoological regions, the Ethiopian is isolated not by water but by sand. The vast Saharan and Arabian deserts restrict and insulate southern Africa and Arabia from the Palearctic avian tribes. The warm climate and varied land forms make the Ethiopian second only to the Neotropical in species abundance, with more than 1,500 kinds of birds. The six endemic families, fewer than in the much smaller Australian, indicate that the

184

desert is a less effective barrier than water to birds' travels. The Ethiopian shares with the Palearctic many species that migrate to this region in the nonbreeding season, but this region has a surprisingly high number of tropical families in common with the Oriental region. Passerines are common here, with many species of weaverbirds and larks; other common birds are hawks, honeyguides, thrushes, finches, and doves; the Ostrich, *Struthio camelus,* Secretary Bird, *Sagittarius serpentarius,* and mouse birds, among others, are peculiar to this region.

The Oriental region includes India, southern China, continental southeast Asia, and the affiliated islands of Java, Borneo, and the Philippines. The line of demarcation between Oriental and Palearctic is the northern extent of the tropical and subtropical climate, clearly defined by the east–west orientation of the Himalayan Mountains, but less clear-cut in China. In the south, the straits that separate the Celebes and Moluccas islands mark the end of the Oriental and the beginning of the Australian. These boundaries do not create the isolation characteristics of the other three zoological regions, resulting in more of a mixture in the north, the thrushes, accentors, dippers, and tits being shared with the Palearctic, and in the south some species of megapodes are found in the Oriental. This more extensive area of overlap between adjacent regions leaves the Oriental with only one endemic family, the fairy bluebirds. Climatically this region is warm, with extensive tropical forests and savanna land. Among the nearly 970 species found here are an abundance of pheasant, pigeon, crow, barbet, sunbird, and finch species. As with the Neotropical and Ethiopian, the Oriental region is the winter home for many migratory birds.

The Palearctic comprises the vast land area of northern Africa, Europe, and all Asia but that south of the Himalayas. It is diverse in topology and is both temperate and arctic in climate. Although more than 1,000 species are found in this region, for its size it is poorly developed in number of species. This area is dominated by passerine species, many of which are forced to migrate south to the Ethiopian or Oriental with winter coming. Another large portion of the species in the Palearctic are water birds, which are also highly migratory. Typical species in this region are owls, hawks, woodpeckers, crows, ducks, and small shore birds; the only endemic family in the Palearctic is Pruellidae, the hedge sparrows.

North America, excluding tropical Central America and the Caribbean islands, is considered the Nearctic region. Similar to the Palearctic in climate, the Nearctic is also rich in migratory passerines and water birds. The region has 750 species and no endemic families, making it the poorest in species number and diversity. The forty-eight families the Nearctic shares with its larger neighbor are here because of the land bridge that formed between Siberia and Alaska at several intervals in geologic time. In fact, the similarities between the two regions are so strong that writers sometimes lump both into the inclusive Holarctic region. When so considered, these temperate regions harbor five endemic families: loons, grouse, auks, waxwings, and hedge sparrows. The Nearctic, however, does have a distinct element not found in the Palearctic: the New World vultures and flycatchers, vireos, wood warblers, and mockingbirds.

The last major avian element we consider are the birds that inhabit the world's oceans. Although these species are found in the zoological regions during the breeding season, for them the land provides only a nesting site, for their lives are tied to the sea. About 260 species of birds are truly marine, and of these 150 are pelagic. Marine species such as gulls, terns, cormorants, frigatebirds, and pelicans are composed mainly of coastwise birds that rarely occur beyond sight of land, whereas penguins, tubenoses, boobies, gannets, and auks inhabit the open ocean. Although these species make up only 3 percent of the world's birds, they range over 70 percent of the earth's surface, but, as with land birds, they are generally restricted to specific regions either by contrary winds that do not facilitate their movement, or by wide bands of foodless water. Serventy (1960) recognizes three major marine regions: the Northern, the Tropical, and the Southern.

The Northern marine region extends from the arctic southward to about north latitude 35° in the Atlantic and Pacific oceans. The distinguishing avifauna in this region are the family Alcidae, which includes the twenty-two species of puffins, auks, and murrelets. Also found here, but not restricted to this region, are kittiwakes, petrels, shearwaters, gannets, and, in the Pacific, three species of albatross. The Tropical marine region includes the warm ocean waters that extend 35° northward and southward from the equator. Compared with the world's colder marine regions the Tropical marine is low in its production of open ocean plankton, and as a result many birds that inhabit these waters depend for food on schools of fish that occur close to land. Typical species in this area are tropicbirds, boobies, terns, and frigatebirds. The Southern marine region includes the colder waters in the Southern Hemisphere southward to Antarctica. This vast area of open ocean is highly productive and has the greatest diversity of marine birds: many species of shearwaters and petrels, nine of the twelve albatross species, sixteen of the seventeen penguins, along with gannets, terns, gulls, and cormorants.

These long lists of birds that inhabit regions of the world may seem of limited usefulness, except that such data provide much insight into the origin and evolution of species, families, and orders of birds. From the weight of numbers we may assume that the albatrosses and shearwaters undoubtedly originated and diversified in the Southern marine region. In the Northern marine region, only six of the twenty-two alcid species are found in the North Atlantic, suggesting that the family originated in the North Pacific. The distribution of land species is also telling, the Horned Lark, *Eremophila alpestris,* being the only lark species found in the Nearctic though seventy-five types of lark are found in the Old World. With wrens the numbers are reversed, and only the Winter Wren, *Troglodytes troglodytes,* ranges into the Old World; the other sixty-three are all confined to the Nearctic and Neotropical regions (Welty,1975).

These lists do not tell us, though, why only one wren or lark has been able to extend its range, leaving the others behind. Obviously, proximity of the regions does influence distribution of birds, as do prevailing winds; but, to better understand why some families and species have spread far and wide and others have remained close to their place of origin, we must turn to ideas generated by the science of ecology.

AVIAN ECOLOGY: HABITAT AND NICHE

Ecology is the study of interactions between organisms and their environment. For any species these interactions take place not over the entire extent of its range but only where the organism is generally found, its habitat. Red-winged Blackbirds, *Agelaius phoeniceus,* range over almost all of North America, but this species is usually limited to open habitats with standing water, like a cattail marsh. Habitats are of many types. In the Nearctic, arctic, tundra, alpine meadows, coniferous forests, deciduous forests, grasslands, deserts, and aquatic regions are all major habitats. Each habitat has characteristic groups of birds, some of which are adapted to live only there, though others thrive in a variety of habitats. Simply walking from a forest to an open field in spring illustrates how the habitat affects species distribution. The forest is the home of the Wood Thrush, *Hylocichla mustelina,* and Ovenbird, *Serurus aurocapillus,* but at the edge of the open field these species are left behind and replaced by the Bobolink, *Dolichonyx oryzivorus,* and the Eastern Meadowlark, *Sturnella magna.* These four species share the same range, but the thrush and the warbler are mid-woods birds and the Bobolink and the Meadowlark are birds of open country.

Species that live in the same habitat, however, do not simply share its resources; rather, they divide them up. Different forest-dwelling species interact differently with their habitat, as do species that live in other habitats; they do not share the same food, song perches, or nest sites. Each species then is considered as occupying its own special place in the environment, and this space is called a niche. A niche has been variously described: a species' way of life, or its role in the environment, but the idea is really much subtler, for a niche represents the physical and biological limits of a species. From one point of view, the goal in natural selection is to make the world irrelevant to a species. Outside the species' limits, the world is relevant, and generally intolerable; inside these limits the world is acceptable: this is the species' niche. For any species, the niche must be warm enough, but not too warm, must have enough rainfall of the correct acidity, must have sufficient mineral content in the soil, must have acceptable hours of day length, and must contain enough roosting and nesting sites, as well as song perches and display areas; obviously it must have enough food of the correct type, nesting material, predators from which the species can escape (most of the time), little infectious disease, and lack of competitors for the resources. Only if these requirements are met will the species occupy the niche. For many species, the absence of only one of these factors may make the difference between thriving in or not inhabiting an otherwise suitable area. The Northern Parula Warbler, *Parula americana,* no longer breeds in a habitat that was once suitable in eastern North America, apparently because *Usnea,* a hanging moss that these birds used as nesting material, disappeared, and the species lost an essential aspect of its niche (Bull, 1961).

The concept of niche is clearly shown by feeding habits of five closely related species of New World warblers that breed in coniferous forests. Here the Bay-breasted Warbler, *Dendroica castanea,* and the Blackburnian Warbler, *Dendroica fusca,* spend more than half their time feeding in the upper portion of the tree, the latter species catching insects on the outer branches and in the air and the Bay-breasted feeding closer to the trunk. Both the Cape May Warbler, *Dendroica tigrina,* and the Black-throated Green Warbler, *Dendroica virens,* occupy the middle story in the forests, the Cape May feeding more often on the insects attracted to the sappy bark on the trunk and the Black-throated Green picking insects from the foliage. The Yellow-rumped Warbler, *Dendroica coronata,* spends most of its time in the forest understory, feeding to a height of about three meters. This vertical division of the habitat allows these similar species to live in the same habitat and not directly compete for its resources (MacArthur and MacArthur, 1961).

In other species, however, competition helps define the niche and range of a species. The distribution of the Winter Wren, *Troglodytes troglodytes,* in the Old World and the New illustrates this effect. In North America the Winter Wren is the most northerly breeding wren in its family, being confined to cold, moist forests. In the Palearctic, however, it is found in many habitats that range far south of its Nearctic distribution. The reason for this difference is probably competition with other wrens. The New World has sixty-two other wren species, some of which must compete for the same resources as the Winter Wren; these species have, in effect, forced this species north; if these competitors are not present, as in the Old World, this wren can find its niche in varied habitats. Another example of how competition influences the distribution of birds may be inferred from the range of the four chickadee species in North America. These species probably have overlapping niche requirements and are therefore competitors. Their mutually exclusive ranges on the continent probably result from competition rather than species preference for a habitat. The Black-capped Chickadee, *Parus atricapillus,* has forced the Boreal Chickadee, *Parus hudsonicus,* north, the Carolina Chickadee, *Parus carolinensis,* south, and the Mountain Chickadee, *Parus gambeli,* to the higher elevations in the west. We must remember, though, that once a species is in a different habitat, natural selection molds it to fit the environment, and it then carves out a new niche. Over long periods two competing species may evolve sufficiently different niches that they can coexist in the same habitat.

Competition among species, then, must be seen as strongly influencing the worldwide distribution of birds. Expansion of its range by a species, or establishment of a breeding population in a new region, depends not only on proper

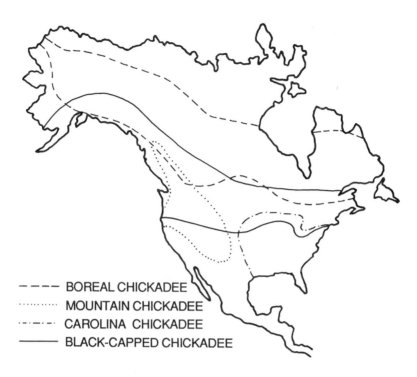

- - - - BOREAL CHICKADEE
.... MOUNTAIN CHICKADEE
- - - - CAROLINA CHICKADEE
——— BLACK-CAPPED CHICKADEE

The ranges of four chickadees found in the United States and Canada suggest that competition defines the extent of their ranges. In geographic areas where their ranges do overlap, not more than one species is found in the same habitat.

environmental conditions, but also on lack of species competing for that niche. We can now see the similarities in avifauna between the Palearctic and the Nearctic as a consequence not only of their proximity and similar habitats, but of Palearctic species' lack of competition as they expanded their ranges into the empty Nearctic niches. An empty niche apparently was ready for the Cattle Egret, *Bubulcus ibis,* when a flock of these birds happened to find themselves a landfall in South America, probably after a very long and errant flight across the Atlantic. Once here these birds found a familiar habitat that fulfilled their requirements for a niche and a lack of competitors. For, although this egret is similar in appearance to many of the New World egrets, it is less aquatic, feeding more on insects flushed from the grass by grazing animals. The lack of competition with local species can be measured by the lack of effect the Cattle Egret's growing population has on populations of similar herons.

An available or an open niche is a vacuum waiting to be filled in an ecosystem; the power of flight gives birds a better chance to fill these spaces than other types of animals have. It is interesting, then, to speculate on the possible expansions of range that some species might have in their future. The Brown Pelican, *Pelecanus occidentalis,* feeds on fish that it spots from the air, then dives into the water to catch them. These birds range south down the east coast of

North and South America as far as the Amazon. The silt-laden effluent from this great river muddies the coastal Atlantic for 160 kilometers eastward, creating an area where these pelicans cannot fish, and hence defining the present southern extent of their range. South of the Amazon River's influence the coastal waters are again clear and competing species are lacking, and so if a flock happened to cross this barrier, it might establish a breeding population that could expand southward all along the South American coast. Three species of albatross breed in the North Pacific, but no species normally occur in the North Atlantic. Accidental sightings in this region have occurred, a Black-browed Albatross, *Diomedea melanophris,* having been seen for many years in succession flying with gannets in the Spitzbergen area (Murphy, 1936). This bird found its niche far from home and was seen attempting to court gannets. If supplied with a mate from its own species, the offspring might be the nucleus for a breeding population here.

Expansion by other species, however, might be inhibited by competition. If New World hummingbirds were to turn up in Africa, they might find a suitable niche, but their ability to establish a breeding population would be inhibited by nectar-eating sunbirds, which occupy about the same niche as hummingbirds. Competition would also inhibit New World flycatchers from expanding their range to the Palearctic because the Old World flycatchers were there already. The African honeyeaters' niche in South America is filled by jacmars, making it unlikely that honeyeaters could survive in the Neotropical region. Probably many other examples of competition among species will be found limiting a species' range.

NICHE SIZE

The size of a species' niche, the organism's range in limits, has always interested ecologists. A bird such as the American Robin, *Turdus migratorius,* which breeds almost the length and breadth of North America and is found in varied habitats, must be considered as having a broadly defined niche, for this hardy species is well adapted to tolerate many temperatures, foods, and nesting situations. Many temperate species are in this condition, for living in a climate that alternately goes boom and bust does not allow them to adapt to only one set of conditions; they must be able to handle many. These species, then, are considered generalists. On the other hand, species specializing in particular types of food in the temperate zones are either seed eaters or migratory species. Swallows, which eat insects, nectar-eating hummingbirds, and fruit-eating tanagers must seek a winter niche in the tropics when their food disappears in fall.

Tropical species have evolved in very different conditions. Their environment remains more or less constant throughout the year. The predictability of these places allows species to adapt to the resources that are available: insect-eating birds can count on their food being present throughout the year; fruit- and nectar-eating birds are equally well provided for. Natural selection in the tropics therefore encourages a species to become more efficient in detecting, catching, and digesting these foods, but in doing so the species loses its ability to live on other foods. The evolutionary direction of tropical species, then, narrows their niche and makes them specialists. Two tropical specialists are the White-tipped Sicklebill, *Eutoxeres aquila,* which is a hummingbird with a sharply decurved bill, well tailored for drawing nectar from the flowers of *Heliconia,* and the Snail Kite, *Rostrhamus sociabilis,* which feeds only on *Pomacea* snails, extracting them from the shell with a strongly hooked beak. These two species have become very efficient in taking food from their environment, but their mastery gives them few options if their food supply fails.

The White-tipped Sicklebill is an example of a tropical specialist.

One consequence of tropical species' narrow niches is that a greater variety of birds can coexist in a tropical forest than in a temperate one. Panama, a country about as big as North Carolina, has nearly 900 species of birds, including 54 species of tanagers, 52 hummingbirds, and 85 tyrant flycatchers (Ridgely, 1976); this wealth compares with 750 species in the whole Nearctic. Tropical species also are usually sedentary; population pressures, and not environmental changes, cause a handful from each of these tropical families to seek a breeding niche in the Nearctic, and the northern representatives of these specialized families are the generalists in the group. All Nearctic species of hummingbirds have straight, medium-length bills, enabling them to feed on various flowers.

The differences between generalists and specialists also help us understand why more temperate families have spread into the tropics than tropical ones into temperate zones. For a northern jack-of-all-trades would find a stable environment more tolerable than a master-of-one would an unstable environment. Therefore, as the Central American land bridge formed, South American species spread as far north as the limit of the tropics, and many more Nearctic forms, such as hawks, owls, woodpeckers, waterfowl, and passerines, moved south into the tropics.

POPULATION SIZE

If the middle and high latitudes are relatively poor in diversity of species, the population of each species is often high. The enormous flocks of geese, ducks, blackbirds, and swallows characteristic of North America and Eurasia are almost absent in the tropics because not only are temperate birds generalists, but entire habitats are as well. Temperate and arctic zones have extensive uniform habitats, such as coniferous and deciduous forests made up of only a few tree varieties, allowing the animals that live there to have extensive breeding habitats. A tropical forest, though, is made up of a bewildering variety of trees; two trees of a species may be one hundred or more meters apart. Birds, being directly or indirectly dependent on specific plants, are discontinuously distributed throughout their ranges. The rich variety of birds in the tropics consists of many species with relatively few individuals.

Through the years, attempts have been made to estimate the population size of species. For species with limited ranges, such as the Whooping Crane, *Grus americana,* simply counting these conspicuous birds on their winter range gives an accurate census, which totaled about 134 individuals in 1989. For species such as the Kirtland's Warbler, *Dendroica kirtlandii,* a less accurate count of singing males done on the same day in spring 1975 revealed 216 males; therefore the population totaled fewer than 500 individuals. In species with extensive ranges and uniform distribution, the size of the population is estimated by determining the average number of birds in a specified area and then multiplying this average density by the entire area of its breeding range. Other ways of approximating the number of individuals in a species are done by estimating the flock size of birds that winter in enormous roosts. These census techniques confirm what most active observers intuitively know: The European Starling, *Sturnus vulgaris,* and the House Sparrow, *Passer domesticus,* are the world's most abundant species; and the Red-winged Blackbird, *Agelaius phoeniceus,* the Red-eyed Vireo, *Vireo olivaceus,* Yellow-rumped Warbler, *Dendroica coronata,* American Robin, *Turdus migratorius,* and the Black-capped Chickadee, *Parus atricapillus,* are the most numerous species in North America, all with populations exceeding 100 million. In Eurasia, species such as the Willow Warbler, *Phylloscopus trochilus,* the Redstart, *Phoenicurus phoenicurus,* and the Tree Pipit, *Anthus trivialis,* like their New World counterparts, all exceed 100 million birds (Mead,

1976). These numbers pale, however, compared with the estimated 3 billion Passenger Pigeons, *Ectopistes migratorius,* which once inhabited central North America.

Joining these temperate-zone land species with large populations are species that inhabit the largest, most uniform habitat on the planet, the oceans. The populations of pelagic species are supported by the almost unlimited resources produced by the sea. And because most of these species are colonial, their population sizes are known with some certainty, but the populations of others are inferred from their high open-ocean densities and their extensive ranges. Among the latter is Wilson's Storm-Petrel, *Oceanites oceanicus,* leading Fisher (1951) to consider this species the most numerous bird in the world. Another abundant species is the Short-tailed Shearwater, *Puffinus tenuirostris,* with an estimated population of 150 million (Peterson, 1948). Counts taken from individual colonies of other marine species show that more than 5 million Dovekies, *Alle alle,* breed in Scoreby Bay, Greenland, alone (Snyder, 1960), and a similar number of Guanay Cormorants, *Phalacrocorax bougainvillii,* were found on one island off the coast of Peru.

BIRDS AND PEOPLE

We have always had a relationship with birds. They were present as we evolved and since that time we have watched them, admired them, envied them, deified them, used them as symbols in literature and art. Judging by our collective actions, however, we seem bent on their destruction. From an avian point of view, this strange naked ape is an enormously potent intruder; we have become a factor in their niche that is ever more difficult to consider irrelevant. And, although one might suppose that the most harmful period in this relationship was when primitive man hunted birds for food, it is at the hands of modern humanity that avian species have suffered most.

Primitive man's effect on birds was probably limited, for as this new species struggled to survive on the African plain, he was rather poorly adapted to do much damage to any one species. An opportunist, he probably caught any birds he could for food; and, a keen observer, he undoubtedly raided nests for eggs. When tools and fire evolved, the human population grew; these tools effectively widened the human niche and gave rise to our cosmopolitan distribution. During this time people abandoned the hunter-gatherer lifestyle for agriculture, significantly increasing the amount of food in their environment.

Probably the first extinction of an avian species at the hand of man occurred between 600 and 300 years ago, when Polynesians colonized New Zealand. These islands, long isolated from other land masses, had no predators and so flightless species had evolved, including the kiwis and the moas. The moas, perhaps seven species in all, were hunted for food until extinct at about the same time as westerners began exploring earth's far-flung reaches. At their hands the pattern and pace of extinctions increased, rapidly doing away with species such as the dodos of Mauritania, the Great Auk, *Pinguinus impennis,* of the North Atlantic, the Passenger Pigeon, *Ectopistes migratorius,* the Labrador Duck, *Camptorhynchus laboradorius,* the Carolina Parakeet, *Conuropsis carolinensis,* and the Eskimo Curlew, *Numenius borealis.* These extinctions were caused by human wasting of the earth's resources. This era of extinction by clubs and guns is now something of the past as hunting is gradually regulated to selected species at specific times of the year. This said, however, we still hear reports about illegal hunting of eagles and hawks from small airplanes: the birds are shot out of the sky after an "exciting" chase (Anonymous, 1971). After reading these reports, one can only wonder about our character and, though some would attribute this behavior to our reverting to our primitive instincts, a more plausible explanation might be that this "sport" comes of alienation from our nature, leading to a decadent and irresponsible abuse of our abilities.

This first assault on avian populations essentially over, birds continue to be confronted by indirect human threats that are potentially far more serious, and come from our massive population and our ability to transform the face of the earth. These threats began with the tilling of the soil in the Fertile Crescent, and continue as chainsaws destroy the tropical rain forests at a rate of perhaps 500 square meters every minute. From an ecological point of view our creating farmland, towns, and cities has simplified habitats. A field of wheat or corn stands in place of forty other species of plants. The wheatfield of course has far fewer niches than the forest or grassland it replaces, in turn decreasing the diversity of species, but allowing those that can survive here huge increases in food, causing their populations to expand; these species are called pests.

The first species to fall victim to destruction of habitat was the Ivory-billed Woodpecker, *Campephilus principalis.* This large woodpecker depended on extensive tracts of forest, in which large dead trees supplied it with insect food and nest sites. When these forests were reduced the Ivory-billed Woodpecker lost a critical portion of its niche and has become extinct since the 1940s. The California Condor, *Gymnogyps californianus,* is on the brink of extinction for a similar reason: this bird's habitat has been so altered and poisoned that none of the species now lives in the wild. And though the Ivory-billed and the California Condor might be considered isolated cases, becoming extinct because of their own somewhat specialized ways, habitat destruction is threatening populations of commoner and hardier species as well. Widespread species such as the American Redstart, *Setophaga ruticilla,* the Kentucky Warbler, *Oporornis formosus,* and the Red-eyed Vireo, *Vireo olivaceus,* have all decreased in numbers in this generation. Most migratory songbirds in North America have shrunk as well because temperate and tropical forests are being destroyed. The most extreme example in this group is Bachman's Warbler, *Vermivora bachmanii;* never a common species, this bird is now very rare in the moist forests in the southeastern United States and in its winter range in Cuba, where its habitat, once tropical forest, is now almost entirely fields of sugar cane. Although destruction of the tropical forest is probably the reason for the general decline in many migratory species, changes in the temperate-zone forest have also been detrimental.

Dividing large tracts of forest into smaller ones forces many woodland species to nest near the forest edge, making their nests more vulnerable to predators such as crows, jays, and cats, which normally do not venture far into the woods. Also, opening up woodland to fields has allowed the Brown-headed Cowbird, *Molothrus ater*, to increase its range and parasitize more species (Wallace, 1986).

The decline in migratory songbird species caused by habitat destruction in the temperate regions is parallelled by a decline in tropical species. But here the problem is potentially more devastating because these species are more specialized and their distribution is limited. The Resplendent Quetzal, *Pharomachrus mocinno,* will become extinct if its mountain-forest habitat is destroyed.

Another habitat that has been threatened by the expanding human population is wetlands. These areas of standing water had little commerical value until they were drained, and were often used only to dispose of the endless waste produced by cities. Our shortsightedness in these activities is clear when we reflect that although swamps and marshes have little monetary value, they are among the most productive habitats in the world, with net productivity three times greater than that of the richest farmland, rivaled only by the tropical rain forest in their ability to convert sunlight into food (Kormondy, 1976). Before the water source of the Florida Everglades was diverted, this extensive wetland supported 1.5 million colonial nesting birds; after the diversion the population dropped to 150,000 (Morgan et al, 1980). These types of habitats also support great flocks of winter waterfowl and other species, but their decrease in size and increase in pollutants have negatively affected wintering and breeding populations of birds.

Overall, simplification of habitats has not been detrimental to all species. Many species of gulls have dramatically increased in population––species such as the Herring Gull, *Larus argentatus,* threaten colonies of other birds in many areas. This imbalance has led to a paradoxical situation in which the National Audubon Society condones destruction of the gulls to save the terns and puffins (Graham, 1985). Species of blackbirds have also increased to the extent that their winter roosts in the southern United States have become so large that they are seen as a threat to grain crops there as well as a possible hazard to human health. To counteract this plague these flocks have been subjected to dousings of soapy water on nights when the temperature drops below freezing, which results in death for many, for the solution removes oil from the feathers and with it their protective insulation (Graham, 1976).

These blackbirds are competitors for human food, and they are encroaching on the niche to which we want exclusive access. Birds, however, are not our major competitors for food—insects are. With their truly staggering numbers, voracious appetites, and very few checks on their population by predators in these simplified habitats, insects can rapidly lay waste to a crop. To combat their threat, we have applied poisons, first with compounds containing heavy metals such as arsenic, mercury, and lead, then with chlorinated organic pesticides, such as DDT and related compounds. These earlier poisons were initially effective in increasing crop yields, but accumulating chemicals such as lead and mercury in the habitat poisoned human food as well. For this reason such pesticides were replaced by the organics such as DDT, which seemed to selectively kill only insects. This promise proved to be false, however, for DDT is a very stable compound and remains in an ecosystem for years. The poison has worked its way up the food chain and increased in concentration as it has done so. Top-order predators such as fish-eating grebes, pelicans, hawks, and eagles began to accumulate very high dosages, killing them outright or causing the species to lay eggs with thin shells that broke before hatching. Its stability has also allowed DDT to be carried far from its place of application, affecting organisms in distant habitats. The Bermuda Petrel, *Pterodroma cahow,* an already endangered species, spends its year on the open ocean far from sources of DDT, but its unhatched eggs show significant levels of DDT (Kormondy, 1976). The detrimental effects of DDT were described in 1962 by Rachel Carson in her *Silent Spring;* but not until such highly visible birds as the Peregrine Falcon, *Falco peregrinus,* the Brown Pelican, *Pelecanus occidentalis,* and the Bald Eagle, *Haliaeetus leucocephalus,* were decimated in population, that her warning was heeded; the Environmental Protection Agency finally banned use of DDT in 1972. The chemical is still produced and widely used in other parts of the world, however, especially in Third-World tropical countries (Leary, 1981).

CONSERVATION

Another story about the relationship between birds and ourselves has a very different theme, a subplot with growing significance, which in the end might redeem our reputation. This story is about efforts individuals and organizations are making to preserve our national and global resources. The theme is conservation, and the plot is about species rescued from the verge of extinction.

Conservation is an apt name for this movement, for it means "to carefully preserve and protect," but the definition fails to include a reason. Therefore, conservation for some means to preserve a species for its own sake, and for others it is a method for protecting their own well-being. This movement, then, places those who detest the squandering of our resources and those who want their children to live in an unspoiled world on the same side as those who feel that organisms have a natural right to continue on this earth. Although this movement has grown many times over since the 1960s, the desire to live in harmony with the environment has always been a part of us. Until recently, however, the environment was considered an inexhaustible resource, and we had little understanding about the effects of our actions . Thus few protested when the Passenger Pigeon, *Ectopistes migratorius,* or the Great Auk, *Pinguinus impennis,* became extinct at our hands. The public reaction to the imminent disappearance of the Whooping Crane, *Grus americana,* was much different. When Robert Porter Allen reported to the scientific world and the national newspapers in 1936 that only fourteen Whooping Cranes were left because of indiscriminate shooting and destruction of habitat, the fires of avian conservation were lit. The public seemed beguiled by these big birds that danced with their mates, and disturbed by the waste that had all but eliminated the species. Such public interest led to national and international commitments to save these very American birds. The Arkansas Wildlife Refuge was established to protect their winter grounds in Texas and, after a long search, the cranes' breeding area in Canada was located and preserved. A captive breeding population was established at the Patuxent Wildlife Research Center in Maryland and a second wild population of Whoopers is being established in Idaho with help from Sandhill Crane, *Grus canadensis,* foster parents. These efforts had brought the Whooping Crane population up to some 196 individuals in 1989, but the cost was millions of dollars. In these same forty-five years, many more millions have been spent to preserve habitats for many other species by creating more wildlife refuges in North America and around the world. Although these efforts stabilized populations in many species, the California Condor, *Gymnogyps californianus,* continued to fail, and in 1985 a controversial decision was made to capture all remaining wild birds and try to promote their breeding in captivity, and at some future date to return a breeding population to the wild.

A similar outcry was heard when the public was informed about the disastrous effects of DDT on the environment in general, but particularly on our national symbol, the Bald Eagle, *Haliaeetus leucocephalus.* This response led to banning of DDT and passage of the Clean Air Act in 1972. This legislation was a statement by the people that the air we breathe and the food we eat must be clean. Because of these actions the populations of Brown Pelicans, *Pelecanus occidentalis,* and Ospreys, *Pandion haliaetus,* are beginning to return to former levels. Encouraged by a program to reintroduce them, the Peregrine Falcon, *Falco peregrinus,* and the Bald Eagle are starting to make a comeback.

Along with these laws the Endangered Species Act in 1973 equalized the odds among species, stating that the federal government could not fund projects that would negatively affect an endangered species. Shortly after its passage, the law was put to the test when the powerful Tennessee Valley Authority was ordered to halt construction of the nearly completed Tellico Dam on the Little Tennessee River because its completion would destroy the then only known habitat of a lowly fish species, the Snail Darter. This law was proving to be not only expensive but inconvenient as well. In 1988 some well-peopled beaches in Rhode Island were closed for most of the summer so that the Piping Plover, *Charadrius melodus,* could have the beach all to itself. In Amherst, Massachusetts, some major roads close on warm spring nights to allow Spotted Salamanders to migrate to their breeding ponds without running the risk of being squashed. With these cases, some now consider the Endangered Species Act a naive if well-intentioned act that is much too expensive to continue. This view ignores history, however, for our own actions shoved these species to the edge of extinction in the first place. Our reckless, only-for-profit development of the planet has led us to a crucial question: What is the price of a species?

Many industrialized nations have begun to struggle with that question, but most of the Third World has not. Some of these countries have moved to establish national parks (some even find that their natural treasures can turn a profit), but poverty and burgeoning populations are directly competing with other species for space. Their "more responsible" neighbors find it easy to point an accusatory finger, but we must remember that the "developed" nations do their share to promote destruction of habitat in the Third World. Costa Rica, for example, is rapidly replacing virgin forest with cattle ranches, and although beef production has more than doubled there, local consumption of beef has dropped, for nearly all the beef is exported to fast-food chains in the United States (Morgan et al, 1980). Wealthy countries must realize that conservation is a global endeavor, and that we must promote preservation, not destruction of habitat in the poorer nations.

Considering, then, the expense, the inconvenience, and the complexities in protecting our world, and considering that many species of birds undoubtedly became extinct before our appearance on earth, that during our stay ninety species, or about 1 percent of present bird species have become extinct at our hands, and yet that whole ecosystems have not yet collapsed (or have they?)—considering these realities—we must ask if saving a species from extinction is worth the cost? The answer must be a resounding *yes* for several reasons. The first is that birds are especially good environmental indicators: their rapid metabolism, rate of reproduction, and high visibility make them the equivalent to environmental litmus paper. An increase in extinct and endangered species signifies growing environmental problems. Just as a caged canary brought into the mines indicated—by dying—the presence of poisonous gases before the miners could detect it, loss of a species indicates an environment that is ever more hazardous to our health.

The second reason is that a species is the end result, and the finest work, of forces greater than ourselves. Call these forces what you will, but to interrupt that work by wastefulness, carelessness, or greed is at least disrespectful if not a crime.

The third reason is that we draw more from the natural world than just food, water, and shelter. Nature is our inspiration; it is a symphony of sound and a canvas of color that keep our spirit alive. For many of us, birds are a link with these intangible qualities, and with the extinction of each species, a variation on a theme, the subtle hue on the canvas is lost, and this loss is forever.

Suggested Reading

The geographic distribution of birds of the world is well documented in the *Encyclopedia of Birds,* edited by Perrins and Middleton, whereas the *Distributional Checklist of North American Birds,* by DeSante and Pyle, gives complete information on birds of the Palearctic. Every year we find more field guides to birds of other countries; even if we never get to use these books in the field, they are informative to flip through. Effects of the environment on birds' social systems, reproductive strategies, and populations are detailed in *Avian Ecology,* by Perrins and Birkhead. For ideas on conservation, *Red Data Book,* published and updated by the International Union for Conservation of Nature and Natural Resources lists endangered species. Maslow's *Bird of Life, Bird of Death* is a chilling account of the ecological problems brewing in Central America. For up-to-date information on environmental problems, read such magazines as *Audubon* and *Sierra*.

Projects

When you travel to other parts of the world, make sure you record the birds you see. Compare this list to the one you keep for the birds you find at home to get some idea about zoological regions of the world. Further comparing the habitat in which the birds on this list are found to those you are familiar with at home may lead to better understanding of ecology. Which species in Europe or Asia replace the American robin as a species that feeds on worms on suburban lawns? or the chickadee at the seed feeder? or long-legged waders in a marsh? Look up the classification describing these species that share the same niches to see if they are in the same genus or family. If they do, they are probably products of a species that has extended its range and then diversified, but if they are not closely related, they may have been created by convergent evolution. As you undertake conservation, the first step is to become aware of local, national, and global issues, and then to stand up for protecting the environment. Make your voice heard at local board meetings, or by writing to your senator and representative. Organizations such as Audubon, Sierra Club, and Greenpeace are active in conservation on many levels, and cannot do without your support.

REFERENCES

Alcock, J. 1970. The origin of tool-use in Egyptian Vulture, *Neophron perc-nopterus. Ibis,* 112: 542.

Alerstam, J., and S. Ulfstand. 1972. Radar and field observations of diurnal migration in south Sweden, Autumn 1971. *Ornis scandinavica,* 3: 99–139.

Allen, R. P. 1952. The whooping crane. *National Audubon Society Research Report No. 3.* New York.

American Ornithologist's Union, 1983. *Check-list of North American Birds,* 6th ed. Washington, D.C.

Anderson, S. H. 1970. Water balance of the Oregon Junco. *Auk,* 87: 161–163.

Anonymous. 1971. A slaughtering of eagles. *Audubon,* 73(5): 72–73.

Armstrong, E. A. 1942. *Bird Displays and Behavior.* Oxford University Press, New York.

Ashmole, N. P., and T. S. Humberto. 1968. Prolonged parental care of Royal Tern and other birds. *Auk,* 85: 90–100.

Bailey, R. E. 1952. The incubation patch of passerine birds. *Condor,* 54: 121–136.

Baldwin, S. P., and S. C. Kerdeigh. 1932. Physiology of the temperature of birds. *Scientific Publications of the Cleveland Museum of Natural History.* 3: 1–196.

Bang, B. G., and S. Cobb. 1968. The size of the olfactory bulb in 108 species of birds. *Auk,* 85: 55–61.

Barklow, W. E., and J. A. Chamberlain. 1984. The use of the tremolo call during mobbing by the Common Loon. *Journal of Field Ornithology,* 55(2): 258–259.

Beletsky, L. D., and M. C. Corral. 1983. Lack of vocal mate recognition in female Red-winged Blackbirds. *Journal of Field Ornithology,* 54(2): 200–202.

Bellrose, F. C. 1957. A spectacular water fowl migration through central North America. *Illinois Department of Registration and Education.* Natural History Survey Division, Biological Notes, no. 36.

Bent, A. C. 1932. Life histories of North American gallinaceous birds. *U.S. National Museum Bulletin* 162, Washington, D.C.

Bent, A. C. 1937. Life histories of North American birds of prey. *U.S. National Museum Bulletin* 174. Washington, D.C.

Berger, A. J. 1961. *Bird Study.* Dover Publications, New York.

Boag, P. T., and P. R. Grant. 1981. Intense natural selection in a population of Darwin's Finches *(Geospizinae)* in the Galápagos. *Science,* 214: 82–85.

Borror, D. J. 1959. Variations in the songs of the Rufous-sided Towhee. *Wilson Bulletin,* 71: 54–72.

Borror, D. J. 1961. Intraspecific variation in passerine bird song. *Wilson Bulletin,* 73: 57–78.

Brackbill, H. 1961. Duetting in the Brown-headed Cowbird. *Auk* 78: 97.

Brodkorb, P. 1955. Number of feathers and weights of various systems in a Bald Eagle. *Wilson Bulletin,* 67: 142.

Brodkorb, P. 1960. How many species of birds have existed? *Bulletin, Florida State Museum Biological Sciences,* 8: 41–53.

Brower, L. P. 1969. Ecological chemistry. *Scientific American,* 220(2): 22–29.

Brown, J. L. 1964. The integration of agonistic behavior in the Steller's Jay *Cyanocitta stelleri* (Gremlin). *University of California Publications in Zoology,* 60: 223–328.

Bull, J. 1974. *Birds of New York State.* Doubleday/Natural History Press, Garden City, New York.

Catchpole, C. K. 1980. Sexual selection and the evolution of complex songs among European warblers of the genus *Acrocephalus. Behavior,* 74: 149–166.

Clapp, R. B., M. K. Klimkiewicz, and A. G. Futcher. 1983. Longevity records of North American birds: Columbidae through Paridae. *Journal of Field Ornithology,* 54(2): 123–137.

Collias, N. E., and E. C. Collias. 1967. A field study of the Red-jungle fowl in north-east India. *Condor,* 69(4): 360–386.

Conover, M. R., D. E. Miller, and G. L. Hunt, Jr. 1979. Female-female pairs and other unusual reproductive associations in Ring-billed and California Gulls. *Auk,* 96: 6–9.

Coulson, J. C. 1966. The influence of the pair bond and age on breeding biology of the Kittiwake Gull, *Rissa tridactyla. Journal of Animal Ecology,* 35: 269–279.

Cullen, E. 1957. Adaptations in the Kittiwake to cliff-nesting. *Ibis,* 99: 275–302.

Dane, B., and W. S. Van der Kloot. 1964. An analysis of the display of the Goldeneye Duck *(Bucephala clangula). Behaviour,* 14(4): 265–281.

Dorst, J. 1962. *The Migration of Birds.* Houghton Mifflin, Boston.

Drewien, R. C., and E. Kuyt. 1979. Teaming up to help the whooper. *National Geographic,* 155(5): 680–693.

Duffy, E., O. N. Creasey, and K. Williamson. 1950. Distraction displays of certain waders. *Ibis,* 92: 27–33.

Ederstrom, H. E., and S. J. Brumleve. 1964. Temperature gradients in the legs of cold-acclimatized pheasants. *American Journal of Physiology,* 207: 457–459.

Emlen, S. T. 1972. An experimental analysis of the parameters of bird song eliciting species recognition. *Behaviour,* 41(1–2): 241–246.

Emlen, S. T. 1975. The stellar-orientation system of a migratory bird. *Scientific American,* 233(2): 102–111.

Falls, J. B. 1969. Functions of territorial song in the white-throated sparrow. In R. A. Hinde, ed., *Bird Vocalizations: Their Relations to Current Problems in Biology and Physiology:* Essays presented to W. H. Thorpe. Cambridge University Press, Cambridge, England.

Fisher, J., and R. A. Hinde. 1949. The opening of milk bottles by birds. *British Birds,* 42: 347–357.

Fisher, J. 1951. *Watching Birds,* revised ed. Harmondsworth, Middlesex.

Fitch, H. S., F. Swenson, and D. F. Tillotson. 1946. Behavior and food habits of the Red-tailed Hawk, *Condor,* 48: 205–237.

Forbush, E. H. 1925–29. *Birds of Massachusetts and other New England States,* 3 vols. Boston: Massachusetts Department of Agriculture.

Frings, H., M. Frings, B. Cos, and L. Peissner. 1955. Recorded calls of Herring Gulls*(Larus argentatus)* as repellents and attractants. *Science*, 121: 318–319.

Frith, H. J. 1956. Breeding habits in the Family Megapodiidae. *Ibis*, 98: 620–640.

Gould, S. J. and N. Eldridge. 1977. Punctuated equilibria: The tempo and mode of evolution reconsidered. *Paleobiology*, 3: 115–151.

Graham, F., Jr. 1976. Blackbirds: A problem that won't fly away. *Audubon*, 78(3): 118–125.

Graham, F., Jr. 1985. Returning the terns. *Audubon*, 87(1): 14–17.

Griffin, D. R. 1943. Homing experiments with Herring Gulls and Common Terns. *Bird-Banding*, 14: 7–23.

Griffin, D. R. 1953. Acoustic orientation in the Oilbird, *Steatornis*. *Proceedings of the National Academy of Science*, 39: 884–893.

Grubb, T. C., Jr. 1972. Smell and foraging in shearwater and petrels. *Nature*, 237: 404–405.

Grubb, T. C., Jr. 1973. Colony location by Leach's Petrel. *Auk*, 90: 78–82.

Gwinner, E. 1968. Circannuale periodik als grundlage des Jahrmeszeitichen funcktions-wandels bei zugvogelen. In *Journal für Ornithologies*, 109(1): 70–95.

Hann, H. W. 1945. *An Introduction to Ornithology*. Edwards Brothers, Ann Arbor, Michigan.

Hartman, F. A. 1961. Locomotor mechanisms of birds. *Smithsonian Miscellaneous Collections*, 143(1): 1–99.

Hartshorne, C. 1958. The relation of bird song to music. *Ibis*, 100: 421–445.

Hatch, D. E. 1970. Energy conserving and heat dissipating mechanisms of the Turkey Vulture. *Auk*, 87: 111–124.

Higuchi, H. 1987. Cast master. *Natural History*, 96: 40–43.

Hohn, E. O. 1969. The phalarope. *Scientific American*, 220(6): 104–109.

Hudson, W. H. 1901. *Birds and Man.* Longmans, Green, London.

Humphrey, P. S., and K. C. Parks. 1959. An approach to the study of molts and molting. *Auk,* 76: 1–31.

Jenni, D. A., and G. Collier. 1972. Polyandry in the American Jacana *(Jacana spinosa). Auk,* 89: 743–765.

Jensen, R. A. C., and C. F. Clining. 1974. Breeding biology of two cuckoos and their hosts in South West Africa. *The Living Bird.* Laboratory of Ornithology, Ithaca, New York.

Johnson, R. A. 1941. Nesting behavior of the Atlantic Murre. *Auk,* 58:153–163.

Johnson, R. A. 1969. Hatching behavior in the Bobwhite. *Wilson Bulletin,* 81: 79–86.

Karplus, M. 1952. Bird activity in the continuous daylight of arctic summer. *Ecology,* 33: 129–134.

Keeton, W. T. 1974. The mystery of Pigeon homing. *Scientific American,* 231(19): 96–98.

Kendeigh, S. C. 1941. Territorial and mating behavior of the House Wren. *Illinois Biological Monographs,* 18(3): 1–120. University of Illinois Press, Urbana, Illinois.

Kiriline, L. de. 1954. The voluble singer of the tree-tops. *Audubon,* 56: 109–111.

Klein, T. J. 1985. *Loon Magic.* Ed. J. Fair. Paper Birch Press, Ashland, Wisconsin.

Koehler, O. 1951. The ability of birds to "count." *Bulletin of Animal Behaviour,* 9: 41–45.

Kooyman, G. L., et al. 1971. Diving behavior of the Emperor Penguin, *Aptenodytes forsteri. Auk,* 88: 775–795.

Kormondy, E. J. 1976. *Concepts of Ecology,* 2nd ed. Prentice-Hall, Englewood Cliffs, N.J.

Lack, D. 1943. *The Life of the Robin.* H. F. and G. Witherby, London.

Lack, D. 1960. The height of bird migration. *British Birds,* 52: 258–267.

Lack, D. 1963. Migration across the North Sea studied by radar. Part II. *Ibis,* 102: 26–57.

Lack, D. 1968. *Ecological Adaptations for Breeding in Birds.* Methuen, London.

Laswieski, R. C., and R. J. Laswieski. 1967. Physiological responses of the Blue-throated and Rivoli's Hummingbirds. *Auk,* 84: 34–48.

Layborne, R. C. 1974. Collision between a vulture and an aircraft at an altitude of 37,000 ft. *Wilson Bulletin,* 86(4): 461–462.

Leary, C. 1982. *The Birdwatcher's Companion.* Hill and Wang, New York.

Leopold, A., and A. E. Eynon. 1961. Avian daybreak and evening song in relation to time and light intensity. *Condor,* 63: 209–293.

Lockley, R. M. 1942. *Shearwaters.* Devin-Adair, Old Greenwich, Ct.

Lord, R. D., et al. 1962. Radiotelemetry on the respiration of a flying duck. *Science,* 137: 39–40.

Lorenz, K. Z. 1950. The comparative method of studying innate behavior patterns. *Physiological Mechanisms in Animal Behaviour. Symposia for Experimental Biology,* vol. 4. Academic Press, New York.

McCabe, T. T. 1942. Types of shorebird flight. *Auk,* 59: 110–111.

MacArthur, R. H., and J. W. MacArthur. 1961. On bird species diversity. *Ecology,* 42: 594–598.

Marler, P. 1970. A comparative approach to vocal learning: Song development in White-crowned Sparrows. *Journal of Comparative Physiological Psychology Monograph,* 71(2) part 2: 1–25.

Marshall, A. J. 1954. *Bower Birds.* Oxford University Press, London.

Maslow, J. E. 1986. *Bird of Life, Bird of Death.* Simon and Schuster, New York.

Mead, C. 1976. *Bird Migration.* Facts on File, New York.

Meinertzhagen, R. 1955. The speed and altitude of bird flight. *Ibis,* 97: 85–116.

Milliotus, P., and P. A. Buckley. 1975. The Massachusetts Ross' Gull. *American Birds,* 29(3): 643–646.

Mohr, H. 1960. Zum Erkennen von Raubvogeln, insbesondere von Sperber und Baumfalk, durch Kleinvogeln. *Zeitschrift für Tierpsychologie,* 17(6): 686–699.

Morgan, M. M., M. D. Morgan, and J. H. Wiersma. 1980. *Introduction to Environmental Science.* W. H. Freeman, San Francisco.

Murphy, R. C. 1936. *Oceanic Birds of South America.* Macmillan, New York.

Nesbet, I. C. T. 1963. Measurements with radar of the height of nocturnal migration over Cape Cod, Massachusetts. *Bird-Banding,* 34: 57–67.

Nesbet, I. C. T. with W. H. Drury, Jr. 1967. Orientation of spring migrants studied by radar. *Bird-Banding* 38:173–186.

Nice, M. M. 1937. Studies in the life history of the Song Sparrow. I. A population study of the Song Sparrow. *Transactions of the Linnaean Society of New York,* 4: 1–274.

Nice, M. M. 1938. The biological significance of bird weights. *Bird-Banding,* 9: 1–11

Nice, M. M. 1943. Studies in the life history of the Song Sparrow. II. *Transactions of the Linnaean Society of New York,* 6: 1–328.

Nice, M. M. 1957. Nesting success in altricial birds. *Auk,* 74: 305–321.

Noble, G. H. 1936. Courtship and sexual selection of the Flicker, *Auk,* 53: 269–282.

Nottebohm, F. 1981. A brain for all seasons: Cyclical anatomical changes in song control nuclei of the Canary brain. *Science,* 214: 1368–1370.

Nottebohm, F., and A. P. Arnold. 1976. Sexual dimorphism in vocal control areas of the songbird brain. *Science,* 194: 211–213.

Odum, E. P. 1941. Variations in the heart rate of birds. *Ecological Monographs,* 11: 299–326.

Orians, G. H. 1969. On the evolution of mating systems in birds and mammals. *American Naturalist,* 103: 589–603.

Papi, F., L. Fiore, V. Faischi, and S. Benvenuti. 1972. Olfaction and homing in Pigeons. *Monitore Zool. Ital.,* n.s. 6: 85–95.

Payne, R. S. 1961. The acoustical location of prey in the Barn Owl *(Tyto alba)*. *American Zoologist,* 1: 379.

Pearson, R. 1972. *The Avian Brain.* Academic Press, London.

Pengelley, E., and S. Asmundson. 1971. Annual biological clocks. *Scientific American,* 224: 72–79.

Penny, R. L. 1967. Molt in the Adélie Penguin. *Auk,* 84: 61–71.

Pennycuick, D. J. 1972. Soaring behavior and performance of some East African birds, observed from a motor-glider. *Ibis,* 4: 178–218.

Perdeck, A. C. 1958. Two types of orientation in migrating Starlings, *Sternus vulgaris* L., and Chaffinches, *Fringilla coelebs* L., as revealed by displacement experiments. *Ardea,* 46: 1–37.

Perrins, C. M., and A. L. A. Middleton, eds.1985. *Encyclopedia of Birds.* Facts on File, New York.

Peterson, R. T. 1948. *Birds over America.* Dodd, Mead, New York.

Pettingill, O. S. 1970. *Ornithology in Laboratory and Field,* 4th ed. Burgess, Minneapolis, Minnesota.

Poole, E. L. 1938. Weights and wing areas in North American birds. *Auk,* 55: 511–517.

Portmann, A. 1950. Le développement postembryonnaire. In Grasse, P. *Traité de Zoologie.* tome XV, *Oiseaux.* Masson, Paris.

Potter, E. F. 1970. Anting in wild birds, its frequency and probable purpose. *Auk,* 87: 692–713.

Richdale, L. E. 1952. The post-egg period in albatrosses. *Biological Monograms,* no. 4. Dunedin, New Zealand.

Ridgely, R. S. 1976. *A Guide to the Birds of Panama.* Princeton University Press, Princeton, N.J.

Ripley, S. D. 1950. Strange courtship of birds of paradise. *National Geographic,* 97: 247–278.

Roberts, B. B. 1934. Notes on birds of central and south-east Iceland. *Ibis,* 4: 239–264.

Roberts, T. S. 1907. A Lapland Longspur tragedy. *Auk,* 24: 369–377.

Royama, T. 1970. Factors governing the hunting and selection of food by the great tit *(Parus major L.). Journal of Animal Ecology,* 39: 619–668.

Salomonsen, F. 1951. The immigration and breeding of the Fieldfare *(Turdus pilaris L.)* in Greenland. *Proceedings of the Xth International Ornithological Congress, Uppsala, June 1950,* 515–526. Almqvist and Wiksells, Uppsala.

Saunders, A. A. 1959. Forty years of spring migration in southern Connecticut. *Wilson Bulletin,* 71: 208–219.

Savile, D. B. 1957. Adaptive evolution in the avian wing. *Evolution,* 11: 212–224.

Serventy, D. L. 1960. Geographic distribution of living birds. In *Biology and Comparative Physiology of Birds,* vol. 1. Ed. A. J. Marshall. Academic Press, New York.

Shy, M. M. 1982. Interspecific feeding among birds: A review. *Journal of Field Ornithology,* 53(4): 370–394.

Smith, D. G. 1972. The role of the epaulets in the Red-winged Blackbird *(Agelaius phoeniceus). Behavior,* 56(1–2): 136–156.

Smith, D.G. 1979. Male singing ability and territory integrity in the Red-winged Blackbird *(Agelaius phoeniceus). Behaviour,* 68: 193–206.

Smith, D. G., and D. O. Norman. 1979. Leader-follower singing in Red-winged Blackbirds. *Condor,* 81: 83–84.

Smith, N. G. 1968. The advantage of being parasitized. *Nature,* 219: 690–694.

Smith, R. L. 1959. The songs of the Grasshopper Sparrow. *Wilson Bulletin,* 71: 141–152.

Snyder, D. E. 1960. Dovekie flights and wrecks. *Massachusetts Audubon,* 44: 117–121.

Starkly, E. E. 1972. A case of interspecific homosexuality in geese. *Auk,* 89: 456–457.

Stresemann, E. 1927–1934. In Kukenthal, W., and T. Krumbach.*Handbuch der Zoologie. Sauropsida: Aves.* W. de Gruyter, Berlin and Leipzig.

Swennen, C. 1968. Nest protection of Eiderducks and Shovellers by means of faeces. *Ardea,* 56: 248–258.

Thielcke, G. 1972. Learning song patterns as pacemaker of evolution. *Proceedings of the XV International Ornithological Congress,* 694. E. J. Brill, Leiden.

Thomson, A. L., ed. 1964. *A New Dictionary of Birds.* Houghton Mifflin, Boston.

Tinbergen, N. 1951. *The Study of Instinct.* Clarendon Press, Oxford.

Tinbergen, N. 1953. *The Herring Gull's World.* William Collins, London.

Thorpe, W. H. 1963. *Learning and instinct in animals,* 2nd ed. Harvard University Press, Cambridge, Massachusetts.

Thorpe, W. H. 1969. In Hinde, R. A., ed. *Bird Vocalizations: Their Relation to Current Problems in Biology and Psychology.* Cambridge University Press, Cambridge, England.

Thorpe, W. H. 1973. Duet-singing birds. *Scientific American,* 229(2): 70–79.

Verner, J., and M. F. Wilson. 1966. The influence of habitat on mating systems of North American passerine birds. *Ecology,* 47: 143–147.

Walcott, C., and R. Green. 1974. Orientation of homing pigeons altered by a change in the direction of an applied magnetic field. *Science,* 184: 180–182.

Walcott, C., J. L. Gould, and J. L. Kirschvink. 1979. Pigeons have magnets. *Science,* 205: 1027.

Wallace, J. 1986. Where have all the songbirds gone? *Sierra,* 71(2): 44–47.

Wedemeyer, W. 1973. The spring migration at Fortine, Montana. *Condor,* 75: 400–413.

Weller, M. W. 1959. Parasitic egg laying in the Redhead *Aythya Americana* and other North American anatidae. *Ecological Monograms,* 29: 333–365.

Welty, J. C. 1975. *The Life of Birds,* 2nd ed. W. B. Saunders, Philadelphia.

Wetmore, A. 1936. The number of contour feathers in Passeriform and related birds. *Auk,* 53: 159–169.

White, S. J. 1971. Selective responsiveness by the Gannet *(Sula bassana)* to played-back calls. *Animal Behaviour,* 19: 125–131.

Wickler, W. 1972. Aufbau und Paarspezifität des Gesangsduettes von *Laniarius funebris* (Aves, Passeriformes, Laniidae). *Zeitschrift für Tierpsychologie,* 30(5): 464–476.

Wiley, R. H. 1973. Territoriality and non-random mating in the Sage Grouse*(Centrocercus urophasianus). Animal Behavior Monographs,* 6(2): 85–169.

Wilson, E. O. 1972. Animal communication. *Scientific American,* 227(3): 52–60.

Wilson, E. O. 1977. *Sociobiology: The New Synthesis.* Belknap Press, Cambridge, Massachusetts.

Woolfenden, G. E. 1975. Florida scrub jay helpers at the nest. *Auk,* 92(1): 1–15.

GLOSSARY

Accipiter Type of hawk with short, rounded wings, long tail, and long legs; represented in North America by Northern Goshawk, Cooper's Hawk, and Sharp-skinned Hawk.

Air sac Part of the avian respiratory system; the sacs direct air to the lung and also dissipate heat and reduce the bird's weight.

Albumen The white of an egg.

Alcid Member of the family Alcidae, which includes murres, puffins, and auks.

Allula feathers Feathers that attach to the "thumb" bone of the bird's wing; used to direct air stream across flight feathers during takeoff and landing.

Alternate plumage Feather coat worn during breeding season in species that molt prior to breeding.

Altricial Helpless condition of the young of a species; among other species, all passerines have altricial young.

Angle of attack Attitude of the wing in relation to the air stream; increasing angle of attack generally increases lift.

Anting Unusual method of feather care: The bird rubs ants on its feather or squats on an anthill, allowing ants to crawl through its feathers. Anting is thought to rid the bird of feather parasites.

Archaeopteryx Oldest known fossilized bird.

Aspect ratio Ratio of the wing's length to its width: Large albatrosses have very long, narrow wings with an aspect ratio of 18 to 1.

Associational learning Type of learning in which stimuli gain meaning by reward or punishment.

Aves Scientific name for the group (class) to which all birds belong.

Banding Method for individually identifying birds by placing numbered bands on their legs.

Barbs Processes that project from the rachis of a feather, the sum of which make up the feather's surface or vane.

Barbules Minute branches off the barb that interlock with barbules of adjacent barbs, forming vane of feather.

Basic plumage Adult plumage in a species; for species that have bright breeding colors (alternate plumage), basic plumage is the winter feather coat.

Biological clock An organism's innate ability to know the time of day or year.

Bristle feathers Vaneless contour feathers that form eyelashes in some species and in others grow around beak or nares.

Brood parasites Species that do not build a nest or care for their young; they lay their eggs in other birds' nests.

Buteo Genus of soaring hawk that includes the Red-tailed, Broad-winged, and Swainson's hawks.

Calamus Part of the central shaft in a feather that is embedded in the skin.

Call Generally a simple vocalization produced by the male, female, or young of a species at any time of year.

Camber Slight arch in the width of a bird's wing; deepening the camber on a wing increases the lift it can develop.

Chalaza Pair of thick, ropelike bands of albumen (white) in an egg that extend on either side of the yolk, that is, hold the yolk in the correct alignment during development.

Cloaca Terminal vent of a bird's digestive, excretory, and reproductive systems.

Clock shifting Research technique that puts a bird's internal sense of time out of synchrony with real time; used to show how a bird uses its internal sense of time and the sun to determine direction.

Clutch All the eggs laid by a bird in its nest.

Contour feathers Outer layer of feathers that make up the body's shape; the flight feathers—primary, secondary, and tail—are also considered contour feathers.

Counter-shading Dark top and light bottom pattern carried by many species; makes the bird harder to see when in full light because the sun lightens the dark surface and the light bottom is darkened by shadow.

Covert feathers Contour feathers that cover base of flight feathers.

Crop Outpouching in a bird's esophagus that holds food until it enters the stomach or is fed to the young.

Crown Top of a bird's head, from eye to eye and forehead to nape.

Determinate egg layers Species that lay a fixed number of eggs in the nest; if an egg is removed from the nest it will not be replaced, as in doves, shore birds, and many passerines (see Indeterminate layers).

Dialect Form of species song that is characteristic of a breeding population of the species.

Disruptive plumage Bold black-and-white patterns on some species, breaking up the body contours and making the bird more difficult to see.

Dominance hierarchy Status arrangement among social organisms in which dominant organisms gain greater access to resources than submissive ones. Commonly referred to as peck order.

Down feathers Short, fluffy feathers that grow under the contour feathers and trap heat close to the body.

Drag Retarding force exerted by air turbulence.

Duet Singing together, observed in some species: A mated pair interchange of calls in quick succession.

Dynamic soaring High-speed flying done by the long-winged sea birds using strong winds on the open ocean.

Egg tooth Hard projection on the front of the beak of hatching birds; used to break the shell when hatching.

Ethology Study of animal behavior in the organism's natural habitat.

Family In classification, labels a group of organisms that have a common ancestor.

Feather sheath Protein covering of a growing feather.

Feather tracks Discrete lines of cells that produce feathers; found in all but the most primitive species, whose feather cells are evenly placed in the skin.

Filoplume Type of feather that has barbs only at the tip; grows near the flight feathers and is thought to help the bird "know" the position occupied by these feathers.

Fixed action pattern Stereotypical innate response by a member of a species to a (sign) stimulus.

Fledgling Stage in development at which young have left the nest but still depend on parents for care.

Flight feathers Primary and secondary feathers on wing and tail.

Fovea Infolded retinal tissue of the eye; most sensitive part of the eye.

Generalist Organism with wide tolerances; found in many types of environments: includes jays and crows.

Genus Group of closely related species.

Gizzard Muscular stomach of a bird; in many species the gizzard contains grit, which grinds up food, acting in place of teeth.

Habituation Simple form of learning, in which an organism stops responding to a stimulus that is not reinforced.

Imprinting Type of learning that takes place during a critical period in early development; enables the young organism to become attached to and learn to recognize its own kind.

Indeterminate egg layer Bird that continues to lay eggs until the nest is full of the species-specific number of eggs; such birds will continue to replace eggs that are removed from the nest: the domesticated chicken is one (see Determinate layer).

Juvenal plumage Contour feathers worn by the young of a species up to its first molt.

Keel Bony process projecting from the sternum of a bird, to which the flight muscles are attached.

Lek Traditional mating area for such species as the Sage Grouse and the Ruff.

Lift Upward force exerted by pressure differences created when air streams across a bird's wing.

Mandible Upper and lower parts of a bird's bill.

Migration Seasonal movement of organisms from breeding area to wintering area and back again.

Molt Loss and regrowth of feathers.

Monogamy Mating system in which one male mates with one female; the commonest mating system in birds.

Navigation Ability to determine where you are in relation to where you want to go, that is, the mysterious map sense that is probably common to most birds.

Nest helpers Arrangement found in species of social birds (such as the Florida Scrub Jay) wherein a breeding-age offspring helps its parents feed and protect their subsequent broods.

Nestling Young bird that is confined to the nest.

Niche Range of tolerances an organism has within its environment.

Ocines Large suborder of passerines that have a well-developed syrinx: the songbirds.

Orientation An organism's ability to align itself with a stimulus such as sunlight or starlight to find a migratory or homeward direction.

Ovum Female reproductive cell, which becomes the yolk of the egg.

Pectoralis Powerful breast muscles of a bird that, when contracted, pull the wings down in their power stroke.

Photoperiod Duration of sunlight in a day; used by many organisms as a cue to initiate behaviors such as breeding or migration.

Polyandry Mating system in which one female mates with more than one male.

Polygamy Mating system in which one sex has more than one mate.

Polygyny Mating system in which one male mates with more than one female.

Powder down feathers Type of down feather that grows continuously at the base and disintegrates at the tip, producing a fine powder that waterproofs the feathers.

Precocial Young that are born feathered and able to run and feed themselves, such as ducks and chickens.

Preening Basic method for feather care, in which the bird cleans, straightens, and, in most species, oils its feathers.

Primary feathers Flight feathers on the "hand" of a bird; responsible for forward thrust in flap flying.

Pygostyle "Tailbone" of a bird, in which the tail feathers are embedded.

Rachis Part of the central shaft in a feather, from which the barbs project.

Radiotelemetry Research technique affixing on an organism an electrical device emitting a radio signal of set frequency that permits tracking the animal by radio receiver.

Range Geographic area within which a species is found.

Ratites Collectively, the ostrich, emu, rhea, cassowary, and kiwi, which were once classified together in the family Ratidae.

Salt gland Organ in the skull between the eyes of species that live on salt water; removes salt from the blood, allowing these species to drink sea water.

Secondary feathers Wing flight feathers that attach to the ulna; the main lifting feathers.

Sexual dimorphism Species with pronounced difference between male and female.

Slotting Spreading of the primary feathers in soaring land birds such as vultures and buteos, forming gaps between feathers; reduces turbulence at the wingtips.

Song Form of vocal communication generally associated with a territorial male during the breeding season.

Specialists Species with limited range of tolerances.

Species An interbreeding group of organisms.

Star compass Ability to get directional information from position of the stars; used by nocturnally migrating passerines to fly north in spring and south in fall.

Static soaring Method of flying using rising currents of air, typified by flight of the vulture.

Structural coloration Color in the feathers caused by structure and not pigment.

Sun compass Ability to use the sun to gain directional information; shown to exist in the pigeon, it is probably common to all birds.

Syrinx Sound-producing organ of the bird, located at junction of bronchi and trachea.

Systematics Science of classification.

Supracoracoideus Interior set of breast muscles, responsible for raising wings on the recovery stroke.

Tarsus Part of a bird's leg between the ankle and toes.

Territory A defended area.

Thermal Column of rising air created by sun's heat.

Torpor Energy-saving adaptation observed in hummingbirds, swifts, and nightjars, reducing body temperature, breathing, and heart rate. Some species of hummingbirds experience torpor almost nightly; in some swifts and nightjars it lasts all during cold spells.

Uropygial gland Oil gland of a bird; found in most species, it secretes an oil that is spread on the feathers during preening.

Wing loading Mathematical relationship between wing's surface area and weight of bird; birds with high wing loading are buoyant flyers.

Zoological regions Six regions on earth defined by distinct group of organisms found in each.

INDEX